BUSINESS
CASE STUDIES
for Advanced GNVQ

Ian Marcousé

and

John Dymott

LONGMAN

LONGMAN GROUP LIMITED
Longman House, Burnt Mill, Harlow, Essex, CM20 2JE, England and
Associated Companies throughout the World.

First published 1994
ISBN 0 582 244757

Design and page make-up by Jordan Publishing Design

Printed in Great Britain by
Butler & Tanner Ltd, Frome and London

The publisher's policy is to use paper manufactured from sustainable
forests.

CONTENTS

Case Studies

ACKNOWLEDGEMENTS

The idea for this book came from Sophie Clark and Jeff Andrew at Longman. The concept was refined through discussion with Tricia Soulsby, the Course Leader for Advanced Business GNVQ at John Ruskin College. Another established GNVQ teacher, John Dymott of Farnham College, was then invited to write the questions and Further Work. As Head of Economics and Business Studies, he received enormous help and support from his team at Farnham, especially Sue Carr, Anne McCabe and Jane Foxwell.

The practicalities of writing involve many hours, printer ribbons, appraisals, re-writes, further re-writes and then the hardest part - thinking of visual material to enliven or explain the text. Many people have helped in these processes. Maureen Marcousé researched, Isobel Dymott typed, Tricia Soulsby commented, Helen Parr edited and the Low family helped illustrate. Many thanks to each of them.

Of all the forms of assistance authors can receive, none is more precious than peace and quiet. For this John and I would like to express the greatest thanks to our families: Isobel, Elizabeth and Laura Dymott and Maureen, Claire and Jonny Marcousé.

Ian Marcousé

HOW TO USE THIS BOOK

Introduction

The Advanced Business GNVQ is a broadly based qualification focused upon the way that business organisations function. This book provides 76 case studies to provide a resource both for direct study and for research purposes. The cases concentrate upon the 8 mandatory units of the course, plus the core skills.

Much of the work in a GNVQ involves student-centred learning to create a portfolio of 'evidence' to meet the performance criteria. The evidence provided by the candidate must be 'sufficient' to confirm their knowledge and understanding in further applications, such as the unit test. This evidence must cover the performance criteria and the associated range statements.

Evidence can be in various forms, including:

- a written report
- a video
- a (witnessed) discussion
- a documented interview

This case study book provides the user with a resource which can be used alongside other activities to fulfil the performance criteria. It can also be a lively and useful way of preparing for end of unit tests.

To students

There are four main strands to completing a unit in GNVQ. These are:

- an action plan
- evidence of coverage of the performance criteria
- evidence of coverage of the range
- a pass in the unit test

This book will help you to achieve these in the following ways:

- The case studies can be used as a source of information in themselves. For example the Just in Time and OKI case studies provide useful background information which could be incorporated into a project looking at Japanese working practices (Unit 5.3).
- The ideas within the case histories can be helpful for your own projects. For example, the case study Constructing a Business Plan clearly demonstrates the key requirements for this task. This will be a valuable resource when you begin to research your own business plan as part of Unit 8.
- The research that you carry out for a particular unit may not provide enough evidence that the range has been covered. You can use the index or the information at the start of each case to select an appropriate case study to fulfil the range requirement.
- Passing the unit tests requires a good grasp of business language. The case studies help by putting business terms into a memorable context. Furthermore, the Questions at the end of each case point to the key business terms that need to be mastered and learned.

To teachers

Business Case Studies was conceived as a flexible resource, providing teachers with access to a wealth of case study material. The cases are arranged in 9 sections: the 8 mandatory GNVQ units followed by cases suitable for the options. Within each section, the cases are arranged in approximate order of difficulty, with the easiest coming first. At the start of each case is an information panel stating the main content of the text and listing the Elements, Performance Criteria and Core Skills tackled within. This should make it relatively easy to select the most appropriate case to cover the syllabus areas or skills required.

This book can be used in six main ways:

1   To introduce students to the concepts and range required for a particular element or unit. Reading the case would act as a catalyst and focal point for discussion.

2   To provide an alternative learning strategy. It would be very time consuming to cover all the requirements of a unit through a wholly student-centred approach. This book gives you a practical alternative, allowing for quicker coverage of the material and therefore making it easier to complete the units.

3   To assist in coverage of the range. While it is expected that much of the GNVQ work will be research based and will involve links with local businesses, such tasks in themselves may not provide enough evidence to cover the range. the cases are arranged by unit and can be selected for this purpose. On page 8–9 is a grid that sets out the key concepts and core skills covered in each case study. This should make it easy to identify the best case to fill gaps in the range.

4   As a starting point for investigative work, Business Case Studies has much to offer. The "Further Work" section at the end of each case suggests ideas for investigations, projects, discussions, interviews or report writing. Providing students with the case history as a starting point should help them tackle these more challenging tasks.

5   Coverage of core skills is provided through numerate, communication and IT tasks placed within the Questions and, especially, the Further Work provided for each of the 76 cases.

6   To develop the skills required to gain a GNVQ merit or distinction, Business Case Studies can offer scope for substantial analysis and evaluation. For example, in the case study Häagen-Dazs UK, question 4 requires the student to evaluate the ethics of using sexy advertising to promote an ice cream. The student could be encouraged to apply a range of criteria to judge the actions of the company – commercial, moral and even artistic. This exercise will encourage students to develop the higher order skill of applying alternative criteria to evaluate actions – one of the grading themes in Advanced GNVQ. Much of the Further Work is designed for students to plan and execute their own research, which may also lead to the award of merit or distinction.

To assist in marking the Questions and to provide ideas on how the Further Work might be tackled, there is an accompanying Answer Guide (ISBN 0582 24477 3).

Grid to show elements and core skills within case studies

Case Study	1.1	1.2	1.3	1.4	2.1	2.2	2.3	2.4	3.1	3.2	3.3	3.4	4.1	4.2	4.3	4.4	5.1	5.2	5.3	5.4	6	7	8	C3.1	C3.2	C3.3	C3.4	AN3.1	AN3.2	AN3.3	IT3.1	IT3.2	IT3.3	IT3.4	IT3.5	Optional Units
1 Panda Wok	•	•																						•							•					
2 The Medicine Business	•	•	•																					•	•	•	•		•				•			
3 Adding Value to Sugar	•																							•	•											
4 Deciding on Factory Location	•	•	•																					•				•		•		•				
5 An Ethical Dilemma	•	•																						•					•							
6 Porsche Cars	•	•																										•								
7 Economic Change as an External Constraint	•	•	•																						•	•			•							
8 Anglo-Japanese Co-operation	•	•	•																																	
9 The Change in Government	•	•	•																					•	•	•	•									RSA 9.3
10 Price Elasticity and Profits	•	•																						•	•											
11 A Pressure Group Triumph	•	•	•																								•						•			
12 Chocolate Soldiers – The Rowntree Takeover	•	•																																		
13 De Lorean Cars	•	•																											•							
14 The New Laser Scanning System					•	•	•																	•												
15 A Day in the Life of Teresa Travis					•	•																														
16 Factory Safety					•	•																			•						•					
17 Personnel Management and Cost Controls					•	•																														
18 Stock Control and Analysis					•																				•	•			•	•			•			
19 BS 5750 and the Quality Fanatic					•																				•											
20 Production Management					•	•	•																		•				•					•		
21 Häagen-Dazs – Dedicated to Perfection									•	•															•				•					•		
22 McDonald's – Marketing Hamburgers									•	•	•														•											
23 The Survival Game									•	•	•																									
24 The Coca-Cola Story									•	•	•																	•								
25 Even Levi's Can Make Mistakes									•	•	•																				•					
26 Let the Buyer Beware									•	•	•																									
27 Häagen-Dazs UK – A Classic Product Launch									•	•	•														•							•				
28 Marketing Majestic									•	•	•														•											
29 Avoiding a Price War									•	•															•			•					•			
30 Body Shop International									•	•																		•			•	•				
31 The Product Portfolio Problem									•	•																										
32 Marlboro and Market Power									•																				•			•				
33 Money and Motivation																	•								•											
34 A Small Business Start-up													•																•		•					B 15.1
35 Personnel Management													•																							B 15.1
36 Bringing in Quality Circles																	•							•												

Mandatory Units | Core Skills Units (Communication 3.1 3.2 3.3 3.4 · A.N.* 3.1 3.2 3.3 · I.T. 3.1 3.2 3.3 3.4 3.5) | Optional Units

Column heading codes (indicated at the head of each case study):

- B 15.2
- B 15.1, 15.3, CG 10.1
- B 15.1, CG 10.1
- B 15.1
- B 9.2, 9.3
- B 12.1, 12.3
- B 12.1, 12.2
- B 11.2
- B 15.1, 15.3
- CG 14.1, 14.2, 14.3 R 9.3
- B 14.1, 14.2, 14.3, 14.4 R 13.2

Case studies:

37 Teamworking – Theory and Practice
38 Management Structure
39 Workforce Performance and the Skoda Supplier
40 Race Discrimination at Work
41 A BMW at Twenty-three
42 The Work of ACAS
43 The Trench
44 Putting Herzberg into Practice
45 British Management Techniques Under Fire
46 Kaizen – Continuous Improvement at OKI
47 Just-In-Time Production – The Japanese Way
48 Whizz Kids
49 The Ford Strike
50 The Sting
51 Credit Factoring
52 Fashion Goes West
53 The Sofabed Saga
54 Liquidity Crisis
55 Investment Within Financial Constraints
56 The Rise and Fall of Laker Airways
57 The 3-in-1 Washing Machine
58 Bombay Pizza
59 Working Capital
60 The Mini-merger
61 Good Management Practice in Retailing
62 Overtrading in Jewellery
63 The Country House Hotel
64 Constructing a Business Plan
65 The Business at the Bottom of the Garden
66 The Prince and the Turnstile
67 The Black Hairdressers
68 Fat Sam's Franchise
69 The Marketing Plan
70 Mrs Ahmed's Cousin
71 A Problem of Production and Stock Scheduling
72 Ford's Model T – the Birth of Modern Industry
73 Budgeting in Harrogate
74 Boomtime for Bankcheck
75 Problems of Pollution in a Chemical Plant
76 Finding a European Location

* AN means Application of Number

Note: Performance criteria coverage is indicated at the head of each case study.

B = BTEC   R = RSA   CG = City and Guilds

9

GNVQ COVERAGE – KEY CONCEPTS AND FURTHER WORK

Case study number	Name of case study	Key concepts	Further work
1	Panda Wok	Government intervention. Demand. Purpose of business.	Report writing.
2	The Medicine Business	Government intervention. Tertiary sector. Demand and supply. Costs. Welfare.	Design an advertisement. Discussion.
3	Adding Value to Sugar	Purpose of business. Needs and wants. Demand and supply. Single product company.	Presentation on factors influencing demand.
4	Deciding on Factory Location	Government intervention. Demand and supply. Trade agreements.	Business letter. Spreadsheet calculations. Discussion.
5	An Ethical Dilemma	Supply and demand. Wealth and welfare. Ethics. Objectives.	Discussion. Report on a sensitive issue.
6	Porsche Cars	Purpose of business. Data sources.	Collecting and recording data.
7	Economic Change as an External Constraint	Demand and supply. Government intervention.	Presentation with a visual aid. Report writing.
8	Anglo-Japanese Co-operation	Role of government. Protectionism.	Use of CD ROM.
9	The Change in Government	Demand. Government intervention. EU policy.	A business letter. Groupwork/discussion. Composing an advertisement.
10	Price Elasticity and Profits	Demand supply. Price elasticity of demand.	Report writing. Presentation.
11	A Pressure Group Triumph	Barriers to competition. Pressure groups. Monopolies and Mergers Commission.	Graphwork. Report/presentation. Writing a sensitive letter.
12	Chocolate Soldiers – The Rowntree Takeover	Demand and supply. Government and EU policy.	EU policies.
13	De Lorean Cars	Location. Elasticity.	How government and EU policies affect business.
14	The New Laser Scanning System	Technology in the workplace. Storing information.	Data protection. Evaluation of systems.
15	A Day in the Life of Teresa Travis	Electronic systems. Enhanced telephone systems.	Advantages and disadvantages of computerisation. Report and visit involving communication systems.
16	Factory Safety	Health and safety. Purposes of systems.	Report on pay systems. Use of file names. Producing a draft version and editing.
17	Personnel Management and Cost Controls	Purpose of systems. Communication systems. Evaluating systems.	Effectiveness of different forms of communications.
18	Stock Control and Analysis	Recording and monitoring performance. Evaluation criteria.	Flow charts. Writing a report.

Case study number	Name of case study	Key concepts	Further work
19	BS 5750 and the Quality Fanatic	Quality.	Visit to a company to study quality.
20	Production Management	Effectiveness of systems. Electronic systems.	IT. Visit to a bank, security routines. Data Protection Act.
21	Häagen-Dazs Dedicated to Perfection	New product development. Product life cycle.	Market research assignment.
22	McDonald's – Marketing Hamburgers	Marketing activities: promotions, advertising, consumer characteristics.	Comparison of marketing activities. Ethics of marketing.
23	The Survival Game	Marketing activities and objectives. Market research.	Comparison of marketing activities. Presentation of a market research report. Drawing up a questionnaire.
24	The Coca-Cola Story	Market research. Marketing activities.	Different research methods. Presentation of own market research.
25	Even Levi's Can Make Mistakes	Market research. Sampling.	Marketing strategy report.
26	Let the Buyer Beware	Consumer trends. Forecasting.	Social grading. Short term predictions.
27	Häagen-Dazs UK – A Classic Product Launch	Market research. Marketing mix. Ethics of advertising.	Plotting a five year forecast on a graph.
28	Marketing Majestic	Consumer characteristics Marketing objectives. Economic information.	Merging text and graphs. Market research report.
29	Avoiding a Price War	Forecasting sales. Promotions.	Numeracy. Solving problems. Making calculations.
30	Body Shop International	Marketing activities, objectives, ethics and mix.	IT: spreadsheet, naming files, paper orientation.
31	The Product Portfolio Problem	Consumption patterns. Product range development.	Line graphs. Forecasting.
32	Marlboro and Market Power	Brand names. Marketing activities.	Discussion on ethical issues.
33	Money and Motivation	Human resourcing. Commission system of payment. Employee relations.	Researching incentive systems.
34	A Small Business Start-up	Interviews. CVs. Letters of application.	Use of IT and non-IT to produce letters and CVs.
35	Personnel Management	Retention. Performance. Trade unions.	Research on falling trade union membership.
36	Bringing in Quality Circles	Japanese working practices.	Presentation and listening.
37	Teamworking – Theory and Practice	Recruitment. Employee relations. Teamwork. Equal opportunities. CV. Interviews.	Discussion. Job description. Job specification. Letters of application. CVs.

Case study number	Name of case study	Key concepts	Further work
38	Management Structure	Organisational structures. Job roles.	Structure of a franchise. Clipart and merger with text.
39	Workplace Performance and the Skoda Supplier	Absenteeism. Employee relations. Workplace performance.	Report. Memo. Discussion.
40	Race Discrimination at Work	Industrial tribunal. Training.	Short report. Discussion.
41	A BMW at Twenty-three	Motivation.	Questionnaire. Desk research on leadership.
42	The Work of ACAS	Trade unions. Demand for labour.	Flexible working. Drawing up a contract.
43	The Trench	Health and safety. Trade unions.	Making estimates and checking results.
44	Putting Herzberg into Practice	Specialisation. Productivity. Wages.	Quality of working life.
45	British Management Techniques Under Fire	Training. Working conditions.	External factors. Report.
46	Kaizen – Continuous Improvement at OKI	Japanese firms. Data sources. Training.	Visit to record workplace performance.
47	Just-in-Time Production	Productivity. Specialisation. External influences.	Research. Flexible work practices.
48	Whizz Kids	Training. Employment trends.	Integrated exercise suitable for an induction to the course.
49	The Ford Strike	Employment features. Industrial relations. Economic factors.	Researching recent changes in working practices.
50	The Sting	Ratios. Share dealing.	Use of spreadsheet to create a balance sheet.
51	Credit Factoring	Receipts and invoices. Cash flow.	Financial documents. Visit.
52	Fashion Goes West	Users of accounts. Simple balance sheet terms.	Cash flow spreadsheet.
53	The Sofabed Saga	Monitoring a business. Percentages.	Calculating ratios.
54	Liquidity Crisis	Users of accounts. Balance sheet analysis.	Bank visit.
55	Investment within Financial Constraints	Forecasting future profits.	Spreadsheet. Profit and loss account.
56	The Rise and Fall of Laker Airways	Cash flow. Asset valuation.	Financial part of a business plan.

Case study number	Name of case study	Key concepts	Further work
57	The 3-in-1 Washing Machine	Direct and indirect costs. Calculation of profit.	Sources of finance for business plan. Cash flow forecast.
58	Bombay Pizza	Cash flow forecast.	Two-dimensional representation of a three-dimensional object.
59	Working Capital	Fixed assets and working capital requirements.	Construction of a 12 month cash flow forecast.
60	The Mini-merger	Profit and loss. Balance sheet.	Trial balance.
61	Good Management Practice in Retailing	Sources of finance for a business plan.	Visit re budgeting and business planning.
62	Overtrading in Jewellery	Forecasting cash flows.	Demand fluctuations.
63	The Country House Hotel	Improving business performance.	Spreadsheet bar chart.
64	Constructing a Business Plan	Financing a business plan. Resources.	A plan from a case study. Spreadsheet cash flow forecast.
65	The Business at the Bottom of the Garden	Business decisions. Insurance.	Presenting a business plan to an audience.
66	The Prince and the Turnstile	Business plan. Resources.	Five part business plan.
67	The Black Hairdressers	Resources.	Flow charts.
68	Fat Sam's Franchise	Franchise. Fixed costs.	Flow charts. Business plan construction.
69	The Marketing Plan	Marketing budget.	Sales and marketing plans
70	Mrs Ahmed's Cousin	Law. Employee rights.	Drawing up a contract.
71	A Problem of Production and Stock Scheduling	Production planning. Stock control.	Drawing a line graph. Using a spreadsheet.
72	Ford's Model T – The Birth of Modern Industry	Mass production.	Plotting a demand curve.
73	Budgeting in Harrogate	Variance. Analysing company performance.	Evaluating IT in the workplace. Budget analysis.
74	Boomtime for Bankcheck	Mismanagement. Communications. Leadership.	Researching leadership styles.
75	Problems of Pollution in a Chemical Plant	Pressure groups. Environment.	Investigate environmental policies of leading companies.
76	Finding a European Location	Decision making. Business in Europe.	Problems of marketing overseas. Preparing for a European option module.

A BUSINESS REPORT

Report formats will vary in different organisations (many organisations have their own house style). However, this section provides help with a possible approach.

As a general guide the report is likely to have the following order:

■ a cover which contains a title and security classification

■ a title page stating who wrote the report, to whom it is addressed, the date of the report and the title of the report. A circulation list may be provided to see who else has a copy

■ an introduction to include the main purpose of the report. In a detailed report the introduction may include the main elements

■ a table of contents; the major sections can be given single numbers (1, 2, 3, 4) and the first level of sub-section a decimal point 1.1.

The length of a report will vary from one or two pages to many pages depending on the subject and nature of the report. You should always aim to keep your reports concise and to the point.

Remember that the report is partly a marketing exercise; you are writing to a specific reader or readers who are going to form an impression about you from the quality of your report. The way in which it is presented may be as important as the contents.

Report writing is an important skill which will be useful for both higher education and employment.

The example below outlines a report on the operational problems at Euro Disney in its first year.

---

1. **Introduction**

1.1 Purpose of report
1.2 Background information

2. **Findings**

Reasons for poor performance
2.1 Economic factors
2.2 Cultural difficulties
2.3 Pricing and other marketing tactics

3. **Recommendations and conclusion**

3.1 An evaluation of the relative importance
    of the problems
3.2 The future of Euro Disney. Where do we
    go next?

- **Visual material.** The actual contents of the report should include visual material. The GNVQ core skills' range refers to the need for diagrams and charts to be inserted at the right place. These 'images' should illustrate complex or difficult points. You should not display too many numbers or graphs, just the significant data. The report must be concise and coherent so do not clutter it with pages of figures. The task of a report is to synthesise detail into a form that will be suitable for the audience. If necessary, detailed figures can be inserted as an appendix at the end of the report.

- **Conclusions and recommendations** bring together material found elsewhere in the report as evidence for an opinion or conclusion. The report's recommendations may have to be in the form of hints, depending on the sensitivity of the topic and the persons reading the report. Conclusions are more objective and based on facts e.g. Euro Disney will have to borrow more money because of the disappointing revenue levels in the first years of operation.

- **Words.** Try to use the language of business as much as possible. If the report is word processed a spell check should always be used to avoid spelling mistakes.

The following case studies include report writing;

Unit 1   1, 5, 7, 10, 11
Unit 2   15, 16
Unit 3   23, 25, 28
Unit 4   39, 40
Unit 5   45

Units 6 and 7 provide opportunities for financial reports and unit 8 involves the production of a business plan and this gives the opportunity for a full report.

A BUSINESS PLAN

A business plan sets out the objectives and forecasts for a firm's medium term future. It is often used to propose in detail the way in which a new business is aiming to be established. It is an exciting document but must also be realistic and achievable.

How to approach the plan

Read through the performance criteria for unit 8 and make sure that you will fulfil these in the objectives and content of your business plan. To achieve all of the criteria you should be prepared to make a presentation of your business plan when you have completed it.

Brainstorm ideas for your business either on your own or in small groups. (There is a list of suggestions below, but it is better to think up your own ideas.)

Once you have decided what business you want to set up, you should investigate a similar business in its early stages. One method of gathering useful information is to undertake primary research by visiting a similar business if there is a possible opportunity. Also read Case 64 on Constructing a Business Plan.

Prepare your action plan so you are clear about the next stages involved in putting together your business plan. Some factors you might want to consider are:

1   Decide on the objectives of your business proposal, and then list them.

2   Prepare an introduction to your business plan which includes these objectives together with a clear statement about the aims and functions of your proposed business.

3   Research the different forms of business ownership (sole trader, partnership and private limited company) and decide which one would be most appropriate for your venture. You should include consideration of the legal and insurance implications of a particular business set up.

4   Think about possible sources of support and use them in your plan. This could include support from within your organisation and from other organisations and individuals.

5   Prepare a flow chart to demonstrate the sequence of operations required to complete your business plan. Show any time constraints or dependencies on your flow chart, for example when the business will be ready to begin trading or when advertising for the new product has to begin in order to make the predicted level of sales. Discuss the feasibility of your flow chart with your teacher or tutor.

6   As part of your production plan, make a decision about the location of your proposed business. Make a note of how you reached your decision, including factors such as available labour and materials supply, competition, and market potential. You will also need to include outline details of the plant (machinery) you will require to produce your product.

7   Think about how you will market your product, taking into account any constraints caused by your marketing budget. Plan the timing of your marketing activity; for example when would be the best time to promote your new product? What sort of marketing approach is likely to be most effective? Think about the factors you will take into account when pricing your product, and how and where you will sell it. Refer back to your business objectives if necessary; for example, a monthly business magazine would probably have a very different pricing policy, promotional plan and distribution outlets to a weekly local paper.

8   Estimate the costs for the first year of running your business. Construct a cash flow forecast, and explain how you will monitor your finance. Prepare a start up balance sheet. What is the amount of capital needed as start up capital? Think about what possible sources of finance are available and add to your finance plan.

9   Will your business survive? Prepare a projected profit and loss sheet for a defined period, for example the year of trading, and a balance sheet for the end of that period.

10 Prepare a presentation of your business plan, including some visuals of your data. Think about the audience you will be presenting to, and make your presentation appropriate for their level of knowledge and understanding.

A BUSINESS LETTER

The core skill element in communications requires the construction of business letters. Element 3.2 states that written material must be prepared on a range of matters: routine matters like handling customers' letters and non-routine matters e.g. a letter on a sensitive issue.

We all have to write a business letter at some stage in our lives. The letter may be to apply for a Saturday job in the local superstore or to ask for an appointment with a bank manager to discuss opening an account.

Guidelines for any letters include the following:

- A letter is a form of communication so make sure that you achieve the objectives in mind when setting out to write the letter.

- Draw up an action plan of the main points you wish to express and arrange them in a suitable order.

- Be businesslike in your style where necessary. Try to use short words and sentences. Brevity and conciseness are to be preferred to long words and complex sentences.

- If writing a letter on a sensitive issue be courteous and honest. A letter can be used as written evidence against you so be careful before making accusations.

- Make sure that grammar, punctuation and spelling follow standard conventions. There should be no excuse for such mistakes if a letter is produced by word processor which can spell-check and grammar-check any document.

Layout and style

One of the main styles is called fully blocked which gives a modern appearance to a letter.

Example of a fully blocked letter with open punctuation

17 Granby Street
Devonport
TORQUAY
D13 TQ2

Your ref 1/3a

12 June 199-

Tesco Ltd
2 Shortheath Crest
TOTNES
Devon
T48 4TN

Dear Sirs

Thank you for your letter requesting me to attend an interview on Tuesday 5th of July at 9.30.

I regret to inform you that I have a GNVQ unit test that morning and will not be able to attend at the time you stated.

Would it be possible to shift the interview to the afternoon or to arrange the interview on an alternative date? I am replying immediately to minimise any inconvenience I may have caused.

I am looking forward to hearing from you again in the near future.

Yours faithfully

Lucy Binfield

A LETTER ON A SENSITIVE ISSUE

Suggestions are made in the Further Work sections of case studies indicating when it might be necessary or appropriate to write a letter on an issue which is non-routine. More suggestions are given below. If you want to obtain a merit or distinction you should independently use this type of letter when you feel it is appropriate.

Unit 1. A letter to the local council complaining, for example, about a company polluting the environment or generally causing a nuisance to the local community.

Unit 4. A letter of rejection to a job applicant. Such letters are difficult to write and should be constructive wherever possible. Aim to highlight some positive aspects or qualities of the candidate. Your letter should also state briefly, if possible, why the candidate was not quite suitable for the job in a sensitive but firm way.

Unit 5. A letter of complaint about poor conditions at work, for example about the lack of maintenance of a piece of machinery or about poor food served in the works canteen.

Unit 6. A letter may be sent concerning a missing item that had been ordered several months before. It may be that the item is vital to the continuation of your business and you have been an important customer for a number of years. Alternatively you could send a letter as a last warning to someone who has not paid their account.

The following is an example of a letter to an unsuccessful applicant for a job at a garden centre.

Bullring Research Centre
Rowledge
BIRMINGHAM
R56 9BI

13th October 199-
Miss Ruth Rahman
12 The Street
Solihull
BIRMINGHAM
S24 5BI

Dear Miss Rahman

Research Officer Vacancies

I am sorry to have to inform you that your application for
the above position has been unsuccessful. The selection
panel had great difficulty in reaching a decision due to the
strength of the candidates for the jobs but, after careful
consideration, the positions have been offered to two other
candidates.

Although I am sorry to have to write to you with
disappointing news, I would like to thank you for your
application and for attending the interview yesterday, and I
wish you all the best for the future.

Yours sincerely

Elaine Thorne
Head of Research

A BUSINESS MEMO

This is the shortest type of report and can be hand-written. It is internal and is usually less formal than a report. A memo is usually sent on a pre-printed form with spaces for To, From, Date, Copies for Circulation to, Title of Memorandum. The sender would either sign or initial the memo.

An example is shown below.

MEMORANDUM

To: All Staff

From: The Chief Safety Officer

Date: 12th July 1994

Fire Drill Reminder

During the next week there will be a fire drill. Staff must take this seriously and make sure they have read the relevant procedures. Fire exits should be used and all windows and doors are to be shut by the last person leaving each room.

Staff should assemble in the carpark and return to their section after a roll call has been taken. The whole operation should take no longer than fifteen minutes. Please see me if there are any matters which need clarification.

Helen Ngati

Helen Ngati

---

1 PANDA WOK

Elements: **1.1** *PC 123*   **1.2** *PC 234*
            IT **3.1** *PC 12345*

Key concepts: Purpose of business, Demand, Government intervention,
Report writing

Panda Wok was started five years ago by Laura Piper and Chris Spence. It was Laura's idea to create a Chinese restaurant with a difference. Customers fill a bowl with ingredients chosen for themselves from a huge range of carefully sliced meats, fish, prawns and vegetables. After adding the flavourings, sauces and cooking oil, they hand their creation to one of three cooks who stand by a huge griddle in the middle of the restaurant. Within three minutes the food is cooked and the onlooking customers take the freshly cooked food back to their table. People are welcome to repeat the process as often as they like.

From its opening day in a blaze of free pandas and free media publicity, Panda Wok was a great success. Chris had planned on **breaking even** in the second or third year, but from the first night the restaurant made money. He was content to enjoy the profits, but Laura was determined to make Panda Wok a national name. Using bank borrowings and the business's cash flow, the company expanded at a furious pace. As the diagram shows, new restaurants were opened with increasing speed. As Laura put it: 'We're steadily turning the country black and white.'

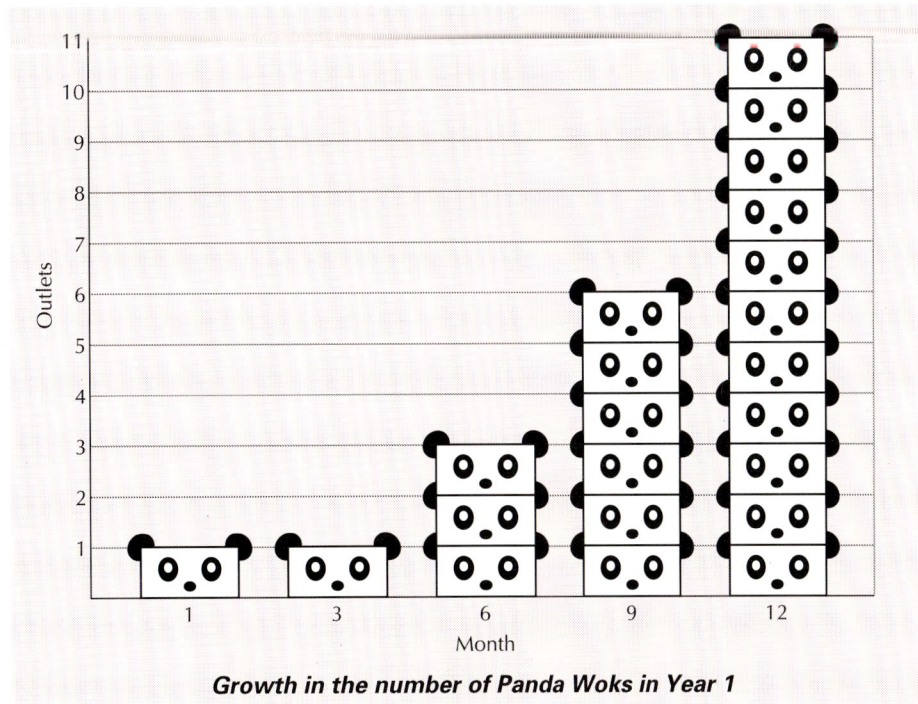

Growth in the number of Panda Woks in Year 1

Just twelve months after day 1, with annualised sales running at £2 million, Chris managed to sit Laura down to talk things over. He knew that she was working from seven in the morning to eight at night, and then going on to visit a different Panda Wok outlet every day. He half-hoped to see signs of exhaustion on her face, but all he detected was shining enthusiasm: 'I want us to be the first national chain of Chinese restaurants…the Marks and Spencer of catering.'

Chris tried to persuade her that their company was not capable of more expansion: 'Our accounting system can't cope, our bank balance goes ever deeper into the red, and we cannot find the time to look carefully at alternative new sites …we must consolidate…we have no **middle management**…if we keep on like this our quality control will go and so will our reputation.'

Chris thought he had got through to Laura, but the buzz of satisfied customers at the Brighton outlet that night switched her back to her growth targets.

It took another two months for the first shock to hit the firm. Panda Wok's bank, with little warning, demanded that its £400,000 overdraft be halved within six weeks. This forced a desperate reappraisal. It quickly became clear that the company's contracts to buy new properties made it impossible to cut back spending so quickly. To avoid **liquidation**, Laura and Chris had to accept a refinancing package which included the bank taking a 40% shareholding in the company. Chris wondered whether this was the time to diversify away from such an income elastic service as a restaurant, but Laura convinced him to keep concentrating on their core skill.

Having survived this phase, Panda Wok returned to its growth path. Its 120 sites were, by now, yielding annual profits of £500,000. Yet this was soon to be dented by a series of difficulties. A direct competitor with better restaurant locations was taking away some trade, while the whole market was affected by a sharp VAT increase on restaurant food. Then came the scandal. The St Albans outlet was prosecuted under the Food Safety Act of 1990 for sloppy hygiene leading to cases of food poisoning. This was picked up by the BBC's Southeast news, and then by the national press. Takings dived. The company almost went under during the following six months, but then began to recover. This time around, Laura was much more cautious. She accepted now that building up the company's quality image was more important than constant expansion.

Questions

1   From this case state three purposes of business.   **(3)**

2   What are the three main industrial sectors? In which sector would you place a
    restaurant?   **(4)**

3   Explain the meaning of: breaking even, middle management, liquidation?   **(3)**

4   Why might demand for a service, like a restaurant, fluctuate?   **(3)**

5   After the first shock how much annual profit was each restaurant earning?   **(3)**

6   Give two examples from the case, of how government intervention can affect
    business.   **(4)**

7   What were the difficulties that the business faced in achieving its purposes?   **(5)**

Further work

1   As part of the introduction to this unit, do some of your own research into the purposes
    of business and the role of the government in business. Working in groups, action plan a
    visit to a small firm and produce a questionnaire to cover the range, including:

    ■   A brief introduction to the history of the business and its legal structure.

    ■   What is the purpose of the business?

    ■   How and why does demand vary?

    ■   What products/services are provided?

    ■   How does local/national government affect you?

    ■   How do European Union decisions affect you?

    ■   What other external factors affect the business?

    Wordprocess your findings in a suitable report format (see page 14 for a suitable format).

2 THE MEDICINE BUSINESS

Elements: **1.1** *PC 1 3 5*   **1.2** *PC 1 2 3 4*   **1.3** *PC 1*
C 3.1 *PC 1 2 3 4*   **3.2** *PC 1 2 3 4*   **3.3** *PC 1 2 3*   **3.4** *PC 1 2 3*
AN 3.2 *PC 1 2 5*   **IT 3.3** *PC 1 2 3 4*

Key concepts: Tertiary sector, Public service, Demand and supply, Government intervention, Costs, Welfare

Mike felt terrific. After three months of looking for his first post, he had been offered a new practice on the edge of Hatfield. It would be the only G.P. surgery for a group of new housing estates in this Hertfordshire town. It seemed a just reward for the five years in university and four years of **vocational training** that he had just been through.

At the interview, the Chairman of the local Family Practitioner Committee (F.P.C.) had warned him that he would not qualify for the £15,000 government grant for setting up new practices. This was because he had not been qualified for the minimum two year period. Yet Mike felt confident that the Committee and the Department of Health would give him all the help he needed; and anyway, in nine years of training he had never been told about problems in starting up a surgery.

Where to start, though? Mike decided to wait until the F.P.C. had sent the lengthy book that sets out the extremely complex arrangements for – and restrictions on – G.P.s' work and remuneration. For whereas many people assume that G.P.s receive salaries, in fact their pay is based upon a series of fees and allowances.

Within a few weeks of his appointment on 30th December 1988, Mike felt he understood enough to get started. The only capital he had was £2,000, so he had to rent premises. As the new estates had nothing suitable, he hired two Portakabins which could be joined to provide areas for a surgery, a waiting room, a reception, and the necessary washing facilities. These were placed on the edge of council land that was still being built on. The F.P.C. would pay the monthly £736 rent, but three months in arrears. In the future, a proper Health Centre was scheduled to be built nearby; Mike would then operate from there.

As he became more aware of the fees, allowances and expenses provided for G.P.s (see **Appendix A**) Mike was struck by how heavily geared they were to existing, large practices. For not only did he require a minimum of 1,000 patients to obtain the full allowance, but also all payments would be received well in arrears. G.P.s receive their earnings quarterly, based upon the number of patients on their list, plus the fees incurred, during the previous three months. As these quarterly cheques apply to the patients on the doctor's list at the start of the quarter, if Mike took patients on in February he would receive no payment for serving them until after 30th June.

However, lateness in payment was only part of the problem. The other was that of getting patients at all. For at that time doctors were not allowed to advertise (this changed in 1990). New practitioners could announce their opening in the local paper, but no more. This had long been agreed between the N.H.S. and the doctors' representatives, because the profession was said to doubt the ethics of attempting to persuade people to switch doctors as they would brands of soap powder.

Despite these difficulties, Mike managed to open the Manor House surgery on 20th February 1989. His bank manager had provided a £10,000 **overdraft** facility, but by decorating and furnishing the Portakabins himself, he had not yet used more than £3,000 of it. The biggest financial outlay was for medical supplies and dressings, on which £2,400 was spent.

Having started the practice, he now needed to generate enough money to pay himself a living wage, and to pay the wages of a receptionist/clerk/book-keeper. The F.P.C. would pay 70% of one employee's salary, but again it would only be paid in arrears. To boost awareness of his practice, Mike decided to get a friend to encourage the local newspaper to write an article about him. When this appeared, other G.P.s in the area complained about his 'soliciting' custom, and he received a stern rebuke from the F.P.C. The same occurred when – some months later – a vicar's wife wrote a piece in the parish magazine praising the quality of care provided by 'this splendid new doctor'.

Mike had always realised, though, that word of mouth would be his most valuable form of publicity. With that in view, he set up various clinics providing preventative medicine for which no NHS fees were available (and were therefore not available at many of the other practices locally). Despite being on call 24 hours a day, seven days a week, he also made a point of sounding sympathetic to night-time calls at home.

Slowly the medicine worked. By 1st April there were 170 patients on his list; by 1st August this had grown to 550. There looked to be the prospect of 1,000 by the end of 1989. Yet Mike's only income in the eight months since he had been appointed had been £903. In July his Building Society mortgage went unpaid, and by August the practice overdraft stood at £8,000. For many months to come the costs that resulted from treating more patients would outweigh the revenues based upon the number of patients three months before. It was clear that careful accounting and a friendly bank manager would be the only way of surviving for several months.

Mike felt an acute sense of grievance against a system that made it so hard to set up a new surgery for any but the well-off. He had many criticisms of the Conservatives' funding of the N.H.S., but applauded their decision to allow advertising in future; he would certainly run **informative advertisements** in the local paper. Yet he also acknowledged the advantages of his position. Instead of joining an established practice where he would be the junior partner, he was able to make all the decisions for himself. Indeed if all went well he would be able to build up a patient list of around 3,000 – which would provide him with a substantial income.

He could not help thinking, though, that after nine years' study to become a G.P. he should not really be expected to teach himself to be a businessman as well.

Sources: *The doctor concerned, and from the magazine Medeconomics. (The name of the town has been changed.)*

APPENDIX A

In 1989, General Practitioners worked to the following package of fees and allowances:

Fees and allowances 1989

BASIC ALLOWANCE	£11,100 p.a.
(doctors with fewer than 1,000 patients receive £11.10 per patient)	
CAPITATION FEES	
(under 65 years old)	£8.95 each
(65–74 years old)	£11.60 each
(over 75 years old)	£14.25 each
NIGHT VISITS	
(first 1 or 2)	£20.25 each
(next 3-5)	£10.13 each
(over 6)	£2.02 each
Vaccinations	£4.45 each

N.B. There were many other specific fees for relatively unusual treatments – too many to list.

(The Department of Health believed that, in 1989, these fees would provide a doctor with the average number of patients [2,000] with an income of £31,105 plus expenses of £14,656 per annum.)

Questions

1 Explain the following terms: vocational training, overdraft, informative advertising. (3)

2 Mike provides a public service and works in the public sector. What is the distinction between the private and public sectors of the economy? (4)

3 Mike is involved in tertiary production. Give two other examples of people who provide a service in the tertiary sector. (2)

4 Work out the annual income that a doctor with 500 patients (all under 65) could expect if 5% of them were vaccinated each year, and if that doctor was called out to a patient on 36 separate nights. (6)

5 Give examples from the case to show how the government intervenes in the health market. (5)

6 How would you compare the objectives of a family doctor like Mike to those of a business? (5)

Further work

1 On a suitable format draw up an advertisement promoting Mike's surgery. Credit will be given for the image being suitable for the subject matter and target audience. The advertisement should provide clear illustrations of the points referred to.

2 To help achieve Communications element 3.1, you could take part in a discussion on the advantages and disadvantages of providing health care through the market.

3 Why has the percentage of the total workforce in the tertiary sector increased over the past 20 years? List four reasons. Obtain statistics from the latest *Social Trends* and draw a pie chart, using a suitable package, to show the percentages of primary, secondary and tertiary sector workers within the UK workforce.

3 ADDING VALUE TO SUGAR

Elements: **1.1** *PC 1245* **1.3** *PC 1*
C **3.1** *PC 1234* **3.2** *PC 123*

Key concepts: Purposes of organisations, Needs and wants, Single product company, Demand and supply

If you laid the 1,000 million lollipops per annum sold by Chupa Chups end to end, they would circle the globe four times. If the firm succeeds in its efforts to set up a joint venture in China, it will lay a claim to be the major lollipop multinational, as it already markets its products in 85 countries.

Chupa Chups is the life's work of a Catalan son of a pastry maker, Enrique Bernat. After working his way up to become the general manager of an overly-diversified food manufacturer, Bernat was given the opportunity to buy the business in 1955. He soon abandoned all the firm's product lines except one; he chose to specialise in lollipops. Given Spain's extreme poverty at that time, concentration on such a frivolous product was a bold step. The attraction, though, was the wide availability and cheapness of the only significant ingredient – sugar. This low input cost gave rise to the opportunity to achieve high added value, in other words a high margin between the cost of materials and the selling price. Lollipops had another financially based attraction – that year-round demand would enable continuous production to be used (chocolate, by contrast, was strongly biased away from the hot summers).

Bernat turned this financial opportunity into a marketing success by building up a highly rewarded, well motivated 400-strong sales force. This was vastly more powerful than that of the rival producers, and by 1960 Chupa was dominant. A later marketing director recalled:

> 'We were almost a monopoly ... so we created our own competition'

With the Spanish market saturated, Chupa looked for a way of adding more value to their modestly priced sweets. Bernat came up with an ideal way – providing a major customer benefit (fun) in a way that appeared to be difficult, and therefore expensive, to produce: lollipops that whistle. That 1962 development spawned various other, ever more musical versions. Bernat also commissioned Salvador Dali to design the distinctive wrappers that have been used ever since.

In the early 1970s, Bernat decided to take advantage of the Dictator Franco's slow opening up of the Spanish economy, by developing exports to the richer European countries. Under the brand name Melody Pops, the premium-priced lollipops became such a success that the company did not have enough plant to meet both Spanish and export demand. With long lead times on building a new factory, and caution about whether the novelty factor might make success short lived, Chupa had to choose between the home and export markets. Confident of their ability to win back the long-established home market, the managers chose to focus on exports. By the late 1970s, Chupa had to stop selling in Spain altogether.

Dozens of small competitors stepped in to supply the Spanish market – often with whistling products. For although Bernat had invented the idea, such an obvious, technically simple process cannot be patented. When extra capacity enabled Chupa to re-enter their home market, they found the going much tougher. Retailers who had been forced to buy from alternative suppliers were reluctant to return – especially while they still held stocks of the rival products. Another massive, highly expensive direct sales campaign was used to regain distribution. Through this, Chupa established a one third market share; well down on earlier levels, but enough to represent a real home base.

Those who meet Enrique Bernat report that – despite being well over 65 – he still talks with optimism about new, revolutionary ways of making ever-better lollipops. Such dedication to a single product flies in the face of text-book advice to diversify. Is his success because of this dedication or despite it?

Questions

1 Research the meaning of these terms: specialisation, value added, market saturation, patent.   (4)

2 What do you think were Bernat's business objectives?   (3)

3 Distinguish between a need and a want. Can a lollipop ever be a need?   (5)

4 Which industrial sector was Bernat involved in?   (2)

5 What factors affect the demand for lollipops?   (4)

6 Why is it difficult to achieve long term success through the production of a single product?   (2)

7 What factors were responsible for determining the number of Melody Pops which could be supplied in a week?   (5)

Further work

1 Use this case study as a starting point for further research into the confectionery market. Divide into groups and prepare a presentation on the factors which influence the demand for one of the following: crisps, soft drinks, chocolate bars, sweets, ice creams. You might wish to contrast demand for one particular brand, such as Walkers, with crisps generally. When another group makes their presentation listen carefully, make notes, and prepare one or two questions to ask them afterwards.

4 DECIDING ON FACTORY LOCATION

Elements: **1.1** PC 1 3 4   **1.2** PC 3 4   **1.3** PC 2 3
            C **3.1**   PC 1 2 3 4   AN **3.1** PC 1 2 3 4 5 6 7   **3.2** PC 1 2 5 7 8
            3.3 PC 1 2 3 4 5 6   IT **3.3** PC 1 2 3 4 5

Key concepts: Trends in UK and Europe, Demand and supply, Government intervention, Trade agreements

In his large office in Hesketh House, London W.1., James Drayton studied the wall-map of Britain. He realised, with some surprise, that he did not know it very well. His twenty years of building up Jarton Electronics had made him familiar with the industrial districts of Japan, Taiwan and South Korea, so he felt he knew Singapore Airport better than he knew Newcastle or Glasgow. Yet having decided to build his first British factory, he knew he must adjust.

Jarton's Projects Director had already done the legwork, and the afternoon's Board Meeting was to discuss whether to choose Site A (Billingham, Co. Durham) or Site B (Rochester, Kent). As Company Chairman, James Drayton's opinion

---

Report to: The Board of Directors
From: D. Springer, Projects Director
Subject: The Costs and Benefits of Sites A and B
Date: April 17th

1 Background and Objectives

1.1 Due to forecast excess demand next year, the Board agreed on 2nd March that a new plant should be constructed. It will produce up to 100,000 video cameras per year at a target cost of £225 each. With worries about the degree of import protectionism towards non-EU goods after the establishment of the Single Market, the Board approved a proposal that the factory should be constructed in Britain.

1.2 This report sets out the costs of each of two alternative sites, broken down into fixed and variable.

2 The Costs

2.1 Based upon the best available evidence, the costs are:

	Site A	Site B
Fixed (per annum)	£000	£000
Rent and rates	1,240	2,100
Salaried staff	3,660	4,500
Depreciation	1,900	1,900
Interest charges	1,200	1,500
Variable (per unit)	£	£
Materials and components	£89.50	£80.00
Piece rate labour	£4.00	£5.00
Delivery costs	£14.50	£5.00
Travel and expenses	£10.00	£4.00

3 Recommendations

3.1 Final conclusions can only be drawn once the marketing department has made a firm sales forecast. The above costs have been calculated on the assumption that 50% of output would be exported to Europe via the Channel Tunnel. If the proportion changes in favour of U.K. sales, site A will become more attractive than suggested above.

3.2 If sales are 100,000 units with about half being exports, site B looks more attractive.

would probably be decisive. The Projects Director started the meeting by presenting a report on the financial implications of each site.

The Chairman asked the Personnel Director for comments, and received the following reply:

'I have severe doubts about estimates such as these. I think they fail to allow for the problem of high labour turnover in the South. There's the measurable costs of staff turnover, of course, such as recruitment and training overheads. But I think it's still more important to allow for the impact on morale of having too little continuity. Both on the production and R & D side, what we need is experienced, loyal staff. In the long run, I'm sure that County Durham with its 12% unemployment will serve us better than Kent with its 5%.'

The Marketing and the Finance Directors both spoke against this view. The Finance Director's views were typical of both:

'To succeed, we need first rate top management. If we set up in the North it will be a struggle to get high-calibre people, because the best ones want to be in reach of London.'

The Personnel Director thought them ignorant and prejudiced. She was feeling rather isolated, and although the Production Director spoke up in favour of County Durham, it was evident that the majority wanted the factory in the South. She tried one last line of argument:

'Are we not being reckless by ignoring the possibility of a slump in demand for our product? After all, if sales fall sharply from 100,000 and perhaps the price slips from the £320 we anticipate, how will we cope with the high fixed costs in the South?'

This suggestion was greeted in silence, with the Finance Director appearing very angry at this stepping over what he regarded as the demarcation line between finance and the rest of the organisation. He reminded his fellow Directors that:

'Our duty is to our shareholders; it is not for us to allow emotion to cloud our judgement just because unemployment is temporarily higher in the North. At 100,000 units, site B will give us £400,000 more profit than site A. I move we vote for site B and then get on with the rest of our agenda.'

Questions

1 State five general factors which influence the location of industry. **(5)**

2 Research three ways in which the UK government could protect its home industry against foreign competition. **(3)**

3 State two disadvantages of restricting imports from the point of view of the consumer. **(2)**

4 Explain in your own words why Jarton felt it necessary to locate a plant in Britain. **(3)**

5 How much would each of the sites cost (per annum) in total fixed costs? Explain why rent, rates and salaried staff costs are higher in the South than in the North of England. **(5)**

6 State two other disadvantages of the southern location, besides the costs mentioned in Question 5. **(2)**

7 Calculate the total variable costs per site if 100,000 video cameras were produced. Explain why, generally, variable costs are higher in the North. **(5)**

Further work

1 In order to attract more industry and employment, most regions have a local authority department that promotes the attractions of its locality. Imagine you are the marketing manager of your local enterprise centre; write a business letter to Jarton outlining the advantages of a location in your area.

2 **a** Set up a spreadsheet, and use formulae to work out profits at site A and profits at site B for the following levels of output: 25,000, 50,000, 75,000, and 100,000 units. Here is a suggested outline of your grid: cell A1 output: A2 25,000: A3 50,000: A4 75,000: A5 100,000: B1 total revenue: C1 total variable costs: D1 total fixed costs: E1 total costs: F1 profits. Produce a hard copy of your spreadsheet.

   b On the basis of your calculations, write a paragraph on which site you would choose. Using the cut and paste facility, transfer your spreadsheet to the same page as your text, and print out a hard copy.

   c In order to meet Communications criteria, discuss in groups other factors that would have to be taken into consideration in a final decision about location.

5 AN ETHICAL DILEMMA

Elements: **1.1** *PC 1245* **1.2** *PC 123* **1.3** *PC 3* **C 3.1** *PC 1234*
AN 3.2 *PC 125*

*Key concepts: Supply and demand, Wealth and welfare, Business ethics,
Government intervention, Objectives*

It was as if someone had spat in the Marketing Director's face. All round the mahogany boardroom table, the smartly dressed men sat stiffly, too shocked to move or speak. Teresa, the only woman present, gulped as she realised that her naive question had ground the meeting to a halt. She knew they were all highly sensitive on the subject, but it had seemed reasonable to ask:

> *'Did you see the World in Action programme last night?'*

Of course, it had been a particularly ferocious attack on the tobacco industry, complete with stomach-wrenching pictures of smokers' diseased lungs, and legs amputated due to failing blood circulation. The programme had even aimed a barb at the man at the head of the table. It pointed out that the International Tobacco Company's Marketing Director had given public assurances that the firm's advertising was never aimed at young people, yet a leaked internal memo signed by him said:

> *'Motor-racing sponsorship may be hard to justify on cost efficiency grounds, but it is the only way we can reach the teenage market.'*

Teresa reflected that in the twenty or so meetings she had attended between International Tobacco Company (I.T. Co.) and her advertising agency, the subject of health – let alone social responsibilities – had never been raised. Yet she had chatted with most of these men on their own over lunch, and knew them all to be caring parents who had thought deeply about the ethical dilemma of being responsible for the advertising of half the country's cigarettes.

One or two felt guilty about their situation, but most had rationalised it away by convincing themselves that their efforts were not persuading people to start smoking, only to get existing smokers to switch from one brand to another. Outside commentators might sneer at this idea, but they comforted themselves that research had never uncovered anyone who attributed their first cigarette to an advertisement.

Fortunately, the spell that had immobilised the meeting was broken by the arrival of tea. After the waitress had left, the advertising agency's Chairman was able to move on to the next item on the agenda: Project Plover. He presented data giving the background to this proposed new product (shown opposite).

Background Research Data For Project Plover

Recent market share trends for low tar brands		Views of smokers of low tar brands	
Last 6 months	22%	Would switch to lower tar if taste OK	52%
6–12 months ago	20.5%		
12–18 months ago	19%		
18–24 months ago	18%	Would switch for 40% less tar	59%
24–36 months ago	17%		

Source: *Ex-factory sales figures*   Source: *ANR Research*

Teresa sat there tensely as her Chairman ran through the presentation that she had written. She had spent four months on Project Plover (a codename used for security purposes), and dearly wanted the I.T.Co. Marketing Director to approve the £200,000 needed for the final preparations before its launch as a new cigarette brand. Inwardly, she applauded her Chairman's clear explanation of the consumer proposition '40% less tar but no less taste than the leading low tar brand'; and his expert account of the middle-class, female niche that this brand would fill in the market.

When he finished, it was the I.T.Co New Product Development Manager's turn. He explained that Plover was forecast to achieve a 1% share of the 5,000 million* pack annual cigarette market, with a gross profit margin of £120 per thousand packs (i.e. 12 pence per pack). Even with a launch advertising budget of £2.5 million, a handsome contribution should be generated. Nor would this be especially at the expense of other I.T.Co. brands, as their competitors held 75% of the low tar market.

'So, what's your opinion, Bob?' asked the agency Chairman.

'Well...' replied the Marketing Director, 'I'm worried at the longer term implications. We've already led nearly a quarter of the market down to low tar and low nicotine cigarettes. If we now encourage them to smoke even weaker cigarettes, are we not just helping them give up altogether? We have a responsibility to think of the company's future. I think we'd better shelve this project.'

Teresa blinked in amazement at what she had heard, and looked round the table to see who would challenge this statement. No-one did. They moved on to the next Agenda item – Snooker sponsorship.

* Apologies for the huge, but realistic, numbers. United Kingdom cigarette sales amount to 5,000 million packs times 20 per pack i.e. 100,000 million cigarettes per year.

Questions

1 What are the main objectives of the International Tobacco Company? (3)

2 The government intervenes in the tobacco industry by putting health warnings on packets of cigarettes. Identify two advantages and two disadvantages of this policy. (4)

3 Name two other means by which the government intervenes in the tobacco industry. (2)

4 Apart from health scares, what other factors explain the decline in cigarette sales in the UK in recent years? (3)

5 The case study mentions social responsibility and ethics. Give definitions and examples of each of these terms. (4)

6 If Plover was to take 1% of the amount of the total annual market of 5000 million packs, how many packs would it sell? (3)

7 How could a tobacco company, based in the UK, respond to falling sales? Suggest one short term and one long term strategy. (6)

Further work

1 Communication core skills element 3.1 refers to taking part in discussions. Arrange a discussion on the issue of whether the sponsorship of sport by cigarette companies encourages people to smoke.

2 Some tobacco smokers are considering legal action for illness suffered as a result of smoking. As the marketing manager write a report to your Managing Director suggesting how cigarette companies could be affected if such cases came to court.

3 Is there a case for removing Teresa from the low tar campaign? Discuss the issues involved.

6 PORSCHE CARS

Elements: **1.1** PC 12345   **1.3** PC 123
AN **3.1** PC 12456   **3.2** PC 125

Key concepts: Purposes of business, Economic relationships, Data sources relevant to the supply of goods

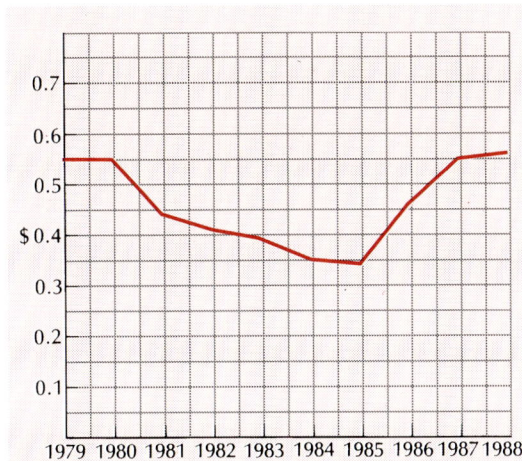

Graph showing $s per DM 1979–1988

The first half of the 1980s were marvellous for the German Porsche Company. A booming US economy was matched by the vast salary increases in the City of London, as the 'Big Bang' generated an upsurge in the demand for City dealers and analysts. The newly acquired wealth on both sides of the Atlantic found an outlet in the most flamboyant status symbol of its time – the Porsche sports car. The strength of the dollar made it possible for Porsche to sell in the United States at very profitable prices. As the United States president Ronald Reagan boasted about the 'mighty dollar', it seemed reasonable to assume that this would continue.

In the early 1980s, the Porsche family had appointed an extrovert German-born American (Peter Schutz) as Chairman. His strategy was a marketing-led one, of developing products and distribution networks that would enable sales to grow rapidly among the new, younger rich. America was booming, so it became the focus of his efforts. A new car, the 924, was designed that would bring the young buyer into the Porsche price range whilst they were not very high up the corporate ladder. Schutz believed that the qualities of their cars would ensure that as they rose in seniority, these people would trade up to the more expensive models. The 924 was priced at £12,000 – far below most Porsches, and comparable with BMWs and Audis. Its profit margins were lower than their other models, but the 924 sold very well in the United States, assisted by the strength of the dollar. By 1985/86, 65% of Porsche sales were in America, and extra factory capacity had been built to cope with record sales volumes.

Then, in 1987, everything turned sour. The dollar had been falling sharply against the Deutschmark, forcing all the German carmakers to increase their prices in the United States. This came at a time when traditional buyers of £30,000 Porsches were becoming dissatisfied with the image portrayed by the young drivers of models that looked similar, yet cost less than half the price. Worse still, in October 1987 came an unexpected and dramatic stock market crash. The sharp falls in share prices led to much lower levels of activity on the stock market, and a more sober approach to spending. Lower salary levels plus the new sense of cautiousness led to reduced demand for sports cars in general and Porsche in particular.

As capacity utilisation dropped and profits disappeared, the supervisory board

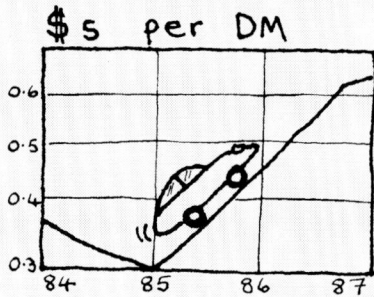

$ s per DM

replaced Schutz with Mr. Branitzki, their former finance director. What followed were swingeing cost and labour cuts, three day weeks in most of their factories, a rapid reassessment of its model and marketing policy, and sharp reductions in output; from 51,000 cars in 1986/87 to 31,000 in 1987/88. This proved sufficient to cut stocks from their pre-cash level of 15,000 cars to just 6,000. Rumours abounded of the firm collapsing under the weight of its problems, and of the chances of the family selling out to a wealthier rival.

By 1989, though, the firm had adjusted to a new, lower demand plateau by slashing its break-even output level. The 924 model was dropped, thereby increasing the average selling price by 10,000 Deutschmarks. New, high performance models were introduced that were tailored for the European market – helping to cut the US share of Porsche sales to 45% of the total. As well as streamlining and improving its product range, the company reconsidered its dealer network in Europe and America, putting the emphasis on specialisation rather than numbers.

Mr. Branitzki was concerned not only to restore the company's exclusive image, but also to prepare for the growing competition from Japanese sports cars in America. In 1988/89, the company spent 24% of its turnover on capital investment, training, and research and development – a considerable act of faith given that profits represented just 1% of sales revenue. By mid 1989, it was clear that Porsche had pulled through, with sales and profits rising once more.

Sources: *The Financial Times; HMSO UN Monthly Statistics Tables*

Questions

1   What is meant by the following: a market-led strategy, a strong dollar, break even level of output? **(3)**

2   What were the objectives of the German Porsche Company? **(2)**

3   Explain how exchange rate changes affected the demand for Porsche cars in the United States. **(3)**

4   What other factors affected the demand for the product? **(2)**

5   What sources of information did the Porsche Company use to help justify its change of policy from October 1987 onwards? **(2)**

6   From the data calculate the reduction in demand for Porsche cars in 1987/88. **(3)**

Further work

1   Part of your core skills in numeracy involves collecting and recording data. Keeping records of economic indicators will help towards Application of Number element 3.1.

Examples of economic indicators are:

■   interest rates

■   FT 100 share price index

■   exchange rates, such as £ against the Deutschmark.

For each of these, describe what it measures, how it is measured and find out its current value. Keep a record of any changes in these indicators for the same day each week over the next three months. Plot these changes on graph paper. Give reasons for any changes or trends. Indicate the source of your statistics on each of your graphs. You could use a computer to draw your charts.

7 ECONOMIC CHANGE AS AN EXTERNAL CONSTRAINT

Elements: **1.1** *PC 1* **1.2** *PC 234* **1.3** *PC 12*
   C **3.2** *PC 1234* **3.3** *PC 123* *AN* **3.2** *PC 1235*

Key concepts: Purposes of organisations, Demand and supply, Government intervention, Economic constraints

Rawsthorn Clothing had enjoyed three years of high profitability, thanks to a consumer spending boom that guaranteed high output and generous profit margins. By the third year it was looking to expand.

From its base in Burnley, the firm had been supplying the womenswear market for eighty years. Now the Directors had decided to diversify into children's clothing, for they thought an opportunity existed for a producer of high quality, classically-styled childrenswear. Despite their recent high profits, it was still necessary for them to borrow a substantial sum to establish a highly efficient, new factory.

This put their gearing up to 40% of capital employed, but the Directors were not concerned because their large retail customers had given enthusiastic verbal support to their scheme. Only the Production Director dissented from the Board's decision, on the grounds that:

'The labour content of a child's garment is only a little lower than that of an adult, yet the price of the finished product is far lower.'

Just five months before the new factory was due to open, however, the economic climate began to worsen. Signs of rising **inflation** had led the Chancellor to push interest rates up quite sharply, and the pound had risen as a result. By opening day, Rawsthorn was starting to detect a reduction in orders throughout its product range. The salesforce made it clear that this was due to three factors:

1 Retailers wanted to cut stock levels to reduce the finance cost;
2 Customers were buying less as rising mortgage rates cut their **disposable incomes**;
3 Those that were still buying tended to buy imported goods that were now more price competitive.

Even more worrying were reports from their overseas agents that Rawsthorn's recent price rises had hit sales more sharply than anticipated.

The poor trading conditions made retailers reluctant to stock Rawsthorn's new childrenswear

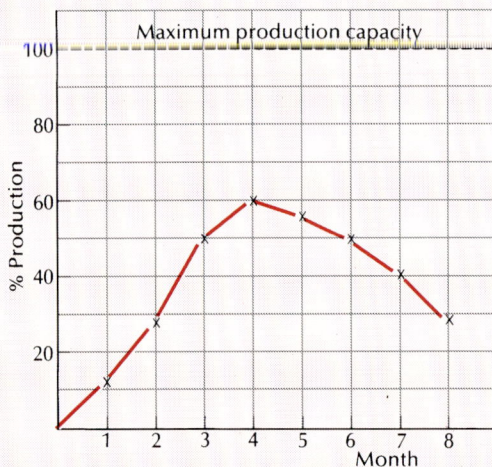

Production of childrenswear

range. The *Financial Times* monthly Retail Survey had just revealed that most shop managers expected weak consumer demand to persist for at least a year. Shopkeepers felt that its high quality, high price proposition was inappropriate to the current marketplace. Eight months after opening, the children's clothing factory was producing at only 30% of single-shift production capacity, causing heavy losses. Even the womenswear division could do no better than to break even, so the company as a whole was trading in the red.

Questions

1 Explain the meaning of the following: inflation, disposable income. **(2)**

2 If VAT were imposed at 7% on children's clothes what would be the new price of a pair of shoes previously priced at £19.99?
   What assumption would you make in carrying out this calculation? **(5)**

3 In the case, one problem is mentioned about the supply of children's wear. What is it? **(2)**

4 What is meant by 'the economic climate'. What could happen to cause the economic climate to worsen? **(4)**

5 How does cutting stock levels lead to a reduction in costs? **(2)**

6 How did the government intervene in the economy to affect Rawsthorn Clothing? Draw a simple flow diagram to show the sequence of events which led to a fall in orders. **(5)**

Further work

1 Outline three approaches which the Directors could adopt to bring the company out of the red. Prepare a presentation, as the marketing department, explaining your solutions. Include one visual aid. To fulfil the criteria your aid should be presented at the right point in your presentation. Be prepared to take questions from the audience.

2 In a period of falling incomes some goods and services may not experience a fall in demand. Discuss types of products and services that might be unaffected and give reasons for your choices.

3 To help meet core skill requirements in communications write a report to the Directors about the effect on the demand for children's clothing of:

   a the imposition of VAT at 7% on children's clothes,

   b a fall in the base interest rate of 2%.

   Your report should have a suitable format with a title, terms of reference, date and recommendations. Assume that these events both take place in the next year. Include the effects that both would have on the firm's various products in the short and long term.

8

ANGLO-JAPANESE CO-OPERATION

FRIDAY JULY 14 1989

Honda to take 20% Rover stake and build UK plant

In 1978, Honda was a minor Japanese producer of cars. It had built up a good reputation for reliability, but its narrow model range and concentration on small family cars meant that its reputation in Britain was undistinguished. British Leyland (B.L.), by contrast, was thought of as a major car producer, with a series of world famous car brands: Jaguar, Land Rover, Range Rover, MG sports cars, Triumph and Rover cars. Many were surprised, therefore, when it was announced that these two firms had signed an agreement to collaborate on the design and production of future models.

However, for B.L.'s new Chairman, Michael Edwardes, it represented an important part of his corporate strategy. He planned to cut back and **rationalise** B.L.'s output by closing loss-making factories, and moving production to relatively few, large plants. These would then have modern, highly automated machinery installed. In this way B.L. would be able to improve its low productivity. Yet the heavy **investment** in labour-saving machinery left insufficient capital for Research and Development on new models. The Ford Sierra, for instance, cost £650 million to develop. So agreement with Honda could spread R & D costs and help overcome this financial problem.

Honda's motive was to get access to the heavily protectionist European market. For although the Common Market provided free trade for members, many of the individual countries imposed import quotas and/or tariffs on outsiders. Italy, for example, limited Japanese car firms to a 1% market share, France to 3%, while Britain set a quota of 11%.

Honda could have tackled this problem by building a complete new factory in Britain or in continental Europe. Shortage of investment capital plus concern about how European governments would respond to this threat to local producers, made the **joint venture** seem more appealing. Furthermore, it would give Honda access to B.L.'s dealer network – the largest in Britain.

The first fruit of the joint venture was the production of Honda's Ballade model as the Triumph Acclaim at Cowley, Oxford. This helped to fill a noticeable gap in B.L.'s product range, and to keep up the level of **capacity utilisation** at the plant. When B.L. attempted to export the Acclaim, the Italian government insisted that it

Japanese investment in UK motor industry

Toyota Burnaston
200,000 cars a year by 1997-98. Carina-type car

Toyota Shotton
Engine plant
200,000 a year by 1997-98

Honda Longbridge
40,000 Honda Concerto cars a year from 1990 produced by Rover

Calsonic Llanelli
Radiators and heaters

Honda Swindon
100,000 cars a year by 1994. New car range

Honda Swindon
Engine plant
70,000 engines a year from 1990 for Honda Concerto, Rover 200/400 rising to 200,000 by 1994

Nissan Sunderland
200,000 cars a year by 1992-93. Bluebird and Micra Aiming for 400,000 by late 90s

IBC Vehicles Luton
(60% GM, 40% Isuzu)
40,000 vans a year rising to 70,000 vans and 4-wheel-drive vehicles by early 90s

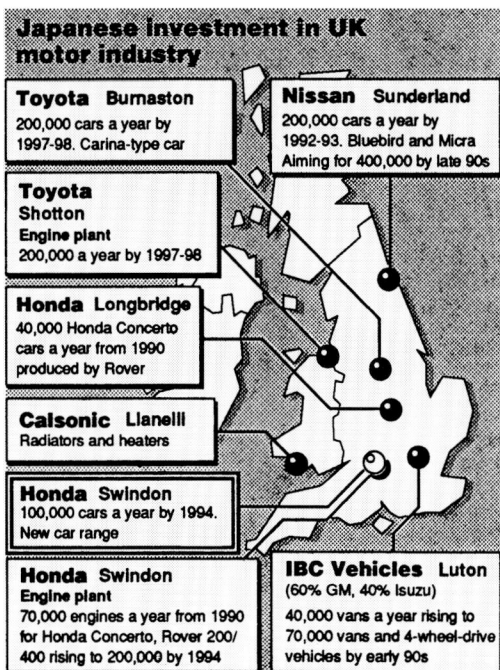

be counted as part of the Japanese quota. For although it had been assembled in Oxford, virtually all the components were Japanese.

As a result the next joint model, the Rover 200, was given a more British identity. British Leyland made some engineering and interior design changes, and fitted a British-made engine to one of the models in the range. It remained the case, however, that the British firm was contributing little to what had been advertised as a partnership.

During the mid 1980s the relationship deepened significantly, as Honda and the renamed Austin Rover began work on their first joint car development programme. This culminated in the launch of the Rover 800-Honda Legend cars in 1986. At the outset Rover was to produce the Legend for Honda while Honda was to produce the slightly differently styled Rover 800 in Japan. This arrangement would minimise transport costs and avoid trade barriers. However the production cooperation broke down in 1988 due to Honda dissatisfaction with the quality achieved by Rover on the Legends built in the United Kingdom. Even more embarrassing for Rover was that despite a large, expensive launch of the Rover Sterling in America, Honda succeeded with the Legend in the United States whereas the 800/Sterling flopped. It began to look as if Honda would not wish to have its name associated with Rover for much longer.

Yet on 13th July 1989 Honda announced that it intended to take a 20% stake in Rover, and would build a new manufacturing plant in the United Kingdom. *The Financial Times* described this as 'a far-reaching expansion of the Honda-Rover relationship'.

Honda's decision to become more heavily involved in U.K. production stemmed from their belief that the development of a single European market in 1992 represented both an opportunity and a threat. The former would come from the ending of separate national regulations on car design, safety and pollution. As a result, longer production runs would be possible to a single European specification. Yet 1992 also posed a threat – that the unified Europeans might decide to erect tough trade barriers, such as those in Italy or France. So Honda followed Nissan and Toyota's lead in deciding to operate within the European Community.

Honda's plan was to invest £300 million in a car assembly plant at Swindon. This would draw in components from Honda's own engine plant next door and from Rover's steel pressings and body panel factory a mile away. Swindon's location on the M4 and near to the M5 would also make it easy to get components from the continent or from the West Midlands. Other important locational factors were its convenience for Heathrow airport, plus its plentiful supply of land.

The objective was to produce 100,000 cars a year at Swindon by 1994, 60% of which would be exported to continental Europe. The process of achieving the objective would be tackled in stages:

Stage 1 Pilot production in late 1991, assembling kits imported from Japan; the Japanese traditionally take great care over this stage, to smooth out any problems before full production begins.

Stage 2 Commercial production starting in Autumn 1992, using 60% local content, and a single shift system.

Stage 3 Full output on a double shift producing 100,000 cars with 80% local content by 1994.

In fact, these targets slipped, so by early 1994 Honda was at least a year away from maximum production levels. This did not concern the Japanese until a bombshell hit on January 31st 1994. Honda's German rival BMW announced that it was buying the 80% of Rover not owned by Honda. This infuriated Honda, which had seen the Rover partnership as a key element in their long-term strategy for Europe. Now it would be inevitable that future Rover models would be based on BMW technology and methods – cutting Honda out.

Yet Honda could reflect upon a highly successful 16 year relationship. In 1978 British Leyland outsold Honda worldwide. By 1994 Honda's sales were four times those of Rover and they had a firm foothold in the UK and European car markets. Rover, meanwhile, had benefited greatly from learning at first hand about Japanese production methods and quality expectations. Such was the strength of Rover's image and model range in 1994, that few worried about redundancies following the BMW takeover. Rover was here to stay.

Source: The Financial Times; Independent on Sunday.

Questions

1 Explain the meaning of the following: rationalise, investment, joint venture, capacity utilisation. **(4)**

2 Identify four factors which influence the demand for a car. **(4)**

3 What were Honda's objectives? Were Rover's objectives any different? **(4)**

4 Give three reasons why Japanese car manufacturers looked for a location in the UK in the 1980s. **(3)**

5 Why did Honda prefer a location in the South of England, whereas Nissan chose the Northeast? **(3)**

6 The joint venture changed from collaboration to competition. Explain what this meant for Rover. **(1)**

7 What is meant by import protection? Give two examples of protection measures. **(2)**

8 Give two arguments for import protection and two arguments against. **(4)**

Further work

1 Part of the range in unit 1.2 requires you to study different approaches to economic management. In the 1980s the government encouraged the free market. What is meant by a free market? Some politicians and economists argue for government intervention in an economy. Using a business studies textbook research the types of measures that a government can take to intervene in an economy.

2 The General Agreement on Tariffs and Trade seeks a general lowering of the level of tariffs. Research the functions of this organisation. If possible use a CD Rom facility to look through the database of a newspaper such as *The Times* or *The Independent*.

3 A command economy is an alternative to a free market or mixed economy. Use an economics textbook to research:

■ a definition and examples of countries which have a command economy

■ the problems of such countries in managing their economies.

Russia and the former Eastern bloc countries have moved to a more market based economy. What does this mean?

Prepare your research in the form of a written report.

9

THE CHANGE IN GOVERNMENT

Elements: **1.1** *PC 1 2 3*   **1.2** *PC 1 2 3 4*   *RSA* **9.3** *PC 1 2 3 4*
C **3.1** *PC 1 2 3 4*   **3.2** *PC 1 2 3 4*   **3.3** *PC 1 2 3*
3.4 *PC 1 2 3*

Key concepts: Demand, Government intervention, Government policy, EU policy

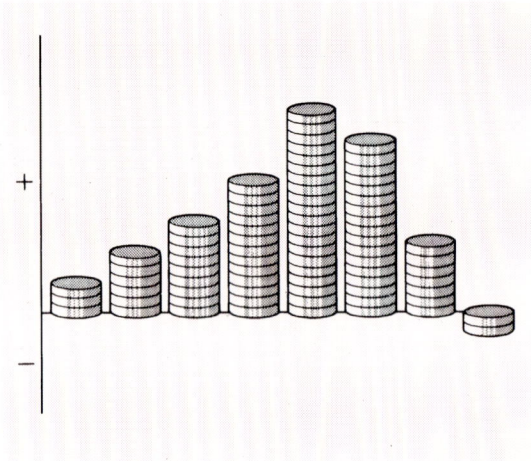

'Nothing's gone right since Labour got in,' said Mr. Martin bitterly. Protex Limited had been very successful in the years prior to the election. Booming consumer demand for home security systems had enabled the firm to increase sales 50% by volume (100% by value) in the previous four years. This had made it appear economic to automate their production methods, as the costs of the new, high technology equipment could be spread over many units of output. Furthermore, the labour-saving aspects of the equipment not only helped to keep direct costs low, but also helped Protex to cope with the coincidental fall in the number of young people within the workforce.

The Finance Director had been the only one to question whether it was wise to borrow substantial sums to finance a mechanisation programme that would be unprofitable if demand fell. The other Directors made it clear that they were confident that the fifteen years of continuous growth in the home security market was not likely to stop. Indeed, the Marketing Director had pointed out that the market had grown from £360 to £840 million over the previous four years. As the Board members took their seats at the start of the meeting, Mr. Martin (the Managing Director) muttered:

> 'Within two days they'd pushed interest rates up to protect the pound. Then came that first budget, with its ending of **mortgage tax relief** above the standard rate – that did for our top-priced, high margin range...'

The Marketing Director took the story up:

> 'Even worse was the decision to make every burglar alarm fitting firm apply for an operating licence. Half of them left the industry – they couldn't be bothered to go through the **red tape** to get their certificate; and of course those fitters were our customers.'

The Finance Director couldn't help wondering if there were other reasons they left the industry, but he said nothing. He wanted to get people onto the main item on the agenda – the cash flow crisis. He reminded everyone that they faced their poorest revenue period (December–February) with an overdraft just £20,000 below the limit set by the bank.

He presented the following figures:

Winter Quarter Cash Budget

Forecast revenues;	£540,000
Gross profit margin:	30%
Salaries and overheads:	£220,000
Interest payments:	£82,000

After they had discussed ways in which the cash shortfall could be funded, conversation returned to the change in the political context of their business operation. The Production Controller warned that a new environmental pollution law would soon force them to invest in £80,000 of filtration equipment, ending their discharges of industrial paints and dyes into the river. Mr. Martin exclaimed 'The Socialists want to put us all out of business! How can we compete with the Japanese with the millstones they place round our necks?'

As they were leaving the boardroom, the Finance Director mentioned to Mr. Martin that he had been glancing, that morning, at the Report and Accounts of Securimax (Protex's main United Kingdom rival).

'How are they doing?' asked Martin.

'Very well,' came the reply.

Questions

1 Explain the meaning of the terms mortgage tax relief and red tape. **(2)**

2 List three ways in which the government affected Protex Limited directly. **(3)**

3 What are the main influences on the demand for home security systems? **(4)**

4 Give two reasons why the government intervenes in the economy by passing legislation like the threatened environmental pollution law. **(2)**

5 Why was the threatened pollution law seen as unfair by Mr Martin? **(4)**

6 The Finance Director was not so sure that the government was to blame for all Protex's problems. What 'mistakes' had Protex made? **(5)**

Further work

1 To contribute towards Communication core skills element 3.2, write a letter from the Managing Director of Protex to the local Member of Parliament complaining about how the government had affected the firm.

2 A local sandpit has been excavated and filled up with domestic refuse. After many years of such a policy, methane gas builds up and causes subsidence in the local area. The methane is burnt off into the air, and 50 people have to be evacuated from their homes. The company responsible wants to take more land to expand the sand extraction area. You are a local resident already concerned with the smell from the sandpit, the rubbish that blows out when there is a strong wind and the general threat to the local area.

Form an action group and arrange to meet the sandpit company representatives. Divide into two groups and write a case for whichever side you are to represent. Arrange a meeting and discuss the issues involved. Research should look at existing laws and the social costs and benefits of the sand quarrying.

3 Within the EU, governments, citizens and businesses are all concerned that there should be common standards, for example on environmental pollution. What are the advantages of this for the EU as a whole? What problems are there in implementing common standards?

4 Businesses are seeking new sources of supply: renewable or recyclable. Devise an advertisement on behalf of the local council, urging people to recycle cans, newspapers and glass; or an advertisement from a business, emphasising its environmental awareness.

10 PRICE ELASTICITY AND PROFITS

Elements: **1.1** *PC 1 2 4* **1.3** *PC 1*
 C **3.1** *PC 1 2 3 4* **3.2** *PC 1 2 3 4* *AN* **3.2** *PC 1 2 3 4 5*

Key concepts: Demand, Supply, Price elasticity

The success of the low-calorie chocolate sector amazed everyone in the industry. It had started so weakly, with a 100-calorie bar with whipped nougat filling, topped with rice and covered in milk chocolate. Produced by a small firm from Finland, it received good distribution from a curious retail trade, but achieved less than a 0.5% market share. When one of the biscuit companies managed a successful launch, however, the three dominant chocolate firms (Mars, Cadbury's, and Rowntree/Nestlé) felt they had to protect their 90% market share.

In the first year after the three major firms launched their low-calorie chocolate bars, supply shortages kept prices high. Then, a series of new product launches made the marketplace increasingly competitive. One firm found that whereas a 2 pence price increase from 40 pence in the first year had cut demand by only 1%, eighteen months later a similar price rise on a 40 pence brand called 'Lo' led to a sales reduction from 50,000 units a week to 45,000. Given that its variable costs were 10 pence per unit, and fixed costs were £13,000 per week, this had quite a serious impact on the brand's profits.

In this new phase, the producers realised they had to look to improve their profitability by cutting costs rather than increasing prices. With low enough costs, they might even be able to increase profits by cutting their prices. Because contribution was already so high, most producers started by looking at ways of cutting their fixed and semi-variable costs. Only one decided to tackle variable costs first, on the grounds that:

> *'As fixed costs don't change, it must make sense to look
> for cuts from the variables.'*

The Finnish originator of the market sector found that its sales had slipped back sharply. Its new Managing Director was alarmed to find that its average total cost per unit was now 4 pence higher than its average selling price, leading to a £4,000 loss per week on its 100,000 units sales. When a Marketing Manager came with a proposal to double sales by improving distribution, he spluttered:

> *'Don't be ridiculous; that'll just double our losses!'*

Questions

1 Explain the meaning of the terms price elastic and price inelastic. **(2)**

2 How did supply and demand change as the market for low calorie chocolate developed? **(4)**

3 State two factors which might explain the initial success of low calorie chocolate. **(2)**

4 If a product has a demand which is price elastic, should a manufacturer increase or decrease the price? Explain your answer. **(3)**

5 Calculate the price elasticity of low calorie chocolate in the first year and compare it with that of the brand called Lo. **(4)**

Work out precisely the impact on Lo's profits. **(5)**

Further work

1 The case study illustrates the problems facing a small firm when its product can easily be copied by larger companies. Imagine that you are the marketing manager for the Finnish company. Write a report to the Managing Director, outlining various strategies that could be used in the face of such intense competition.

2 Manufacturers and retailers try to make the demand for their products as price inelastic as possible. Divide into groups and select one of the following products for each group. Give a presentation, explaining how marketing is able to make demand more price inelastic.

- *The Financial Times*
- Gold Blend coffee
- Fairy Liquid
- a subscription to a Sky Movie channel.

3 In 1993 News International reduced the price of *The Sun* from 25p to 20p, and *The Times* from 45p to 30p. What percentage fall did each of these price cuts represent? Which other newspapers have been affected by these changes and what strategies could they adopt to counter these moves?

11 A PRESSURE GROUP TRIUMPH

Elements: **1.1** *PC 1 2* **1.2** *PC 2 3 4* **1.3** *PC 1*
C **3.4** *PC 1 2 3* IT **3.3** *PC 1 2 3 4*

Key concepts: Government policy, Barriers to competition, Pressure groups,
Monopolies and Mergers Commission

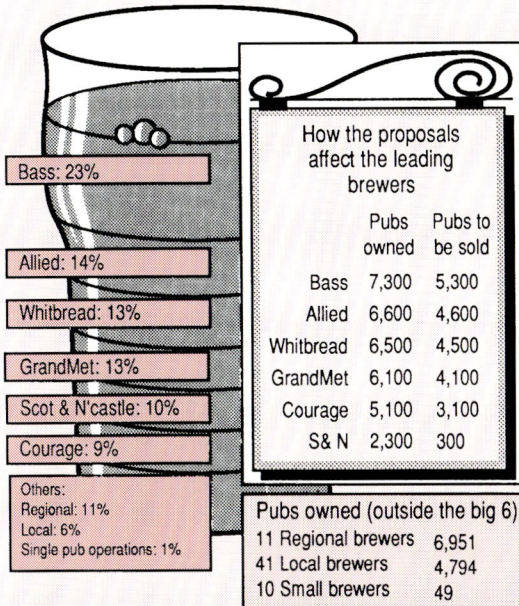

How the proposals affect the leading brewers		
	Pubs owned	Pubs to be sold
Bass	7,300	5,300
Allied	6,600	4,600
Whitbread	6,500	4,500
GrandMet	6,100	4,100
Courage	5,100	3,100
S & N	2,300	300

Pubs owned (outside the big 6)	
11 Regional brewers	6,951
41 Local brewers	4,794
10 Small brewers	49

Bass: 23%
Allied: 14%
Whitbread: 13%
GrandMet: 13%
Scot & N'castle: 10%
Courage: 9%
Others:
Regional: 11%
Local: 6%
Single pub operations: 1%

The big brewers' market shares

During the 1980s, the government prided itself on its challenges to cosy monopoly practices. It took on trade unions, the opticians, direct labour organisations of local councils, and many nationalised industries – and won. Then, in 1989, it took on the breweries, long known to be one of the country's most powerful lobbyists.

The Monopolies and Mergers Commission (MMC) had been asked by the Office of Fair Trading to look into Britain's unique system of 'tied' houses. The system was one of vertical integration, in which breweries controlled many of their outlets (pubs and off-licences). Apart from brewery-owned pubs, tenant landlords were tied into selling just one supplier's beer, spirits and soft drinks. Even apparently 'free' houses were being tied by brewers offering low interest rate loans in return for exclusive selling rights. The MMC estimated that more than 87% of pubs were brewery-controlled.

The March 1989 report described the £16 billion industry as a 'complex monopoly' in which it found 'hostility to would-be competitors and distortions of trade' wherever it looked. The brewers were also judged to have used their monopoly power to impose unjustified price increases. Since 1979 the price of a pint of bitter (excluding VAT and excise duties) had risen by 15% more than inflation generally, as measured by the Retail Prices Index. The Commission was also critical of the 10 pence price premium charged for lager, for which it found no good reason. Indeed, some brewers had lower production costs for lager than for other beers.

According to the MMC, this overcharging was due to the ability of the big firms to keep out the many small, local brewers. Monopoly power was concentrated among the 'Big 6' (see diagram); together they held 82% of the market. Individual market shares appeared quite low, but should be thought of as national averages, hiding the true regional pattern. In much of Norfolk, for instance, Grand Metropolitan held over 40% of the market share; the same was true of Allied (Tetley's) in Yorkshire and Courage in Kent.

The MMC's recommended solution proved more sweeping than the industry

had expected:

1 A ceiling of 2,000 pubs per brewer. This would only affect the 'Big 6', forcing Bass, for instance, to sell off 5,300.
2 A ban on any more loans made in return for sales of a particular brewer's beer.
3 Every publican to have the right to buy a 'guest beer', not produced by the brewer owning the pub.
4 Greater security of tenure for tenant landlords.

To enormous approval from the Consumers' Association and from Fleet Street, Trade Secretary Lord Young said that he was 'minded' to accept the proposals. He showed his backing for the report by stating publicly, on 21st March, that:

> *'The MMC conclude that this complex monopoly restricts competition at all levels, against the public interest.'*

The 'Big 6', through the employers' pressure group The Brewers Society, then set about demolishing the MMC's case and recommendations. A massive £6 million advertising campaign was launched. It held out the grim prospect of quaint countryside locals being sold off, if the Commission was successful. Journalists and MPs were bombarded with worried letters from small brewers, all claiming to be acting independently of the Brewers Society. Other independent breweries welcomed the MMC report, and claimed that the 'Big 6' were putting pressure on the smaller firms. The President of the tenant landlords' group went even further. He declared that breweries were threatening to sack landlords who failed to support the fight against the MMC.

Even more significant was the pressure the brewers managed to put on Lord Young from the government's own back benches. By early May, fifty Conservative MPs had signed a Commons motion congratulating 'this highly competitive industry' on its huge investment in improvements to pubs. The powerful Conservative backbench 1922 Committee summoned Lord Young to quiz him on his plans. Given the anti-monopoly stance of so many Tories, it was unclear why such support was being given to the brewers. Labour Party claims that the Tories were looking after their paymasters were countered by Conservatives who stressed that they were simply passing on the concerns of their constituents. Soon afterwards, newspapers began writing stories about Department of Trade meetings with the brewers, and about probable concessions.

On 10th July, Lord Young published his plan for dealing with the beer market. It represented a remarkable climb-down from what he had been 'minded' to accept just four months before. The *Financial Times* commented that 'the beerage has won hands down'. Under Young's compromise plan:

1   Brewers would not have to sell off any pubs, but half of those above the 2,000 level would have to become free houses; owned by the brewery but (in theory) free to buy from any supplier.

2   All tied and tenanted pubs must sell at least one cask-conditioned ('real ale') guest beer.

3   A review of the licensing system which restricted the opening of new pubs to those for which a local 'need' could be demonstrated (the brewers used this to limit competition).

The value of brewery shares jumped up in response to this heavy dilution of the original proposals. Opposition MPs claimed that Lord Young had caved in to the brewers and their strong political lobby. With cruel timing, several brewers announced price rises of up to 8 pence a pint the following day. This gave Young's opponents more ammunition to fire at him. It is not known if this brush with the power of the brewery vested interests contributed to Lord Young's resignation from the government a month later.

Sources: *The Financial Times; The Independent; The Publican; The Times*

Questions

1   The breweries are keen to control off-licences and pubs. Give three advantages to the breweries of this control.   **(3)**

2   Explain the broad aims of a pressure group.   **(2)**

3   What practices were taking place to cause the brewers' monopoly to be reported to the Monopolies and Mergers Commission?   **(3)**

4   How could the companies attempt to explain the 10% price premium for lager?   **(5)**

5   Firms in the private sector may try to profit maximise. What other objectives are apparent from the breweries case study?   **(2)**

Further work

1   Produce a diagram to illustrate 'The big brewers' market share', preferably using a suitable computer package. Include an appropriate title, key and scale.

Write a brief description of how the market would be affected if Bass took over Whitbread.

If your text is wordprocessed, transfer it onto the same page as the graph.

2   Use this case study as a basis to carry out your own research into how a pressure group can influence and lobby a government either in a local or national context. You may wish to research Greenpeace, a Trade Union, or the Consumers' Association. A report or presentation could investigate history, objectives and successes.

3   Communications element 3.4 includes the need to respond to a letter on a sensitive issue (this is covered on page 20). Imagine that you are the public relations manager of a large regional brewery. You receive a sensitive letter from a neighbour of one of your tied outlets, complaining about the noise levels from the local public house. Draft a suitable reply, stating the steps that you would take to ensure that there will be no repetition of the high level of noise.

12 CHOCOLATE SOLDIERS – THE ROWNTREE TAKEOVER

Elements: *1.1* PC 12345   *1.2* PC 1234   *1.3* PC 1

Key concepts: Demand, Government and EU policy, Reasons for government intervention, Supply, EU policy

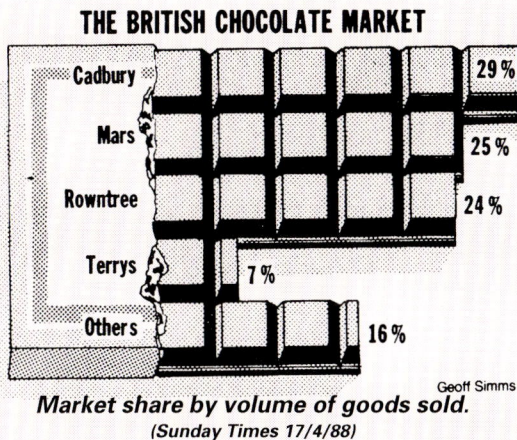

THE BRITISH CHOCOLATE MARKET

Cadbury	29%
Mars	25%
Rowntree	24%
Terrys	7%
Others	16%

Geoff Simms

Market share by volume of goods sold.
(Sunday Times 17/4/88)

At 8.30 a.m. on 13th April 1988, the Swiss chocolate group Suchard launched a '**dawn raid**' on the shares of Rowntree. In a thirty-five minute buying spree they bought £160 million of Rowntree's shares in the London stock market – 14.9% of the British firm's share capital. This was achieved by offering shareholders 630 pence for shares worth 475 pence the previous day. Suchard made it clear that their objective was to build a 25% stake in Rowntree; few doubted that it would soon be used to launch a full take-over bid.

Rowntree's Chairman said: 'Suchard may need Rowntree, but Rowntree does not need Suchard.' Although he was clearly shocked at the threat to the York firm's 130-year history, the Chairman seemed confident that he could fight off a competitor of a similar size to Rowntree itself. As he proclaimed:

'*Rowntree, the largest confectionery business in the United Kingdom, has one of the best **portfolios of brand names** in the world... Kit Kat, Smarties, and After Eight have taken years of investment.*'

Two weeks passed before the real hammer blow – a full take-over bid at 890 pence cash from the huge Nestlé group (the world's biggest food company). This valued Rowntree at £2.1 billion.

ROWNTREE

share price

APRIL

Source: Datastream

The Swiss giant made it clear that in the run up to 1992, it was not willing to allow Suchard to gain such a strong position in the European chocolate market. A City analyst maintained that:

'*Nestlé cannot afford to allow Rowntree to fall to Suchard. Rowntree is a dead duck.*'

The latter view came from examination of Nestlé's balance sheet. This showed that the Swiss multinational had bank deposits worth £2.7 billion. So it could swallow Rowntree from, in effect, its petty cash. With sales and profits more than 500% higher than either Rowntree or Suchard, Nestlé could not be stopped in the marketplace. So action switched to the only other forum for determining the outcome – the government and its Monopolies and Mergers Commission.

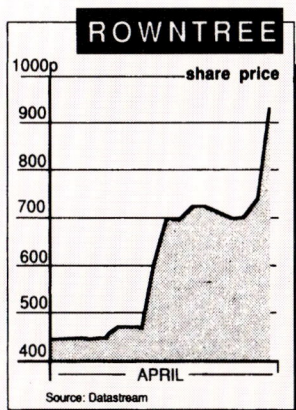

For Rowntree's management there appeared to be 3 possible ways of persuading the government to intervene:

1   On the grounds that merger would be anti-competitive, given Nestlé's substantial share of the European chocolate market.

2   That as Swiss laws enabled its companies to protect themselves from being taken over, it would be unfair to allow a Swiss predator to buy up a British firm.

3   That Rowntree's unusual position of being a major British company based in the North meant that keeping it independent was important for **regional policy**.

Rowntree's problem with the first possibility can be seen in the table below. Neither Nestlé's 3% nor Suchard's 2% of the U.K. chocolate market would add sufficient to Rowntree's market share even to match that of Cadbury's. Many politicians suggested that with the onset of the single European market in 1992, the proper consideration should be European market shares, but the British government rejected this view.

European chocolate confectionery market shares

	UK	Austria	Belgium	France	Italy	Netherlands	Switzerland	W. Germany	Total
	(% by sales value)								
Mars	24	4	6	11	1	23	9	22	17
Suchard	2	73	82	13	–	–	17	15	13
Rowntree	26	–	2	17	–	13	–	3	11
Ferrero	2	–	5	6	34	–	–	16	10
Cadbury	30	–	–	8	–	–	–	–	9
Nestlé	3	5	3	10	5	–	17	8	9

Source: *Henderson Crosthwaite (Financial Times 27/4/88)*

Rowntree's chose to present an upbeat image as a caring employer, a solidly northern firm, and the developer of world markets for such British products as After Eights and the Lion Bar. The latter became an important part of Rowntree's defence. For, despite its weak performance in Britain, the Lion bar had become a notable success in the rest of Europe. Rowntree's management was keen to get across the notion that the sleepy Swiss producers of solid chocolate bars were desperate to buy a firm with proven skills in the marketing of the growing chocolate 'count-lines' sector (single, hand-held bars such as Mars, Flake, and Lion).

The battle of the brand names

Rowntree	Nestlé	Suchard
Kit Kat	Nescafé	Toblerone
Quality Street	Carnation	Milka
Aero	Crosse & Blackwell	Cote D'Or
Black Magic	Findus	
Rolo	L'Oreal	
After Eight	Chambourcy	
Smarties	Libby's	
Yorkie	Milky Bar	

Suchard's Chairman was quite open about the attractions of Rowntrees:

> *'Rowntree is an excellent company with a fascinating range of brands. Brands are the most important thing.'*

Behind the scenes, Rowntree carried out extensive lobbying of M.P.s, Ministers, and the employers' organisation, the Confederation of British Industry (the C.B.I.). Public Relations schemes were devised to promote the idea: 'Hands Off Rowntree'. In early May the C.B.I. recommended that the takeover be referred by the government to the Monopolies and Mergers Commission. That would ensure the suspension of the bid for many months while its likely impact was investigated. This source of pressure on the government was silenced, however, when the C.B.I. gave in to Nestlé's public threat to cancel its membership.

The Rowntree unions were also active in supporting the existing management. For the Rowntree family had established at the turn of the century a pattern of **paternalism** that led to the early introduction of a shorter working week, a pension scheme, and good working conditions. Recent managements had tended to maintain these traditions, so the workforce were especially loyal to the company.

By mid May, over two hundred M.P.s had signed motions of support for Rowntree. They were thwarted, though, by the government's desire to be seen to be welcoming to foreign firms, in the hope of attracting investment into extra production here. On 25th May, Lord Young announced that the Department of Trade would not be recommending that the bid be investigated. Although the Labour Party's Bryan Gould described this as a 'betrayal of British industry', many commentators accepted the government's stance that:

> *'Intervention by public authorities in lawful commercial transactions should be kept to a minimum since... decisions of private decision makers in competitive markets result in the most desirable outcomes for the economy as a whole.'*

The following day Suchard challenged Nestlé with a £2.32 billion counter-bid at 950 pence a share. This may well have been no more than a ploy to push Nestlé into paying more for Rowntree shares. For Suchard already held over a £100 million profit on the shares they had bought for 630 pence just six weeks before. It convinced Rowntree's largest union that the end was near, however, for on 1st June its Executive urged the management to end their opposition to the bids, and to start negotiating with both of the Swiss firms. The union believed it essential that the new owners should view their Rowntree division with favour, not hostility.

The battle ended, as expected, with a knock-out blow by Nestlé. On 23rd June Nestlé offered 1075 pence (£2.55 billion), which Suchard accepted was more than it could afford. Having accumulated a 29.9% stake in Rowntree, Suchard could sell its shares to Nestlé at a profit of more than £200 million. Nestlé announced that they had given assurances that York would continue to be the centre of Rowntree activity, and that the firm's employment policy and practices would be respected. Nevertheless, the Swiss would not give any job guarantees to Rowntree's 13,000 U.K. workers. Within a few days Nestlé had won the acceptance of the Rowntree Board and shareholders.

Following Nestlé's success, two issues continue to be hotly debated:

1   Is it right to allow successful, profitable, well-managed firms like Rowntree to be taken over unless the bidder can demonstrate some clear social or economic benefit?

2   Do company accounts give sufficient weight to the enormous value of the 'goodwill' represented by the value of brand names? For one of the reasons that Rowntree was 'a dead duck' was because the Swiss rivals were able to offer Rowntree shareholders such a large premium over the pre-bid value of the shares.

Sources: *The Financial Times; The Guardian; The Independent; The Observer; The Sunday Times*

Questions

1   Explain the following terms: dawn raid, portfolio of brand names, regional policy, paternalism. **(4)**

2   Give four reasons why Suchard wanted to buy Rowntree. **(4)**

3   Nestlé also wanted to buy Rowntree. Were the reasons for their interest different from Suchard's? Explain your answer. **(4)**

4   Study the diagram showing Rowntree's share price. What were the causes of the April changes in price? **(3)**

5   If 1,000 Rowntree shares were bought on April 12th how much would shareholders have received if they sold them on:

   a   April 13th

   b   June 23rd? **(4)**

6   Suchard lost the battle to take over Rowntree, but gained financially. Explain why. **(3)**

7   The government did not intervene in the takeover. Explain why the takeover was left to the market. **(3)**

Further work

1   To complete element 1.2, there should be an awareness of EU policies. Using reference books in your library, describe and explain how any two of the following EU policies affect business organisations:

- creation of a single integrated market
- freedom of movement of goods
- the movement towards single standards and harmonisation of laws.

13 DE LOREAN CARS – 'FROM COW PASTURE TO PRODUCTION'

Elements: **1.1** *PC 2* **1.2** *PC 234*
AN 3.2 *PC 12345*

Key concepts: Government intervention, Price elasticity of demand, Location

On 3rd August 1978, Mr. John De Lorean announced agreement with the Labour government on a financing package for the establishment of a new sports car factory in Belfast, Northern Ireland. De Lorean, an American former vice-president of General Motors (the world's largest car producer), was to invest £20 million, with government funded bodies such as the Northern Ireland Development Agency (NIDA) putting in £45 million. NIDA would have an equity stake worth £15 million, and would also provide grants and loans.

Sceptics pointed out that the Irish government had already turned the scheme down, believing it to be too risky. Their doubts hinged on the sales forecasts being put forward for an untried product, and on technological factors. De Lorean's prototype called for construction methods never before used in the motor industry.

Mr. Roy Mason, the Northern Ireland Secretary of State, was understandably jubilant, however. It had long been his belief that the sectarian violence in Northern Ireland was connected with the high unemployment. Indeed violence and economic underdevelopment seemed to form a vicious circle. Now he could announce a factory to be sited next to one of Belfast's largest Catholic housing estates, where male unemployment stood at 35%. Its projected employment of 2,000 people could help break through that circle.

De Lorean announced that:

> *'We aim to move from cow pasture to production within eighteen months.'*

Some regarded his choice of this **'greenfield' site** as risky, because the lack of local car production meant that his workforce would be completely inexperienced. De Lorean countered this by stressing the potential benefits of a workforce with no traditional **restrictive practices**.

The car, to be designed by the Italian Giugiaro, would have a body shell of glass fibre-reinforced plastic bonded to a stainless steel outer skin. Although technologically novel (and therefore potentially troublesome) it conformed to an essential element in De Lorean's marketing proposition. He was famous in the United States as the man who quit General Motors, and then exposed that company's practice of 'built-in obsolescence', i.e. they used materials and components with a relatively short life-span, so that customers would need to replace their car regularly. De Lorean had long promoted the notion of an 'ethical' car that would last fifteen years, not five. He claimed that this new car would be completely rustproof, and therefore the body could last for ever. It was to be marketed in the United States alone, as that was where De Lorean's standing meant that dealers were prepared to invest in the project. And at an anticipated $14,000 it would be priced below General Motor's Corvette – the biggest selling sports car in the United States. Hence the expectation of sales of 30,000 cars a year.

By August 1980, 'technical problems' had caused sufficient delays for De Lorean to have to warn his U.S. dealers that the car's launch would have to be put back from November to early 1981. It also meant that extra funds were needed, which the firm managed to get from the (by now, Conservative) government.

On 21st January 1981, De Lorean drove one of the first finished production cars off the assembly line. He announced that a batch of 700 cars would be delivered to U.S. dealers in April. Cars were said to be coming off the line at a rate of three per day, rising to thirty per day by the end of the following month. The U.S. dealers' worries about the supply delays were compounded by the company's ever escalating view of the car's price tag. In August 1980, De Lorean declared that his pricing strategy was that the car should sell for just under $20,000 – about the same as the Corvette. Now, in January 1981, he was speaking of 'the mid $20,000s', i.e. around 20% more than the U.S. produced rival. A major Kansas City car dealer said that the price was pressing up against the threshold at which consumer resistance could be expected: 'If it goes above $24,000 we have a problem'. De Lorean blamed the price escalation on higher inflation in the United Kingdom than in the United States, and the unexpected strength of sterling (see Appendix A).

By the end of January it was plain that the De Lorean Motor Company (DMC) had a major cash crisis. Successive governments had already invested £70 million in the project, and now the firm wanted a guarantee of a £10 million bank loan to 'help resolve a short term working capital requirement'. The problem was that a series of production hitches had delayed the launch by six months. So continuing production expenditure, a wage bill of over £100,000 per week, plus steady stockbuilding were all draining cash at a time when none was coming in. In February the government provided the £10 million bank guarantee, but stated that no more public money would be made available to the project.

The crisis of confidence in DMC during January evaporated by May. Motoring journalists gushed over the 2.8 litre V6 engine, the gull-wing doors and the fifteen year life-span of the bodies. They referred to the 12,000 cars expected to be sold in the United States during 1981 at $25,000 each, and the resultant royalties of £2.4 million that the U.K. government could expect to receive (£185 on each of the first 90,000 cars, and £45 on each subsequent one). Throughout the media there was a feeling of admiration for DMC's achievement in creating a car factory from nothing; and a fervent wish that its success would boost Belfast. So when, on 22nd May, the government announced a guarantee of a further £7 million, it received little criticism for changing its mind on increasing its financial commitment.

By August 1981 more than 2,000 people were employed at the Belfast plant. The firm claimed fifty to sixty cars were being built per day. Demand in the United States was said to be phenomenal. Yet in early 1982 DMC was put on a three day week and output was halved from 400 to 200 per week. It emerged that low demand had led to a stockpile of 2,500 unsold cars. De Lorean blamed this on the fierce recession in the U.S. market for new cars; some of the dealers felt that the very poor standard of finish on the cars was the key factor.

The true market potential of the De Lorean car began to come under serious scrutiny. DMC's construction, production and cash flow difficulties had always been presented to the public in the context of an apparently guaranteed level of demand. It had been suggested that the firm's U.S. dealers had placed firm orders for the first two years' production (40,000 cars). Also, the original government investment had been made after the McKinsey management consultancy had forecast demand for 30,000 units per year. What had not been revealed was that McKinsey had analysed the likely price elasticity of the car. At approximate price parity with the Corvette, demand should be for 30,000; but at $25,000 for a De Lorean against $20,000 for a Corvette the McKinsey formula forecast demand of just 15,000 units. Furthermore the forecasts were based on a healthy U.S. car market, whereas 1981 proved the worst in twenty years. Sports car sales were hit especially hard as recession mentality took its grip on sales of luxury items. Of the 7,000 cars built by DMC in 1981, only 3,000 were actually registered to owners.

With DMC's problems becoming evermore public knowledge, rumours began to be reported in the press about De Lorean's 'Concorde lifestyle'. For the head of a publicly funded business in severe financial difficulties, his high profile in New York's social scene was disturbing. Especially as it became clear that De Lorean himself had never invested much capital in the project: a later Report by the Public Accounts Committee of the House of Commons showed that his total capital investment amounted to less than £1 million. On 28th January 1982 the Labour M.P. Bob Cryer said bitterly:

> *'This particular venture appears to be a rip-off for the directors and a disaster for the workers.'*

The following day 1,100 redundancies were announced at the plant, bringing the workforce down to 1,500. But this could not prevent the firm from insolvency. On 19th February, 1982 the company went into voluntary receivership. It owed £31 million to its suppliers and had an unsold stock of 3,000 cars. The Receiver said he would keep the business going and look for a buyer. The hoped-for upturn in U.S. demand during the Spring sales peak failed to materialise, however, and wave after wave of redundancies cut the workforce down to a few maintenance staff by the Autumn. With no buyer for the firm and no customers for its products, virtually all the government's investment was lost. Attempts to retrieve some from John De Lorean (on grounds of fraudulent diversion of funds) faltered in the United States courts.

To Mrs. Thatcher's government it was proof that governments should not get involved directly in business activity. The Labour opposition preferred to think of it as an example of how greedy and cynical entrepreneurs can be. Perhaps all it proves, however, is that the internal constraints upon the successful establishment of a new manufacturing firm are troublesome enough; the external factors make it a matter of luck as well.

Sources: *The Financial Times; The Guardian; The Times*

APPENDIX A: UK & US Exchange rates and Inflation rates 1978–1982

	US $ per £	UK inflation %	US inflation %
1978	1.90	9.0	6.8
1979	2.10	13.0	11.4
1980	2.30	18.0	13.6
1981	2.05	12.0	10.4
1982	1.75	8.0	6.4

Sources: *HMSO Annual Abstract of Statistics; U.N. Statistical Yearbook.*

Questions

1 What is meant by the terms greenfield site and restrictive practices? (2)

2 How did successive governments intervene and help the De Lorean car factory? (3)

3 If sales were expected to be 30 000 cars at $14 000 and 12 000 cars at $25 000, calculate the total revenue at each of the prices. (2)

4 Calculate the price elasticity of the De Lorean car according to the McKinsey report. (4)

5 What factors caused the price of the car to reach $25 000? (4)

6 What were the difficulties involved in locating the car plant in Northern Ireland? Was the project doomed from the beginning? (5)

Further work

1 To complete the range on element 1.2, you need to have an understanding of the impact of EU and UK government policy on business. In groups, action plan a visit to a local business to find out how it is affected; areas of enquiry could include:

■ export and imports of materials/products

■ foreign exchange dealings

■ EU rules and regulations.

2 To help complete the range and prepare for the unit test it would be useful to look at back copies of newspapers to locate examples of UK government and EU policies which affect business organisations. Take cuttings from the last two or three weeks and explain the type of intervention and the reason for it. For each example give a date and name the source of information. If you have access to a CD Rom facility this could be used. The range statements include the following reasons for intervention:

■ to support competition

■ to eliminate barriers to competition

■ to eliminate inequality of opportunity

■ to sustain employment

■ to give subsidies.

14 THE NEW LASER SCANNING SYSTEM

Elements: **2.1** *PC 1 2 3 4 5* **2.2** *PC 1 2 3 4 5* **2.3** *PC 1 2 3 4 5*
C **3.1** *PC 1 2 3 4*

Key concepts: Storing and using information, Effects of technology in the workplace

When the laser scanning system was first mentioned, Suzanne felt the same sense of mild anticipation as the other check-out staff. The management explained that because it would do away with individual item pricing, it would prevent friction with customers over missing or incorrect prices. Furthermore, the fact that it was modern technology might make it easier to get another job in the future.

In the lead up to the changeover, all the staff went on a two day training course. This was interesting and gave Suzanne a chance to get to know her fellow workers far better than ever before. So by the time it was installed, her attitude to the system was very positive. This was strengthened further in the early weeks, when managers came round regularly to ask her how it was going, and when customers chatted about their likes and dislikes of the high-speed service.

The first moment of doubt came when she overheard managers discussing 'IPMs'. The store manager was telling the personnel manager that:

> *'Three of the staff are so far down on their IPMs that they're dragging the store average down. You must sort them out.'*

It soon became clear that IPM stood for Items Per Minute, and that the computerised tills not only checked out groceries, but also checked on staff. When managers realised that information was spreading on the grapevine, they called a meeting to explain how this information was to be used. All the staff were given a copy of the computer print-out from the previous week, as shown below.

Week 4 Summary Of Checkout Operator Productivity (Rear Of Store Operators Only)

Operator	Hours worked	Total items	Average IPM	Operators variance from their average	
				IPM in in best hour	IPM in worst hour
Trudy S.	22	31,680	24	32	17
Simon G.	36	38,880	18	33	13
David W.	14	14,280	17	23	14
Tracy F.	35	52,500	25	30	21
Sonal S.	35	48,300	23	26	20
Suzanne P.	18	31,320	29	38	22
Jane H.	35	40,000	19	23	16
Steve H.	24	31,700	22	34	13
Eileen L.	38	57,000	25	36	16
Mutlu M.	20	25,200	21	27	17
AVERAGE	27.7	37,060	22.3	30	17
U.K. AVERAGE	24.5	36,450	24.8	30	20

The ten check-out staff were told that head office set a minimum IPM target of 22 per head. Any who failed to achieve this would be retrained, moved to other duties, or have fewer requests to work extra hours. Steve asked if there was any way the till could give them a running score of how they were doing, but apparently there was not. At the end of the session, the personnel manager asked Jane, Steve, Simon and David to stay behind.

Suzanne felt pleased to see how well she had been doing, and wondered whether the company might introduce a bonus scheme based upon IPM performance. She did feel disturbed, though, to think that this clever monitoring device had been sprung upon them. What came as a shock, however, was the pressure she found herself under at break time. Steve and Simon (both students at her college) told her bitterly that their performance had been compared directly with hers. Simon finished off by saying:

> 'What are you doing it for? They're making massive enough profits anyway. You ought to stop crawling and think of your mates.'

Over the following weeks Suzanne tried to slow down her workrate, but she found this surprisingly hard; she preferred to work at her natural, fast pace. Nevertheless, anything was preferable to poisoning her relationships with her work and college friends.

After four weeks, Steve and Simon had pushed their productivity level up to 22, while Suzanne's had slipped back to 25. The store managers held another meeting, though, because they were getting pressure from the Regional Manager to boost the IPM score up from the 22.8 level it had now stabilised at. The Deputy Store Manager showed clear signs of stress as he shouted:

> 'We've flogged ourselves sorting out all the teething problems with the new system. You don't know the half of it. All you have to do is to work reasonably hard. We're the ones with the hassles – don't make me pass them on to you.'

As Suzanne's productivity slid back up towards the 30 IPM level, she began to realise how much her back ached after a busy Saturday. During a dull Geography lesson the following Monday, she scribbled some numbers down on paper.

Over the following months several of the original staff left. Many complained about back pains; some also said that migraines were ruining their evenings. All felt that the scanning machines had made their job even more repetitive than before. With new, inexperienced staff being recruited, the IPM average for the store worsened. The Deputy Manager began to pressurise the older hands to work more hours; and when Steve slipped back to an IPM of 19 in the week of the mock A-level exams, the same manager bellowed at him. It was all too much, Suzanne handed in her notice that night.

Saturday hours

8 30 – 12 15 am =	3 ¾ hours
1 00 – 3 15 pm =	2 ¼ hours
3 30 – 6 00 pm =	2 ½ hours
	8 ½ hours

8½ hours × 60 mins = 510 mins

510 × 30 IPM = 15 300 items

15 300 × (say) ½ lb = 7650 lbs

7650 lbs = 1440 lbs

= 5·3 tons a day !!

5·3 tons lifted for wages of £23·80 !

Questions

1 State three initial advantages to the workforce of the new technology. **(3)**

2 Give three possible reasons why the management introduced this new laser checkout system. **(3)**

3 To what extent was the management responsible for the problems involved in the new system? **(3)**

4 How could the management deal with the imbalance of checkout operator productivity using a more sympathetic approach? **(4)**

5 Examine the summary of checkout operator productivity. Describe and give possible reasons for any operator variations. **(5)**

6 Give two possible reasons why a supermarket may change from counting items per minute to items per hour. **(2)**

Further work

1 In order to meet the performance criteria it would be valuable to arrange a visit to a local business or other suitable organisation to analyse and evaluate systems used. An example from a supermarket visit might include a report on the following:

- A description of systems used, for example: stock control, deliveries, a part-time staff rota, checkout operations.

- To what extent are the systems computerised?

- How well do the systems meet the needs of the organisation?

- What problems are involved in implementing new systems?

- Which systems are not capable or worth computerising?

- How does the Data Protection Act affect your record keeping?

(Other suitable visits could be to a library or a building society.)

2 Certain colleges have introduced a swipe card reader to register students. A typical system costs nearly £10,000 to purchase and install. Discuss the advantages and disadvantages of the system for:

a the student

b the college.

15 A DAY IN THE LIFE OF TERESA TRAVIS

Elements: **2.2** *PC 12345* **2.3** *PC 1245*
C **3.2** *PC 1234*

Key concepts: Communication systems, Electronic systems, Enhanced telephone systems

Teresa sat down at her desk and switched on the PC. It flashed up two memos, one from the accounts department and another from the Manchester office. As she read them, her assistant came in with coffee and the mail. 'Deal with Manchester please, Anne,' she said, nodding at the screen.

Anne went over to her desk and called up the memo, to puzzle over its contents and a suitable response. As usual, Teresa had handed on a task that Anne knew little about; and if she quizzed her boss about it there was likely to be a sharp retort about 'showing responsibility'. The manager of the Manchester office wanted to know the progress being made on the job for Graylink plc, as the deadline for completion had passed two days ago.

Meanwhile Teresa had rummaged through the post to find a letter from her biggest client. It was a message of congratulation for his satisfaction with the new Sales Director that Teresa had found. She scanned the letter into the internal computer network, to circulate it to her fellow Directors, then composed an elegant reply to the client. Teresa enjoyed great success at 'Park Lane Headhunters', the recruitment agency for senior management personnel, and was not shy about keeping others informed.

Before she had been through the rest of her letters, a telephone call from the Managing Director summoned her to an emergency meeting. A letter had arrived from a long-standing client threatening legal action for negligence over a disastrously unsuccessful appointment. The absence from the meeting of the executive responsible showed the extent of the Managing Director's displeasure. Teresa put forward the view that even though their contracts with clients denied liability for their recommendations, they could not afford the bad publicity generated by a court case. Both of her fellow Directors agreed with this, but the Managing Director eventually said: 'I don't think we can afford to set a precedent. We'll have to brazen it out.'

Back at her desk, Teresa went through the rest of her post, then called up the computer's 'Pending' file. It contained the names and phone numbers of the firms she had decided to contact that week. Part of her job was to press for new clients and therefore extra sources of sales revenue. Teresa decided which companies to try, while Anne phoned to find out the right person to contact and then sent a standard introductory letter. This was later followed up by Teresa phoning to suggest a preliminary meeting, possibly over lunch (depending upon how promising the contact sounded). She decided that she would try three of the numbers that morning.

The first of the contacts was in a meeting, but the second proved promising. Yes, he often needed to appoint senior staff, and indeed newspaper advertising often failed to get the right calibre of applicant, and yes he was free for lunch next Thursday. The third call was to the Personnel Director of a large construction company. It began well, but started to go wrong when the Director referred to: 'The necessity for higher job quality delivery within the Field Installation section and the Attachment Materials Pipeline'.

As Teresa was grappling mentally with this, he asked whether she had experience in finding 'Unix-based Quality System Auditors'. She mumbled an apology and rang off.

It was with some relief that she went off to her lunch appointment with a long-standing client. Nahdia Khan ran a chain of fifteen exclusive, high fashion clothing outlets. Teresa recounted her story of the construction company to hoots of laughter from Nahdia, setting the tone for a relaxing lunch. Over coffee it was interrupted, however, when Teresa's mobile phone rang with an urgent message from the Managing Director, demanding that she return to sort out 'the Manchester problem'.

The afternoon turned quite unpleasant as Teresa blamed Anne for being unable to deal with 'a minor query from Manchester'. The atmosphere worsened when Teresa saw a copy of the fax that her assistant had sent. It made it plain that work on the Graylink account had all but ceased. It was honest but hardly tactful. Teresa phoned the head of the Manchester office to apologise for Anne's 'bizarre' fax, and to assure her that several contacts looked promising. The remainder of the day was spent in a frustrating and fruitless chase for Graylink's new head of finance.

To round off Teresa's day, just as she was about to leave a call came through from the accounts department: 'About that memo…'.

Questions

1 Describe the different forms of communications used in the case study. Include internal and external, electronic and face-to-face. (4)

2 Why did Teresa communicate much more effectively with Nahdia than with Anne? (4)

3 State two advantages and two disadvantages of verbal communications. (4)

4 The Data Protection Act safeguards information stored on computers. When was this Act passed?

If you were an executive listed on the database at the recruitment agency, what rights would you have under this Act? (4)

5 Identify the main barriers to effective communication within the case study. (4)

Further work

1 Computers are a part of the workplace and they will be with us for future generations, but there are disadvantages associated with them. These disadvantages affect the efficiency of an organisation.

Research the following criticisms and say how organisations can overcome them:

a Staff become isolated at workstations and talk to computers, not to one another.

b Some staff fear that they will not be able to cope with the new technology.

c There are technical problems of viruses, compatibility, hacking and support services.

2 The telephone network is developing enhanced systems. (British Telecom's education department have details on such systems.) What would be the advantages and disadvantages to an organisation of the following features:

a a stacking system for phone calls

b a screen showing to whom one is talking

c mobile car phones.

3 To help you complete element 2.2, contact a recruitment agency or an estate agency near you and arrange a visit. Investigate the communication systems used and write a report on your visit with a title, date, and suitable headings.

■ What communications systems are used? (Give a brief description, for example: fax, computers.)

■ What inter-office communication systems are used?

■ What new technology has been introduced in recent years?

■ How does the agency ensure that any communication system is accurate, cost effective, and secure?

16 FACTORY SAFETY

Elements: **2.1** PC 1 2 3 4 **2.2** PC 3 5
IT **3.1** PC 1 2 3

Key concepts: Legal requirements, Health and safety, Communications systems,
Purposes of systems

'Not another accident! That's the eighth this week, and the day shift haven't had a single one.' As Production Manager of PowerMo Lawnmowers, Mike was responsible not only for safety but also for output, and he knew each production line accident lost him an average of 60 units. He was a great believer in **delegation**, so he left the Night Shift Manager to get on with things. Though, as Mike admitted to himself, he had not seen much of him lately, so they ought to meet to discuss the situation. The night shift would not be in until five o'clock, so Mike spent the morning digging out figures on the accident rate by shift over the past year. He passed them over to his management trainee for comment, who turned them into the bar chart shown below.

Meanwhile, Mike consulted his six day-shift **foremen** about the monthly variations in safety. One explained:

> *'Well, you're always going to get peaks before holiday times when you're on **piecework**, aren't you? The lads are aiming to get a good 20% more in July and December than they do regularly. And, if you work 20% faster on those grinding machines, it's not surprising that you get sloppy.'*

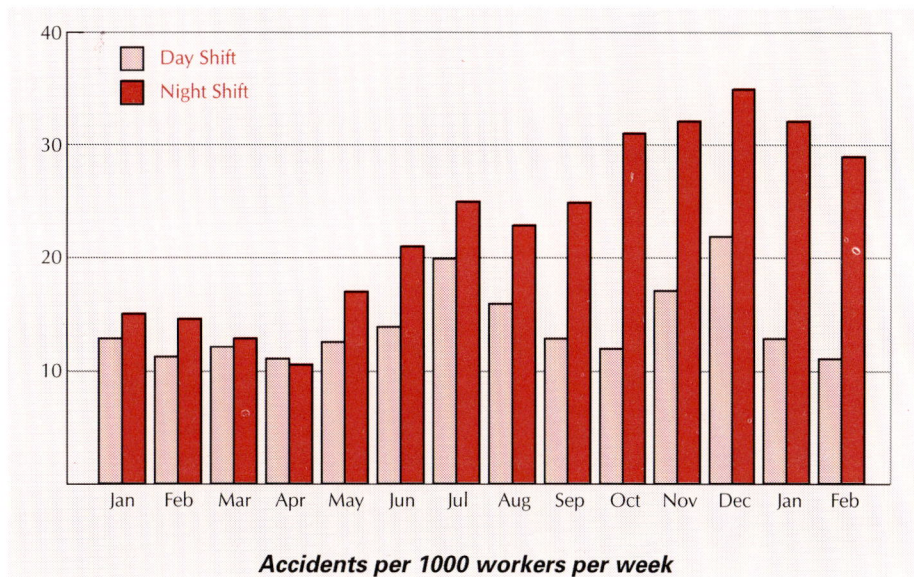

Accidents per 1000 workers per week

All agreed that there seemed no reason for the long-term accident rate to be rising, and that all seemed well for the coming Spring sales peak.

A quick check on the night shift's productivity figures revealed that there had been no improvement since last May, so there was evidently some other cause. Instead of talking to his night shift manager that afternoon, Mike decided to call in unannounced that evening. It occurred to him that he had not actually been there at night since just after the shift manager's appointment last May.

The afternoon's monthly management meeting proved sticky. The sales manager presented a report on customer feedback, which showed dissatisfaction with product quality and with delivery reliability over the past six months. Mike defended his department stoutly, blaming the 'second rate materials and components bought in by purchasing' (whose manager was away that day). Yet he found it harder to fend off the following implied criticism from the financial controller:

> *'I cannot understand how we have let the reject rate rise 50% in the last year. If it's due to faulty components, why are they not checked before wasting labour time on them? This has put our variable costs up to £1.40 per unit instead of the budgeted £1.32, which has cut our contribution per unit by 8 pence to 32 pence. So now our **break-even** point has risen to 100,000 units.'*

Mike's evening visit proved more illuminating than he had anticipated. During the day, the factory was a hive of purposeful activity. Now, he observed men shouting out conversation, even jokes, above the mechanical din. They were working on dangerous machinery, and supposed to be producing products to exact specifications, yet concentration levels seemed low. Mike looked in vain for the night shift manager or his foreman, until he found them in the office. He kept calm enough to find out that neither man knew of any problems. Both assumed that the safety, productivity, and wastage figures were quite satisfactory; they had heard nothing to the contrary.

It was the trainee, the following day, who completed the misery of Mike's week. He had heard from a secretary that the shop stewards for the night shift had asked for an urgent meeting with Mike's boss.

Questions

1 What is meant by these terms: delegation, foremen, piecework, break-even? **(4)**

2 Why were there more accidents on the night shift? **(2)**

3 Give three possible causes of accidents in the workplace. **(3)**

4 Why should firms be concerned about a healthy and safe environment? **(4)**

5 What are the main requirements of the 1974 Health and Safety at Work Act? **(2)**

6 What are three of the costs involved in providing a safe and healthy environment? **(3)**

7 How could you record each person's output at Powermo? **(3)**

8 To what extent was Mike's failure to communicate a cause of the high accident rate and poor quality standards? **(5)**

Further work

1 Payment systems vary from organisation to organisation. As human resources manager, write a report to the Managing Director on the effects of changing a pay system from piecework to a timerate system. Your report should include:

- a description of the different pay systems
- advantages and disadvantages involved in changing to a new system
- how employees will be told about the new system
- an explanation of the use of information technology to assist in the changeover.

To help you fulfil core skills in Information Technology, wordprocess your report. When you produce your report, show that you can use suitable file names for saving work, and print out a specific page of the document, for example payment systems. Produce a draft version, edit this and then make a final copy.

17 PERSONNEL MANAGEMENT AND COST CONTROLS

Elements: *2.1* PC 1345   *2.2* PC 134
             C *3.2* PC 1234   *3.3* PC 123   AN *3.2* PC 1235

*Key concepts: Purposes of a system, Routine and non-routine tasks,
             Communication systems, Evaluating systems*

Dreeman Limited is a manufacturing firm employing forty factory and thirty administrative/managerial staff. It is a major producer of smoke detectors, which it designs, assembles, tests, and markets.

It regards itself as rather progressive in its personnel policies, with its close links with local colleges, and its **single status conditions** of service. So, whereas in many firms only the factory workers have to clock in, and have no sick pay and no company pension, at Dreeman the shop floor staff enjoy the same rights as the white-collar staff. This system was introduced three years ago, when four factory workers with eighty years' service between them, refused to clock in any more. Now the Managing Director believes there is much more mutual trust and respect between workforce and management.

Each year, Dreeman make over 100,000 smoke detectors, in twenty-six different models. The largest selling line – with 12,000 units – is produced continually, the remainder in batches. Having so many lines produced by **batch production** in the same factory and largely by the same people, makes it hard to keep track of how long it takes to produce each item. Without accurate information, it is then impossible for the accountant to decide the true production cost; this matters because 60% of the firm's direct costs are on labour. In turn, it makes pricing a hit-and-miss affair. The other need for accurate production time information is to enable the supervisor to judge the output per worker. Annual bonuses can be based on this information, as can decisions to give warnings of dismissal to those considered inefficient.

At present, Dreeman's approach is two-fold:-

1   **Standard Costs** are calculated when a new line is introduced. This entails a lot of work in measuring precisely how long it should take to carry out each task, plus the estimated wage, material, and fuel costs per unit. Yet it has the advantage of providing a yardstick against which shop floor performance can be measured. Unfortunately, shop floor resistance to the sight of anyone with a stopwatch means that once an item is in production, the Standard Times do not get updated. Some are as much as ten years old.

2   The second element in their costing system is time-sheets, on which the factory workers are supposed to record how long they spent on each batch of work. If this was completed accurately, it would be possible to calculate precisely the time spent per unit on each line made. This could then be compared with the Standard Times to assess efficiency. Unfortunately, the shop floor workers regard timesheets either as pointless bureaucracy or as a threat, so they fill them in only when the supervisor pressures them – too infrequently for them to be accurate.

Now a new Personnel Manager has been given the task of setting up a computerised system of time-sheet analysis that would print out actual production times per unit. Although a computer novice, he knows enough to warn the Managing Director that: 'Computerising a defective system can only speed up the mess.'

When he starts talking the problem over with the two factory supervisors, he is surprised to find out that not even they knew how the information is used to work out production costs and prices. What is clear, though, is that shop floor resistance to the system is deep-rooted. One supervisor suggests:

> 'If you want a system that my crew will work properly,
> you've got to make it so that it cannot be used to measure
> their own performance. They can't abide snooping.'

In fact, it is the Personnel Manager's secretary who suggests the solution that is adopted. She suggests a time sheet that follows the batch round the factory floor, and is filled in anonymously by those who spend time on the batch. In that way, no one need object to filling it in, and therefore a training session on its importance should ensure that it will be completed with fair accuracy. As she says:

> 'Better to have valid information on one thing than
> worthless information on two.'

Questions

1 What is meant by the following terms: single status conditions, batch production, standard costs, white collar and blue collar workers? (5)

2 What is the purpose of a clocking-in system? What are two disadvantages of such a system? (4)

3 Give two examples of routine and non-routine tasks involved in smoke detector production. (4)

4 Why was it difficult to monitor and record batch production? (4)

5 What is the average output for the batch-produced lines? (4)

6 What was the advantage of standard costing to management? (2)

7 Why were the workers less enthusiastic about standard costs and standard times? (3)

8 Explain in your own words why computerising the system would not make the organisation more efficient. (4)

Further work

1 One of the basic problems of introducing a new system, highlighted by the case study, is resistance to change. What are the causes of such resistance for this, or any other, workforce? How can any fears or barriers be overcome? Imagine that you are the Managing Director of Dreeman Limited. Write a letter to your Chairman on this sensitive issue, explaining how you could ensure that the process of change would be introduced gradually, with as little disruption as possible.

2 Look at workplace communications in your school or college, or any organisation with which you are familiar. Arrange to interview two members of staff from your chosen organisation.

   ■ What methods of communication are used?

   ■ What are the problems of communication?

   ■ How could communication be improved?

   ■ How do people feel about the effectiveness of different means of communication?

You could record your interviews on tape, or work in pairs with one interviewing and one taking notes. Make a written or oral presentation of your findings.

3 To help you to obtain core skills in Communication, examine the following means of communication used by organisations: telephone, fax machine, business letter, notice board, meetings.

Using secondary sources, research the effectiveness of the different forms. You could work in groups, studying one form each, and then reporting on your findings. In your report include a sketch, diagram or chart. State when each form of communication would be appropriate or inappropriate.

18 STOCK CONTROL AND ANALYSIS

Elements: **2.1** *PC 12345* **2.3** *PC 123*
C **3.2** *PC 1234* AN **3.3** *PC 1234*
IT **3.3** *PC 1234*

*Key concepts: Supporting human resources, Recording and monitoring
performance, Evaluation criteria, Stock control*

Lockware Plastics is part of the Lockware Group, a medium-sized Public Limited Company. In its latest financial year, the group made a pre-tax profit of £2.1 million – a big recovery from its awful performance of recent years. The plastics division enjoyed a 10% sales increase, but this was still 46% below the levels of four years before (see below). In his recent report to shareholders, the Chairman said:

'Our recent difficulties have been due to the severity of the economic recession in our main operating markets. Now we are fit, lean and eager to take advantage of the improving world economy.'

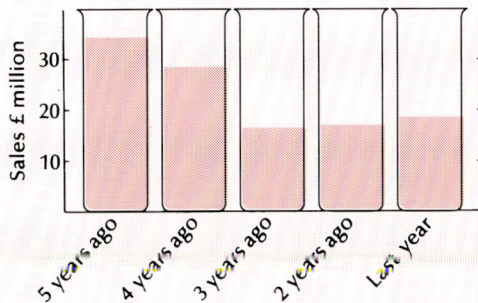

Sales revenue for Lockware Plastics during the last 5 years

Lisa had her doubts. She was stuck in a dingy plastic moulding factory, wondering how a management trainee with four weeks' experience could be expected to sort out a mess like this. The production director had evidently been surprised to see her that Monday, and had only spent twenty minutes with her before telling her to 'get the machine spares system into shape'.

It took her a day to find out that he meant the Engineering Stores section, where spare parts were held in stock in case any of the manufacturing machinery broke down. Lisa found the storeman unhelpful as she tried to learn about the system and its problems. Fortunately a young maintenance man took an interest, and her education began.

She learned that a recent stock check recorded £60,000 of machine parts held in the warehouse. As the book value of the machines themselves was only £40,000, this seemed very high. Furthermore, the maintenance man assured her that the 49 large moulding machines broke down frequently, and despite the warehouse full of supplies, the right part was often missing. Lisa was assured that there was usually at least one machine idle on any one day for just this reason. So, on the face of it, Lockware had the worst of all worlds – large stockpiles of some parts and none of others.

Lisa discussed with the cost accountant the implications of a machine being out of order. She found that if a machine was out of action for a whole week, the lost contribution amounted to £16,000 on average (production is 'round the clock' seven days a week). Due to the non-stop, three shift production, machine downtime can never be made up, so it puts back delivery times.

Already, Lisa had enough information to appreciate that she had quite an important task on her hands. She tried again to talk to the warehouseman, and this time had some success. He said:

'We've got four different types of machine here; with 498 separate parts between them. The four machines each come from different suppliers, two British, one German, and one American. If we run out of an American part, it can take eight weeks to get a replacement. The problem is that the maintenance lads just help themselves if I'm not around, so I think we've got spares when we haven't. Then they bad mouth me when they come for a spare and I haven't got any.'

He went on to explain that re-ordering was undertaken when the number of parts reached a minimum level. The level differed according to the turnover of the part; the higher the usage/turnover, the higher the minimum level. These minimum levels were not recorded anywhere. The warehouseman said proudly that he knew which parts had a quick usage and which were needed rarely. Lisa was astonished to learn that re-ordering was so dependent on his personal judgement. She wondered what happened when he went on holiday, and what chaos there would be when he retired. No less surprising was that he had the authority to re-order any number of parts, yet he had no knowledge of any budget to which he should be working.

Lisa set out to check on the efficiency of this system. She found a file of **stock record cards**. A typical one is shown below.

Stock Record For Previous Year – Omron Light Switch

Quantity delivered	Delivery date	Unit cost	USAGE Quant.	Date	Stock	Physical count	Date of count
3	2/1	£28			3		
			1	4/3	3		
			1	12/4	1		
			1	11/6	NIL		
			Stock check		NIL	NIL	30/6
2	8/7	£30			2		
			1	25/7	1		
			1	14/9	NIL		
2	24/9	£30			2		
			Stock check		2	1	31/12

She felt that this confirmed her suspicions of the warehouseman's competence. Especially when she heard from a maintenance man that the lack of this item had held up production on one machine for three days last September.

Lisa tried to talk things over with the production director, who was supposed to be in charge of her six week 'training programme in manufacturing'. As he still seemed unwilling to find any time for her, she decided to prove her worth by conducting a full analysis of all 498 machine parts. She found the stock records for each part for the last three years. She intended to place each part in a category that reflected its frequency of use. To virtually guarantee that no part would ever be out of stock, each part was categorised depending upon its highest (rather than its average) annual usage:

e.g.   Year 1   Year 2   Year 3
                 6   4   16

The part would be placed in category 4 (below).

Category	Frequency part used in a year	Proposed minimum stock level	Proposed maximum stock level
1	0–5	1	2
2	6–10	1	2
3	11–15	1	3
4	16–20	2	4
5	21–25	2	4
6	26–30	3	5
7	31–35	3	6
8	36–40	4	8
9	41–45	4	8
10	46–50	5	10
11	51+	5	10

The categories emerged as a result of Lisa's three weeks' study of the stock record cards, as did the proposed **minimum** and **maximum stock levels**. This study also showed her the scope for increasing the efficiency of the firm's stock control system. Among the many peculiarities she found one part costing £78 that had not been used once in the last three years; fifteen were in stock, so over £1,000 had been tied up quite unnecessarily for three years.

After another week of careful calculation, Lisa was able to prove that her system would, on average, cut Lockware's stockholding from £60,000 to £36,500. Furthermore, if it was implemented fully, it would ensure that parts were virtually never out of stock. The cost accountant had been able to calculate for her that machine downtime had cost £85,000 of lost contribution (and therefore profit) in the past year. Careful use of probability theory enabled her to show that her method would lead to an average of just £5,000 of lost production per year, so she appeared to have a watertight case for change.

With her six weeks nearly over, Lisa asked the personnel director (who had recruited her originally) if he would arrange a meeting with the production director for her to present her findings. This duly occurred, and Lisa impressed the personnel director and herself with her clear presentation of such complex material. The production director was less happy, however. He summoned her the following day and could barely control his fury as he told her, 'You betrayed my trust, prying without my authority, and then humiliating me in front of a fellow director. Get out and don't ever return to my patch.'

Lisa could never quite get over that, and left Lockware as soon as her year's training was completed. Five years later, she was production director for a firm with a fine growth record. It overtook Lockware's sales turnover soon afterwards.

Questions

1   What is meant by a stock record card, minimum stock level, maximum
stock level?   (3)

2   State two routine functions involved in a stock control system.   (2)

3   Giving two reasons for each, state why too much or too little stock can be a problem
for a firm.   (4)

4   Draw a graph showing the stocks of Omron light switches over the previous year
(inevitably the dates will be approximate). On what grounds were Lisa's suspicions
confirmed?   (10)

5   What was the system for reordering parts? Give two reasons why it was inefficient.
How could it be improved?   (6)

6   Describe Lisa's new system. Why was it an improvement on the old system?   (5)

7   What are three of the costs involved in any stock control system?   (3)

8   The Omron light switch stock record has a physical count. Give two reasons why
this is necessary.   (2)

Further work

1   Imagine that you are Lisa. Write a report to the Production Director explaining how the system of stock control is not helping the company to be 'leaner and fitter' and achieve its objectives. Evaluate the present system in terms of security, efficiency and cost effectiveness.

2   Part of core skills in Communication involves preparing written materials on routine matters. Administration is often concerned with devising efficient systems. What is meant by administration? Devise an administration system for an organisation's outgoing mail. First of all discuss your college system with the office staff. Take notes and then produce a flowchart showing the stages involved. Is there a logbook procedure for outgoing mail? How does it work? Your flowchart could be produced using a suitable software package.

BS 5750 AND THE QUALITY FANATIC

19

Elements: **2.1** *PC 1234*
             C **3.2** *PC 1234*

Key concepts: Administration systems, BS 5750, Recording business performance

The management of the Kimber Wetsuit Company (KWC) had been considering adopting the BS 5750 quality standard for some years. What clinched it was when the Ministry of Defence turned down KWC's quote for 1,000 suits for Royal Navy divers. They lost the order to BJ Diving, which had just received its 5750 certificate.

As a former professional diver, KWC's Managing Director (Jim Stewart) had always been fanatical about quality. This had helped in his development of a substantial export business, accounting for 75% of sales turnover. The level of quality that the overseas buyers looked for had been instilled by Jim into his workforce. So he found it hard to see what the British Standard could do to improve on the reliability of his wetsuits. Nevertheless he decided to hire a consultant to advise how to proceed.

The advisor spent a day following an order through from design, to materials ordering, cutting, bonding, assembly, styling, quality control and packing. Every piece of documentation was checked, as was the communication system and document storage method. The following day Jim Stewart received detailed feedback on what the firm would have to do to achieve the BS 5750 standard. He was horrified at the focus on paperwork, which included specific recommendations for at least twelve new pieces of record keeping or record storage. He told his wife after work: 'Not once did the clown mention the quality of craftsmanship or the care taken by every worker in my factory'.

After a few days, however, Jim calmed down and set about reading the documentation from the British Standards Institute, and re-reading the consultant's report. This enabled him to write his own report (shown overleaf), which he sent to every member of his staff.

Jim decided that the best way to proceed was not through outside 'experts' or even as a purely management-based exercise. His approach was to be bottom-up, i.e. employee-centred.

The whole KWC staff received a huge boost when they heard, four months later, that the Navy had cancelled its order with BJ Diving on the grounds that the wetsuits delivered so far did not meet the Navy's standards. Gossip soon reached them that BJ's approach to obtaining BS 5750 had been so bureaucratic that the company was weighed down with paperwork systems. The process of producing high quality wetsuits had become secondary to producing high quality paper.

With BJ Diving rejected and KWC well on the way to its 5750 quality standard, it was no surprise when Jim received a telephone call from the Ministry of Defence. Within a fortnight KWC had the contract for producing the remaining 500 Navy wetsuits.

Report to: All members of staff
From: Jim
Subject: Applying for the British Standard 5750 quality award
Date: March 17th

1 Background

We have recently lost out on a Royal Navy order that would have added 50% to this year's sales. BJ Diving won it because they hold the BS 5750 certificate that the Navy insists upon. As we all know, our quality is considerably better than theirs, so it would be foolish of us to allow this to occur again.

2 Proposal

I intend that we should achieve the required standard within nine months. The Italian Navy contract comes up then, and it is my plan that this should form the stepping stone to a far stronger presence in the European market. The BS 5750 is the same as the internationally accepted ISO 9000, so this should help our cause.

3 Detailed requirements

In order to be successful, we will need to cover four main areas:

3.1 Management responsibility: an organisation chart will be needed to set out the responsibilities of all staff who manage or carry out work associated with the quality of the product and customer service. Quality procedures must be written down in full detail.

3.2 Contract review: each customer's requirements must be defined and documented to establish that the necessary resources are available.

3.3 Process control: requiring documentation of how the process is to be carried out. Written instructions must be given to each employee involved and the process must be monitored. (Note to all: I do not know how this may affect our policy of self-checking.)

3.4 Document control: we must produce quality and procedure manuals to be kept in designated locations. Any changes to the system must be logged in the manuals.

4 Conclusion

I am as appalled as any of you at the amount of paperwork this will generate. It will cost us a great deal and will probably be very irritating to work with. Nevertheless, if important customers want us to hold this certificate, we must not only get on with it, but also trust that our customers are not fools. I will be very surprised if we do not learn a great deal from this process, and emerge an even stronger company as a result.

Questions

1 Why are firms so keen to obtain a BS 5750 certificate? **(3)**

2 BJ Diving's approach to obtaining BS 5750 was described as being too bureaucratic. Explain what this means. **(2)**

3 What do you think will be the benefit to the workforce from going through the procedures to obtain BS 5750? **(3)**

4 Jim Stewart decided to implement the BS 5750 requirements through a bottom-up approach. What is meant by this and how might it be achieved? **(6)**

5 According to John Oakland, Exxon Professor of Total Quality Management, there are three main components of Total Quality Management:

- a documented quality management system
- statistical tools and techniques
- teamwork.

To what extent did Jim Stewart fulfil these three criteria? **(6)**

Further work

1 Compare this company and the way it obtained its BS 5750 certificate with a company in your own area. Your evidence could be in the form of a report following an interview. The company you study may not have a certificate, however it may still be possible to study how it works towards achieving quality.

20 PRODUCTION MANAGEMENT

Elements: **2.1** *PC 12345* **2.2** *PC 12345* **2.3** *PC 12345*
AN **3.2** *PC 1235* *IT* **3.4** *PC 1345*

Key concepts: Purposes of systems, Effectiveness of systems, Effects of computer technology

Scott's arrival from the United States as the new managing director came after eight redundancy programmes within the previous ten years. So the workforce of York International was understandably defensive, and **job demarcation** was rife. As a producer of air conditioning equipment, the firm's sales were dependent upon the highly cyclical construction industry – hence its hire-and-fire record. The poor morale among the eight hundred workers showed in the firm's poor delivery and quality performance. Sixty-one per cent of all deliveries were over twenty days late, and quality costs of £1.5 million a year were accounting for 14% of the total manufacturing bill. The major element in the quality cost was warranty claims, which implied further customer inconvenience and therefore dissatisfaction.

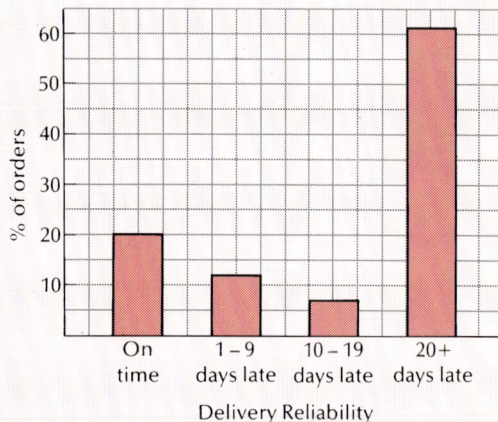

York delivery record before introduction of 'Order out of Chaos' programme

Scott's first statement to his staff was to promise no more redundancies, and to announce a three year programme for 'Order Out of Chaos'. At first, **middle management** was as sceptical as the workforce. The first action that made people take notice was Scott's order to the sales department to aim for steady growth. They were to refuse orders that would beat their sales targets, since that would disrupt the attempt to reorganise the production system. His second action was to set the factory the objective of establishing an efficient system of production control so that the whole production monitoring process could be computerised in twelve months' time. For Scott had quickly appreciated that York's fundamental problem was that it was locked into a chaos spiral.

Disorganisation undermined production control, which reinforced the disorganisation; and low morale had become both cause and effect. The greatest surprise for the staff was that the third step was not to dictate how this objective should be achieved, as the previous management would have done. Instead, he encouraged middle management to work in teams with engineers and shopfloor workers to decide on the correct strategy.

The building of order required certain key building blocks.

1 Training was needed on the purpose of monitoring systems, so that it was possible to obtain accurate data. Before, maintenance men would have helped themselves to spare parts from the stores; now careful recording took place.

2 Meaningful production plans were needed to schedule people's work for each

day. Variance analysis was used to check the accuracy of the planning, and major variances by individual workers were discussed openly between worker and foreman.

Within the twelve month target, York had production information of an accuracy that it had never enjoyed before; and production planning had emerged from the old-style **crisis management**. By the time the Manufacturing Resource Planning (MRP) computer was installed, Scott suspected that they had already achieved 80% of all the possible gains.

The computer monitored all material inputs and stocks, all production in each section of the factory (plus wastage) and finished goods quality and stock levels. It could also match this information with customer order quantities and delivery dates, enabling managers to anticipate when completion of a particular order would need to be speeded up. Within a year of the MRP computer's installation, on-time deliveries had risen to 85%, from 20% just two years before.

In the longer term, though, the computer's simulation capacity proved its most valuable facility. It enabled production engineers to get quick answers to questions such as 'What if we replace the four hand-operated pressing machines with one automated one?' The computer could show not only the direct cost implications, but also the impact on **work-in-progress**, on factory layout, and on overheads.

Scott's managerial skill was to use such print-outs not as a blueprint, but for discussion with the relevant engineers and workers. Often it was found that there were better ways of using the existing equipment (perhaps using conveyor belt transfer of components). This encouraged the workforce to participate in decision making, and therefore to work to prove that the decision they had initiated or backed was the right one. The higher motivation of the workforce showed through in product quality. From representing 6.5% of the total manufacturing bill, the cost of guarantee claims fell to 1%.

The next stage in the company's production-led revival came with the appointment of an expert in Just-In-Time manufacturing as the production director. When interviewing, Scott made sure that candidates were not only qualified technically, but were also committed to a bottom-up approach to employee involvement. Authoritarian, top-down managers were rejected. For Scott was convinced that active participation by the workforce was essential if further changes to working practices were necessary.

Source: *Machinery and Production Engineering*

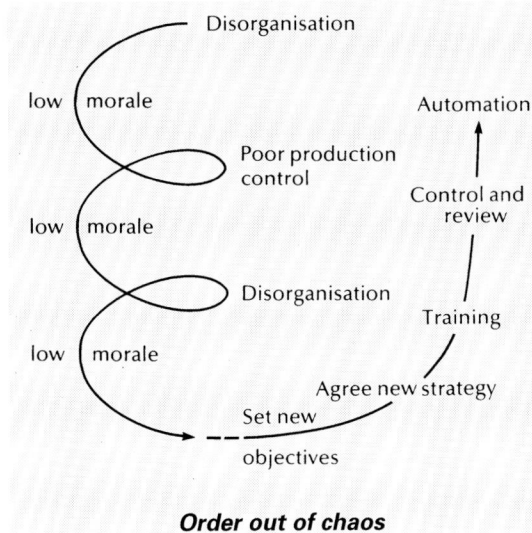

Order out of chaos

Questions

1   What is meant by these terms: job demarcation, middle management, crisis
management, work-in-progress?   **(4)**

2   Before Scott came to York International, what was:

   a   the total manufacturing bill

   b   the amount of the total manufacturing bill spent on the cost of guarantee claims? **(5)**

3   What were the problems that Scott inherited at York International?   **(3)**

4   How did the new computer support the functions of the business?   **(3)**

5   The case study shows that the way technology is introduced is critical to
whether it will be successful or not. How did Scott win the workforce over to
his system?   **(5)**

Further work

1   In order to cover the range for unit 2, a visit to a local bank or building society would be
valuable. The visit would also enable you to cover element 3.4 (core skills in
Information Technology) which deals with security routines and improvements in day-
to-day working. In recent years, financial institutions have been implementing new
systems.

Describe at least two different administrative and information processing systems .

- What are the purposes of the systems?

- How well do the systems support the running of the company?

- What is the effect of technology on customer service and staff?

- How do financial institutions cope with the problem of security in their information
systems?

- How are they affected by the Data Protection Act?

Finally, you could ask about the cost effectiveness of new technology, and raise the issue
of job losses.

21 HÄAGEN-DAZS – DEDICATED TO PERFECTION

Elements: **3.1** *PC 1 2 3 4 5*   **3.3** *PC 1 2 3 4*
              C **3.2** *PC 1 2 3 4*

Key concepts: New product development, Product life cycle,
*   Marketing mix*

In the 1950s a New York manufacturer of an ice cream brand called Ciro's decided to extend its distribution from ice cream parlours to supermarkets. Reuben Mattus had spotted that rising affluence plus freezer ownership encouraged consumers to buy ice cream all year round. Not surprisingly, this distribution strategy was soon imitated by larger rivals. They were able to offer incentive deals to the retailers that Mattus could not match, so sales of Ciro's slipped back.

Thwarted by his competitors, Mattus decided to try a different approach. Using fresh cream, all natural ingredients and with less air blown into the mix, he produced an ice cream with a finer flavour and texture. To distinguish it from other ice creams, he gave his new product a Scandinavian sounding name and packed it into pint pots instead of the usual 2 litre packs. In 1961 the first Häagen-Dazs ice cream was sold in New York delicatessens.

With its high ingredients' cost and small-scale production, the price of Häagen-Dazs had to be high to be profitable. This was off-putting to shopkeepers, who feared that customers would refuse to buy it. So Mattus visited shops personally, giving staff a taste of the product and promising to buy back any product that did not sell. By removing the shops' financial risk, gaining distribution became more possible. Slowly but steadily Häagen-Dazs spread to New York grocers, then supermarkets and later to national store chains.

Without the desire or the finance to promote the product through advertising, Mattus relied upon word of mouth to generate customer demand. Fortunately, Häagen-Dazs customers loved talking about the product. By the mid-1970s the ice cream's popularity was such that remaining Ciro ice cream products were phased out to turn the production capacity over to Häagen-Dazs. Mattus developed the theme 'Dedicated To Perfection' as a focus of staff training, materials purchasing and production control. He was determined that growth would not be at the expense of the product quality that he had sought and found in 1961.

At the same time Mattus's daughter came up with the idea of creating a 'dipping store' in which vanilla ice cream bars were hand-dipped in melted milk or plain chocolate to create a hand-made choc ice. From this 250 Häagen-Dazs stores were developed in America, each offering an opportunity for people to sample the products they could then buy from supermarkets.

By the early 1980s Häagen-Dazs had become established as *the* super-premium ice cream throughout America. In 1983 the company was sold off to the Pillsbury Company, with a condition of sale being that the company's quality standards would always be maintained. Pillsbury, the multi-national owners of Burger King, were looking to develop Häagen-Dazs internationally. In 1984, after signing an agreement for it to be manufactured in Japan, Häagen-Dazs grew to become that country's best selling super-premium ice cream.

Three years later, with sales levelling off in America, Pillsbury started to look seriously at the European market. Little progress had been made by 1989, however, when Pillsbury was itself bought up by the British company Grand Metropolitan. The American firm with the Scandinavian sounding name was now British owned, and was soon to launch its product in Britain (see Case Study 27).

Meanwhile, by 1992 American sales were slipping under pressure from a strong competitor. Ben and Jerry's produced high quality ice cream at high prices, but differentiated itself from Häagen-Dazs by containing bigger chunks of chocolate, almonds or toffee. It also had a livelier image, as epitomised by the name of one of its flavours, Cherry Garcia. Häagen-Dazs responded to Ben and Jerry's success by introducing comparable products within a new range called Exträas. This revitalised Häagen-Dazs sales. For thirty years, the company's dedication to perfection had been enough to succeed; modern markets might require still more.

Sources: *The Financial Times; Häagen-Dazs UK Ltd.*

Questions

1 What are three different ways of distributing ice-cream? (3)

2 What were the distinctive features of the marketing mix of Häagen-Dazs that made the product up-market? (4)

3 How did Mattus try to avoid the risk of failure? (3)

4 a What is meant by a product life cycle? (4)

   b Sketch a product life cycle diagram to show the stages in the development of Häagen-Dazs in America, using the dates provided. (6)

5 Use this case study to explain why firms have to look continually at new product developments. (5)

Further work

1 The case study acts as an introduction to the ice cream market. Imagine you are the manager of an ice cream company. Do some market research, involving the general public, on types of ice cream bought, where ice cream is bought and how much is bought in terms of money and volume. Your objective is to establish whether there is a market for an 'up-market' type of ice cream, and to find out how much money people would be prepared to pay for such a product. It would be best to work in groups to interview at least 80 suitable people. Analyse your data and write a report of your findings for the Marketing Director of your ice cream company.

22 McDONALD'S – MARKETING HAMBURGERS

Elements   **3.2** *PC 1234*   **3.3** *PC 12345*
         AN **3.2** *PC 125*

Key concepts: Marketing activities, Promotions, Product life cycle, Advertising, Consumer characteristics

In 1954, a salesman of milkshake machines paid a call on a customer in Southern California. It was a small drive-in restaurant that sold a limited range of products at unusually low prices. The salesman (Ray Kroc) was impressed with its **assembly-line production** method, and even more by the queues of customers. Although the hamburgers sold for just 15 cents each, this one outlet had annual sales over $300,000.

Kroc saw the potential of the business, and offered the owners an arrangement which would give him sole rights to franchise their name, production method and **logo** throughout the United States. The owners (Richard and Maurice McDonald) would receive a quarter of all Kroc's **franchise** income, which was to be 1.9% of all the franchisees' sales revenue. The golden arches which formed part of Kroc's original restaurant design structure were turned into the familiar 'M' trademark.

During this period, customer demand stemmed from McDonald's low prices, rapid service, and dedication to service and cleanliness. Its appeal was to families at a time when rival drive-ins attracted the smaller teenage market. Growth proved rapid, and by 1960 the 225 McDonald's franchises provided annual sales of almost $50 million. In 1961, Kroc bought the McDonald brothers out for $2.7 million. Had they held on to their 0.5% royalty they would have earned over $400 million by the late 1980s.

Following the buyout, the McDonald's Corporation profits flourished due to increasing numbers of outlets, and new contracts that took a much higher percentage of the franchise operator's income. However, annual sales per store were static at around $200,000 so the individual franchises needed ways to boost their own revenues. Some focused on the limited menu (and were responsible for creating the Big Mac in 1968 and the Egg McMuffin in 1973), while others concentrated on publicity.

In Washington, a clown character was being used with success on local television: renamed Ronald McDonald he became used nationally from 1965. Franchise operators found that T.V. advertising caused immediate sales increases, and that it helped overcome the traditional takeaway sales slump during the harsh northern American winter. So they agreed to contribute 1% of McDonald's $260 million sales in 1966 to a national advertising fund. This helped sales per store to jump to $275,000 from around $200,000 in the early 1960s.

It was at the local level, too, that sales promotions originated. Some became enormous successes nationally, including a mint-green Shamrock Shake sold on St. Patrick's Day, and scratch cards yielding instant prizes of Big Macs. Better promotions were capable of boosting short-term sales by 6%, and adding some novelty to the customers' visit.

Throughout this period of local initiative the McDonald's Corporation made surprisingly little contribution to the marketing effort. Only in 1968, at a time when rivals such as Burger King were closing the gap on McDonald's, did they form a marketing department. Its head decided to base his objectives on Ray Kroc's view that 'We're not in the hamburger business, we're in show business'.

Advertising agencies were invited to compete for the account by answering ten questions, including whether McDonald's possessed a 'unique selling proposition'. One agency replied no, McDonald's had only a unique sales personality, for its proposition differed 'depending on whether we're talking to moms, dads, or kids'. The agency recommended building up personality into one of warmth, fun, relaxation – and won the account.

The new campaign focused on the emotional pleasures of eating out: family togetherness, fun, and a sense of reward. Prolific use of television advertising was seen as the key to doubling revenues per store to $620,000 by 1973.

Although other factors were involved, the importance of advertising was also evident in Britain. The first British outlet to open (in Woolwich, London in 1974) started poorly. In its first year its revenue of $300,000 was too small to prevent losses of $150,000. The second outlet proved no better. Yet when profitable West End stores justified television advertising, the situation turned into one of runaway success. By 1986 the U.K. operation was so profitable that it cost the Corporation $38 million to buy out its British subsidiary.

During the 1980s, the enormous scale of the world-wide McDonald's operation was making local initiative harder to incorporate into the marketing process.

It was the Corporation itself that devised the hugely successful introduction of Chicken McNuggets in the early 1980s, and the massive T.V and promotional campaigns throughout the decade. By 1985, McDonald's controlled 20% of the $45 billion fast food market in the United States and enjoyed rapid growth in its many overseas markets. Ray Kroc had died the previous year, but his successors saw no need to change the McDonald's system.

Source: *'Behind The Arches'; J.F. Love.*

Questions

1 What is meant by: assembly line production, a logo, a franchise? **(3)**

2 Explain the term marketing. **(2)**

3 How do promotions differ from marketing? **(3)**

4 Give two reasons why TV advertising boosted sales so heavily in the UK. **(2)**

5 Research the meaning of the product life cycle.

    a Draw diagrams to show your estimate of the present position on the product life cycle of a Big Mac, a Shamrock Shake and Chicken McNuggets. **(5)**

    b What is meant by the mature phase of the life cycle ? How do companies like McDonald's try to prevent their products going into decline? **(3)**

Further work

1 Advertising agencies base many of their decisions on consumer characteristics.

Describe the characteristics of McDonald's customers in relation to their age, gender, lifestyle, and conscience spending (for example, green spending).

Use the Annual Abstract of Statistics to research the demographic changes likely to occur in the UK over the next 25 years. How will these affect organisations like Burger King and McDonald's?

2 To meet the criteria for element 3.3 you are required to compare the effectiveness of marketing activities undertaken for two competing products. You could compare McDonald's with Burger King or Pizza Hut. Action plan a visit to a branch of each organisation as a start to your comparison. Describe any ethical issues relating to the marketing activities of the two organisations.

3 TV advertising is very popular for the following reasons: it reaches virtually the whole population, it has great scope for creativity, and it has the ability to demonstrate how a product works. To help you to fulfil the range of element 3.3, list all the TV commercials shown within a two hour period mid-evening. Use this research to account for the type of products advertised on television at this time. This task could be developed to cover Application of Number element 3.1.

Elements: **3.1** *PC 12345*   **3.2** *PC 1234*   **3.3** *PC 1234*
C **3.2** *PC 1234 AN* **3.1** *PC 125* **3.2** *PC 125*

Key concepts: *Marketing activities, Objectives of marketing, Consumer
characteristics, Market research*

The Survival Game was first played in June 1981 in the woods of New Hampshire, USA. Two teams – each armed with paint pellet guns – attempt to infiltrate the other's base camp, capture their flag and return it to their own base. It proved to be a huge success and by 1988 it had become a $150 million industry.

Survival Game U.K. Limited was formed in 1984 to establish this new sport in Britain. Its owners identified two markets: weekend leisure for sporty types and a weekday business market training course in teamwork. In 1985 the company achieved 2,500 customers. Word of mouth plus television coverage pushed demand up rapidly to 60,000 players by 1988. This sales explosion was accommodated by Survival Game U.K. setting up three of its own sites plus twenty-one franchised outlets. Each site covers over twenty acres of partly wooded terrain, and is usually rented from a large landowner or local authority.

Allan Burrows is an enthusiastic Survival Game player, whose £15,000 redundancy payout has tempted him to become the twenty-second franchisee. He has been having to make a 100-mile round trip to travel to the Norwich site, and so sees potential in developing one in Ipswich. A phone call to the firm's London offices reveals the following information:

1   Franchise fee – £10,000 for an eight year contract to manage the sole Survival Game U.K. site in Suffolk. Included would be all the equipment needed to start, including 50 'Splatmaster' pistols and 12,000 Splatballs (filled with washable orange paint).

2   Training and promotion – full training is given to all franchisees, not only in the running of the game but also in accounting and publicity techniques.

3   Back-up services – including supplies, national marketing and public relations.

4   Financial projection (assuming 40 players for 75 days in the year, i.e. 3,000 customers) – as follows:

Sales revenue

	Game fee	£48,000
	Paint pellets	£30,000
	Other revenue	£10,000
	Total sales:	£88,000

Cost of sales

	Paint pellets	£20,000
	Other costs	£5,000
	Total direct costs	£25,000

Overheads

	Site rent	£3,750
	Wages	£6,500
	Other overheads	£19,750
	Total overheads	£30,000
	Pre-tax profit	£33,000

Allan was impressed, and decided to contact a local landowner to see if a suitable site could be rented per day. There proved to be a thirty acre wooded site available at a daily rate of £80. He also wanted to consider catering facilities before committing himself. Allan knew that he and his friends found food the only disappointment about their trips to Norwich. After a morning's action one wanted a substantial and enjoyable meal. So Allan negotiated with a local caterer to provide a hearty, barbecued meal for £8 per head. He felt he should charge his customers no more than £5 for this, so he had to build this loss into his profit projections. Apart from the fact that he realised that high local labour costs would add 50% to the wage bill, Allan was happy about the rest of Survival Game U.K.'s forecasts.

A fellow game-player sounded a note of caution, however. He said that Survival Game magazine had been carrying advertisements offering a complete set of 'Splatmaster' guns and equipment for just £1,200. As he said: 'Anyone could start up in this business now'. Furthermore he knew the editor of the magazine, and had learned that its circulation had levelled off after its sharp rise in recent years. Allan phoned Survival Game U.K. about these points and was reassured to hear that they attributed the magazine's sales hiccup to its editorial weaknesses, not to flat demand for the game itself. In fact Survival Game U.K.'s managing director said that:

'In the first six months of this year there have been 10% more game players than in the same period last year. So business is booming.'

Questions

1 State three advantages to Allan of taking out a franchise. (3)

2 How would you advertise and promote the Survival game to the two different market sectors, business and leisure? (5)

3 One of the key elements of the marketing mix is place. What factors should Allan consider when deciding on the location of his Survival site? (6)

4 Calculate the annual pre-tax profit Allan could expect if he went ahead with the Survival Game UK operation. (5)

5 Why should Allan be cautious about going ahead with the franchise? Your answer should include evidence from the text as well as any other external factors you feel may be relevant. (6)

6 How could Allan increase the number of people playing the Survival Game? (5)

Further work

1 The market for games is very large: analyse two or three games that you know, and look at the 'secret of their success'.

You could choose Scrabble, Monopoly, Cluedo, Pictionary and so on. Compare marketing activities for two of these competing products, and look at their effectiveness in achieving objectives like increasing sales, increasing market share, and enhancing product image. Marketing activities include product pricing, packaging, advertising, promotion.

2 A marketing assistant in your company has devised a new golf board game. You are aware that golf is a growth sport, and wish to test the product in a small market.

How would you use market research to establish a name for the new product, to identify whether there is a potential demand, and to establish price, packaging and distribution? Draw up a questionnaire to help you in your research. Decide whether a random or quota sample would best meet your requirements. Explain the basis of your choice. Ask a sample of people what they feel about the new game. Analyse the data, draw your conclusions and present a report on the findings of your market research.

3 Several sports and leisure pursuits have experienced revivals or have been newly introduced in recent years. In order to meet the criteria for element 3.2, action plan a visit to one of the activities, and draw up a questionnaire for the marketing manager.

Answer parts a to d for any one of the following: ten pin bowling, ice skating, dry slope skiing, aerobics, karate, gymnastics, or fitness training.

a Identify the characteristics of typical consumers.

b Analyse economic information that may have an effect on consumption in your local area, for example, unemployment, level of income, standard of living.

c Attempt a forecast of sales and market demand for the next five years.

d Which of the above activities are likely to be still in demand in 25 years' time ? Give your reasons.

To help you meet Communications core skills element 3.3, give a presentation, including a graph, to show projected demand for the next five years.

24

THE COCA-COLA STORY

Elements: *3.1* PC 23   *3.2* PC 23   *3.3* PC 12345
AN *3.1* PC 123456

Key concepts: Market research, Marketing mix, Objectives,
            Marketing activities

Coca-Cola was first sold on 8th May 1886 by a pharmacist called John Pemberton. He had devised the syrup as a headache remedy, but found that it mixed well with soda water. The first advertisement for the drink appeared in the *Atlanta Journal*: 'containing ... the wonderful Coca plant and Cola nuts'. The name proved memorable but Pemberton wanted a stylish trademark. He found it when his book-keeper wrote the brand name with a flourish in an accounts ledger. That script was registered as a trademark in 1893 and has been used ever since.

Yet it was not Pemberton who created the Coca-Cola business empire. In 1886 only nine drinks were sold per day at just 5 cents per glass. So he sold the name, the formula and the manufacturing equipment to a wealthy trader, Asa Candler, for $2,300. In 1892 Candler founded The Coca-Cola Company, and his capital plus his understanding of distribution ensured that the drink spread rapidly. Candler's marketing strategy was to sell the drink through soda fountains rather than through shops. So the syrup was transported in (red) barrels from Atlanta, and mixed with soda in a glass at the point of sale. By 1899 sales had progressed to 281,055 gallons.

Then came the real revolution. Two young lawyers saw the opportunity for Coca-Cola to be made more widely available by selling it in bottles. In 1899 they arranged to meet Candler and asked him for a bottling contract for the whole of the United States. To their surprise he agreed – and set a price of 1 dollar on the contract. This established the franchise structure that has operated throughout the world ever since. The Coca-Cola Company supplies a concentrated essence to bottling firms that turn it into syrup, add carbonated water, then bottle and distribute it. So the Atlanta head office is responsible only for producing and delivering the concentrate, and for marketing the brand. The new approach generated sales growth to 6,767,822 gallons by 1913.

Drink Coca-Cola

6,000,000 drinks a day

The original 1899 bottle had no special shape or design. By 1913 the success of Coca-Cola encouraged many imitators to offer 'Cola Sola' or 'Pepsi Cola' in similar bottles. So the owners of the Coca-Cola bottling franchises contacted various glass manufacturers to hold a competition to design a distinctive new bottle. In 1916 the characteristic glass Coca-Cola bottle – still used today – was patented and launched. Sales pushed ahead still further, to 18.7 million gallons by 1919.

That year two other important events occurred. The Candler family sold the company for $25 million to a group led by Ernest Woodruff, whose son Bob became Coca-Cola's chief executive for the next 40 years. He was responsible for turning this soft drink into a world-wide symbol of the 'American Dream'. Helping him finance that was the other event of 1919 – the onset of Prohibition in the United States. For although it is remembered mainly for its encouragement of the illegal production and sale of alcohol, the law-abiding majority turned to soft drinks. Coca-Cola sales grew ever faster, and its distinctive name and bottle made it increasingly possible to sell it at a price premium.

Bob Woodruff's approach to leadership was to set standards and strategies, and to ensure that everyone knew they were being followed as firmly at the top as elsewhere in the organisation. He viewed the company as a force for good, not just a force for profit. For example he insisted that Coca-Cola delivery drivers 'must always set a good example in the way they drive'. He tried to give a sense of purpose, of mission, to all his employees, as can be seen in his three short 'commandments':

1   Absolute loyalty to the product and the Company.

2   All partners must earn a good salary.

3   Simplicity of the product (one drink, one bottle, one price).

If the third point is reminiscent of Henry Ford, the first two are more akin to the style of the Marks and the Sieff families at Marks and Spencer.

That third statement was stuck to until the 1950s. So for over 40 years Coca-Cola meant just one product. This narrow focus may have been important in the company's success, because the drive to diversify often attracts a firm's most talented executives, and much of its investment capital. Only when Pepsi gained market share during the 1950s as a result of the launch of a larger pack size did Coke allow itself to break its rule. From then on, The Coca-Cola Company redefined itself as a soft drinks company, which encouraged it to launch Fanta in 1960 and Sprite in 1961.

The 1960s might have seen the end of the apparently unstoppable rise of Coke. Not only was it a 70 year old product at a time when youth and experimentation were fashionable, but also the product had developed a rather staid, middle-aged image. The following advertising slogans show how this had come about:

Coke Time

'The friendliest club in the world'	1946
'For home and hospitality'	1951
'Refreshment through the years'	1951
'Sign of good taste'	1957
'Happy pause for the youth of all ages'	1958

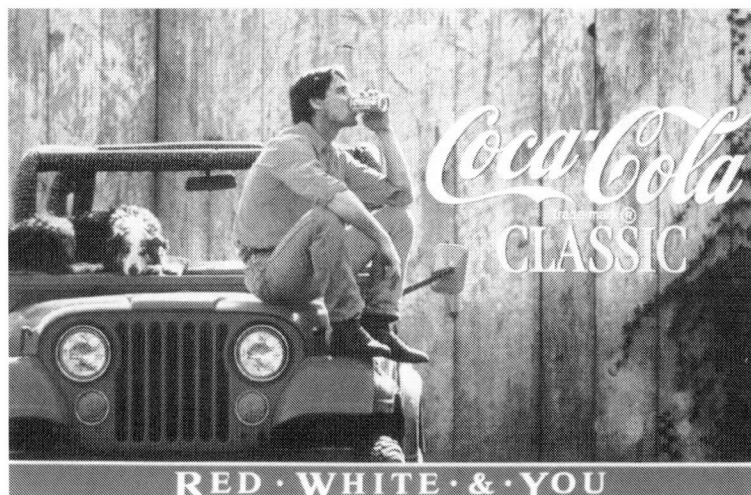

At the end of the 1950s Coca-Cola appointed a new, younger advertising agency. During the 1960s the marketing strategy became increasingly youth orientated. This not only meant new catchphrases such as 'Things go better with Coke', but also visual imagery became focused on young people having fun together.

By 1984 world-wide sales of The Coca-Cola Company were worth $7.4 billion (representing about 283 million cans per day). It was the biggest soft drinks producer in the world by a considerable margin. Yet its market share had slipped from 22.5% to 21.8%, while that of Pepsi had increased by 0.1%. Coke's new Chairman considered this a threat, especially as research showed that younger people were particularly prone to favour Pepsi. His worry was that he was presiding over the classic break within a product's life cycle between growth and decline. So a new formula drink was concocted, and then tested in great secrecy among a staggering 190,000 sample. The taste of the new Coke appeared to beat the old by 61% to 39%, so its launch was prepared.

In April 1985 it was announced to a horrified public that, after 99 years, Coke was to be relaunched with a 'Great new taste!' An immediate rush to try the new formula was followed by a barrage of criticism. Within a few days 'USA Today' published an opinion poll that showed 59% of consumers preferred the old Coca-Cola, 25% Pepsi, and only 13% the new Coke. The new was derided for being sweeter and less fizzy – 'like a Pepsi left open'. The outcry forced the company to backtrack, so on 10th July it announced that the old Coke would be reintroduced as Coca-Cola Classic.

Pepsi had gloated over Coke's original decision, as it appeared to confirm their long standing claim that in the 'Pepsi Taste Challenge' their product was preferred to Coke. Yet the whole episode proved more beneficial to Coke than Pepsi. The wave of nostalgia for 'the real thing' plus the publicity about the sweetness of both new Coke and Pepsi strengthened Coca-Cola's traditional image. By the end of 1985 Coke's share of the United States cola market had grown by four percentage points.

From 1886 to 1986 Coke's sales progress was almost uninterrupted. Health trends were met by low calorie or caffeine-free versions and changing consumer habits by family-sized bottles, multipacks, or automatic vending machines. The key to the firm's success has always been in the magic of its image, as captured in the two slogans: 'The real thing' and 'Coke is it!'. For just as Levi's are not just **a** pair of jeans, Coke is not just **a** cola. The brand name, the logo, its status as the original, and its distinctive bottle have all been woven into a decisive marketing advantage. An advantage that not only enables Coke to outsell other colas decisively, but also enables the Atlanta firm to charge a price premium. For profitability, Coke is it.

Sources: *'The chronicle of Coca-Cola'; The Conran Foundation: 'Coke!'; The Financial Times; 'Coca Cola Superstar': F.S. Palazzini*

'Coca-Cola' and 'Coke' are registered trade marks which identify the same product of The Coca-Cola Company.

Questions

1. What are the four main elements of the marketing mix? **(4)**

2. Give examples of three different objectives pursued by Coca-Cola. **(3)**

3. Which elements of the marketing mix were used most by Coca-Cola to increase sales? **(4)**

4. What is a product life-cycle? Draw a diagram to show the positions of Coca-Cola and Diet Coke on a product life-cycle, at the moment. **(5)**

5. Give three reasons why Coca-Cola geared their marketing to the younger generation in the 1960s. **(3)**

6. Explain the reasons for the diversification since 1960, ie the launch of Fanta, Sprite, low calorie and caffeine-free versions. **(3)**

7. Why was it a fault in marketing research to test the taste of Coke secretly? **(3)**

8. What is meant by quota sampling? How would you set about obtaining the right quota for a survey into the type of people who consumed Coke? **(5)**

Further work

1. Describe the main market research methods used by companies and advertising agencies. Why may an agency be preferred in some cases?

   There are different methods of carrying out research: by post, telephone, and personal interview. What are the advantages and disadvantages of each of these methods?

2. Part of the Application of Number core skills involves designing and using a questionnaire to survey opinion. There are very few products around today that were with us 100 years ago. Do you feel that Coca-Cola will always be with us? Undertake research into why people purchase Coke. Your research should include a questionnaire with at least ten questions, and it should include examples of both open and closed questions. Draw up recommendations to the Coca-Cola company as to what strategy you would adopt to ensure that people will still be consuming the product well into the 21st century. Identify any social or demographic trends that may affect the demand for the product. You should survey a minimum of 20 people. Use a suitable table or graph to display some of your numerical material.

3. In some less developed countries Coca-Cola has been accused of introducing unnecessary sugar into diets and of paying its workforce very low wages. As a sales manager how could you defend the Coca-Cola company in the face of these accusations?

25

EVEN LEVI'S CAN MAKE MISTAKES

Elements: **3.1** *PC 12345*   **3.3** *PC 3*
AN **3.2** *PC 12345*

*Key concepts: Market research, Quantitative and qualitative methods, Types of
research sample*

During the 1980s, Levi's US division was looking at ways of diversifying away from its heavy dependence on a jeans market that appeared to be saturated. They had already introduced Levi's shoes, shirts and socks, which sold quite well among people who were already buying Levi jeans. Now they wanted to move into the market for higher priced clothes, in order to attract a new type of customer to the Levi Strauss brand. As menswear had always been their biggest seller, it was decided to concentrate on the male market first.

To decide how to meet this objective, a market research company was commissioned to investigate mens' purchasing habits and attitudes to clothes (a Usage and Attitudes study). A large quantitative survey was conducted among a quota sample of 2,000 men who had recently spent at least $50 on clothing. When analysed, the survey revealed that the entire menswear market could be segmented into five types of buyer:

- Type 1 **Traditionalist** (probably over 45; department store shopper; buys polyester suits and slacks; shops with wife)
- Type 2 **Classic Independent** ('a real clothes horse'; 21% of market, yet buying 46% of wool blend suits; buys at independent stores; expensive tastes)
- Type 3 **Utilitarian** (wears jeans for work and play; 26% of the market; Levi loyalists)
- Type 4 **Trendy Casual** (buying 'designer', high fashion clothes; might buy 501's, but usually considers Levi too mass-market; 19% of the market)
- Type 5 **Price Shopper** (buys whatever and wherever the lowest prices are found; no potential for Levi; 14% of market)

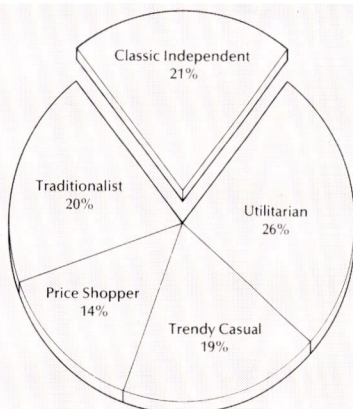

Menswear Market Segmentation

As the Type 2 Classic Independent men fitted in with Levi's objective, the research company was asked to computer analyse the findings so that the behaviour and attitudes of this specific group could be split out from the rest of the sample. The large total number of interviews made it possible to have confidence in the reliability of the data from this sub-sample. It emerged that Type 2 men wanted traditionally styled, perhaps pinstriped, suits; that they liked to buy through independent clothes shops or tailors, rather than at department stores; and that they liked to shop alone, whereas others liked having their wife/girlfriend with them.

To tackle this segment of the market, Levi's decided to introduce 'Tailored Classics', a range of high quality wool suits, trousers and jackets. The research showed that these buyers valued quality and fit rather than low prices, so they decided to price their range 10% above that of the competition. To avoid direct product comparisons – and to ensure that not too large a salesforce was needed – Levi chose to distribute through department store chains.

Having decided on this strategy, its acceptability to the target market was tested via a series of group discussions. These were conducted by a psychologist who was to look for the real motivations behind respondents' opinions or behaviour. The psychologist reported that the Type 2 men had two misgivings: first, they were concerned that the garments would be in standard fittings, and so would not provide the tailoring they wanted; second, although they could believe that Levi's could make a good suit, they still felt uncomfortable about the Levi's name. One said:

> '*When I think Levi I think jeans. If they're making suits I have to be convinced.*'

Another felt that:

> '*If I went to work and someone said: "Hey, that's a good suit, Joe, who's it by?" I wouldn't feel comfortable saying Levi.*'

The company's marketing executives responded to this by deciding to concentrate on the separate jackets and trousers in the launch advertising, and let suits 'slipstream'. The Director of Consumer Marketing felt certain that:

> '*The thing that's going to overcome Levi's image for casualness as no other thing can, is a suit that's made by Levi that doesn't look like all the other things we've made. Once that gets on the racks people will put an asterisk on the image that says: "Oh, and they can also make a good suit when they put their mind to it".*'

Soon after this decision, salesmen started contacting retail buyers. After four months of selling to the trade, it was clear that the range's sales targets would not be met. Even a price cut did little to redeem the situation, and Tailored Classics achieved only 65% of its modest sales targets.

Levi's could only find consolation if they could learn why they went so badly wrong.

Sources: *Channel 4: 'Commercial Breaks'; The Financial Times*

Questions

1   Give two reasons why Levi's chose to use a separate company to undertake research, rather than do it in-house. **(2)**

2   What is a quota sample? Name one other type of sampling method which could be used in market research. **(3)**

3   Why was a quota sample appropriate in this case? **(2)**

4   **a**   In constructing the pie chart, how many degrees within the circle should be given to the Type 2 segment? **(2)**

   b   The US menswear market was then worth $4,000 million. If Levi's had achieved a 10% share of the Type 2 segment, what sales value would this have represented (show your workings). **(3)**

5   What were the messages within the research findings that Levi's chose to ignore? **(2)**

6   Distinguish between quantitative and qualitative research by using examples from the case study. **(4)**

7   Market research reduces the risk of failure. Why did it not work in this instance? **(2)**

Further work

1   Describe the concept of the product life cycle. Sketch a diagram to show where you would place Levi's jeans in that cycle? Write a report to the Managing Director of Levi's UK Ltd on a marketing strategy to increase sales to the youth market.

2   Divide another market into the relevant segments of buyers. For example, you could use the market for paperback books, board games or the holiday market.

   Imagine that you wish to launch a new product into one of these market segments. How would you market the product? What constraints would there be on the marketing department?

26

LET THE BUYER BEWARE

Elements: **3.1** *PC 1* **3.2** *PC 1234* **3.3** *PC 4*

Key concepts: Consumer trends, Forecasting, Economic information, Marketing activities, Social trends

It had all happened by chance. Melanie had been moaning to a friend about the problems of running her small design company. The friend knew of another woman (Cathy) who was thinking of selling a business. So they arranged to meet.

Cathy started the firm seven years ago, by finding a manufacturer who could mass-produce her design of baby and toddler footwear. In her first year the turnover was only £7,342 but retailers seemed to like her products, so she kept going. Two thousand pounds was spent on display stands at the Junior Fashion Fair at Olympia in the following two years, and orders began to pour in. Stockists soon included shops such as Bentalls, Children's World, and many independent babywear outlets.

By the fourth year, the Babyboots range of products had expanded to four size bands (0-6 months; 6-12 months; 12-18 months; and 18-24 months), and within each band were eight different colours, four different linings, and four different fabrics. The range has not really altered since. That year, sales were £78,780 and Cathy was making a £13,000 profit even after paying herself a small salary. Given that she did little more than take orders, pack them, carry them to the Post Office, and then phone the factory for new supplies, this was good money. Her office was (and is) a small room at the back of her house, and the stockroom the house's basement.

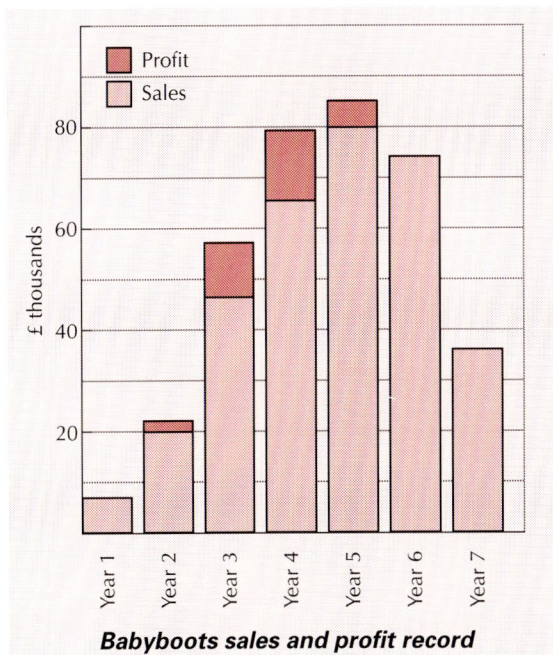

Babyboots sales and profit record

Early in the fifth year, though, Cathy had a baby and began to find it hard to find the time and energy to keep the business going. 'I realise now that I should have sold it then', she told Melanie.

Over the two years since the baby, Cathy has done nothing active to market her products. She has relied on existing customers, plus three agents who sell her goods on commission. Two operate in the South-East footwear trade on a 5% commission, but provide very little business. The third is in Scotland, and sells to chemist shops for an 8% commission. This man sold £10,000 worth of Babyboots last year – more than the six Bentalls department stores.

Now Melanie is trying to decide if she should make an offer for the Babyboots business, and if so, for how much? In making up her mind, she has to decide what she would do to revitalise it. For 'the books' reveal that sales slumped from £74,000 to

£35,900 in the latest year. Cathy maintains that this is a temporary result of her neglect, but could it be due to factors that would have longer term implications?

Melanie's questioning reveals that Babyboots not only have competition from a British firm (Padders), but also from Korean suppliers who sell at half the price charged by the two British rivals.

The attempt to find out more financial details is hampered by the fact that no full accounts have been prepared for this year or last. Nevertheless, the information below gives a lot of useful data – all provided willingly by Cathy. She also explains that she buys from her manufacturer at £1.55, spends three pence per display bag, and charges her customers for postage. The list price of Babyboots is £2.05, though half her customers are paying an average price of £1.95 (this includes the agents' commission).

Babyboots Sales And Profit History

	Latest Year	Year 6	Year 5	Year 4	Year 3	Year 2	Year 1
Sales £000	36	74	85	79	57	22	7
Contribution £000	–	–	20	23	17	6.5	2
Gross profit margin %	–	–	23.7	29.3	29.6	29.4	29.0
Overheads £000	–	–	15	9.3	6.4	4.4	2.4
Profit £000	–	–	5	13.7	10.6	2.1	– 0.4

Questions

1 What is a sales agent? State two advantages and two disadvantages of using agents to increase sales. **(5)**

2 Describe the main trends in Babyboots' sales and profits over the past seven years. **(4)**

3 Give three possible reasons for the decline in sales during the past two years. **(3)**

4 If you were Melanie, what possible marketing strategies would you suggest to boost profit in the coming year? Explain which you favour most and why. **(5)**

5 Based on the trends and economic information provided, write a short report to Melanie, as a potential buyer of the firm, on whether she should buy the business if the asking price was £12,000. **(8)**

Further work

1 Consumers can be classified in many ways. Certain groups are then targeted by the market researchers. One such classification is based on social grading. There are six main categories: social group A – upper middle class; B – middle class; C1 – lower middle class; C2 – skilled working class; D – working class; E – lowest level of subsistence.

For each class, give three types of occupations you would include. How would the following business sectors use social grade categories: the newspaper industry, tourist industry and supermarket chains?

2 Analyse present market trends and make a short-term prediction (1–5 years) of consumer trends and a sales forecast (1–5 years) on any of the following:

- organic food sold in supermarkets
- the number of satellite dishes and viewers of Sky TV in the UK
- the number of people visiting EuroDisney in France
- the number of people using the Channel tunnel.

Economic information that you would need to help forecast would include unemployment rates, economic growth, and inflation statistics. You may wish to make a best and worst scenario about the statistics and adapt your sales figures accordingly.

27 HÄAGEN-DAZS UK – A CLASSIC PRODUCT LAUNCH

Elements: **3.1** *PC 2 3* **3.2** *PC 1* **3.3** *PC 1 3 4 5*
IT **3.2** *PC 1 2 3 5 6 7*

Key concepts: Market research, Marketing mix, Ethics of advertising

In 1989, in a strategic decision to move into the fast food business, the British firm Grand Metropolitan bought up Pillsbury, the American owners of Burger King and other food brands. It is said that Grand Metropolitan only 'discovered' Häagen-Dazs after they had bought it. No time was lost, however, in developing its potential in the British market.

As a catalyst to consumer awareness of the brand, a lavishly appointed Häagen-Dazs outlet was established at London's Leicester Square in mid-1989. Long queues quickly became the norm, despite price levels 50% higher than other ice cream parlours. This was testimony to the quality of the product and proved that a gap existed in the market for a super-premium brand. Yet might it only be a market for lavish treats when out for the evening, or was there a wider, retail market opportunity? And if so, how could it best be exploited? These were questions for an advertising agency to answer.

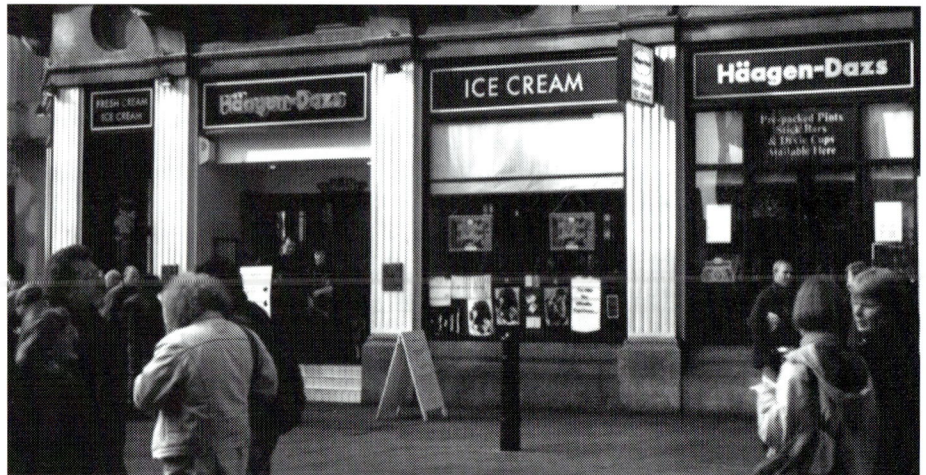

After talking to several different agencies, Häagen-Dazs UK decided upon Bartle, Bogle and Hegarty (BBH), best known for the Levi 501s advertising. The agency's brief was to help Häagen-Dazs create a new 'gold standard' and become the ultimate ice cream in the market. At the time a premium sector existed in which Loseley and New England were the most prestigious and expensive brands. Häagen-Dazs UK decided to open up a new super-premium sector, with ice cream priced at £2.99 per half litre. This was three to four times the price of standard dairy ice cream and 50% higher than its two closest competitors.

The first task was to provide the background research upon which long-term, strategic decisions could be based. A large-scale survey showed that the target market for premium ice cream sold through retail outlets was 25–44 year olds with high disposable income but without children. These became the criteria for selecting the sample for the group discussions that followed.

These groups of six to eight men and women were prompted into discussion by each being given a half-litre tub of Häagen-Dazs Vanilla to eat as they talked. The interviewees were asked when and where they could imagine consuming the product. Usually the answer was eating it alone, as a reward or as a 'dream-like' compensation for a bad day or date. The big step forward came, however, as the group leader asked when they might share their Häagen-Dazs. Customers talked of sharing a spoon with their partner, feeding each other, and of 'mellowing out' together in front of their favourite video. Products such as Cadbury's Flake had long portrayed themselves as a self-indulgence. Häagen-Dazs now had a unique way of advertising a food product: as a sensual pleasure to be shared.

The research provided the material for BBH's account planner to write the creative brief. From this the creative department would be able to consider how best to advertise the product. It was decided that the brief should be met by the use of press media rather than television. For not only is television an expensive way of reaching affluent adults, it also lacks the subtlety of mood that BBH wanted. So the agency's media department was asked to plan a campaign aimed at affluent adults in their moments of relaxation. This led to spaces being bought in the weekend colour supplements and womens consumer press.

Meanwhile, a parallel survey had been researching into the suitability of the American pack design within the British market. In a large scale quantitative survey consumers found the pack significantly different to other ice-cream brands. Group discussions showed that once people tried the ice cream they could identify with the package as authentic high quality. So the company and the agency decided to leave the imported packs unchanged.

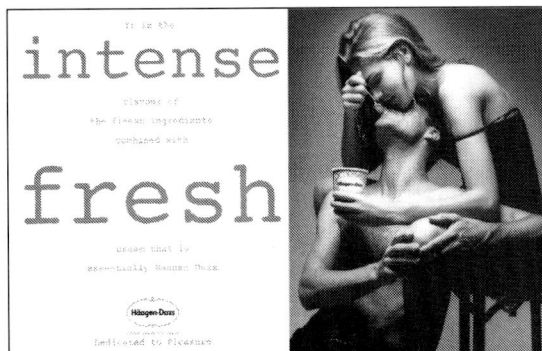

It is the **intense** flavour of the finest ingredients combined with **fresh** cream that is essentially Häagen-Dazs

Häagen-Dazs

Dedicated to Pleasure

On Sunday July 21st 1991 the first advertisement appeared – one of four black and white photographs that juxtaposed product messages with sensual imagery, with the slogan 'dedicated to pleasure'. The launch advertising burst lasted eight weeks and cost a little over £300,000. A further three-week campaign before Christmas took the year's spending to £450,000.

From the start, editorial coverage of the launch was considerable. Much of it represented marvellous free public relations. Some of the newspaper reporting focused upon the ethics of advertising ice cream through sexy images. Did it exploit women? Did it meet the Advertising Standards Authority yardstick of 'Legal, Decent, Honest and Truthful'? Whatever the answers, sales kept rising.

The financial impact of the advertising was dramatic, with sales doubling between June and July 1991. In 1991 as a whole, sales were five times their 1990 level. Häagen-Dazs went from a 2% share of the £50 million premium ice cream market in October 1990 to 22% by October 1991.

The diagram below relates the launch advertising bursts to Häagen-Dazs sales to retailers.

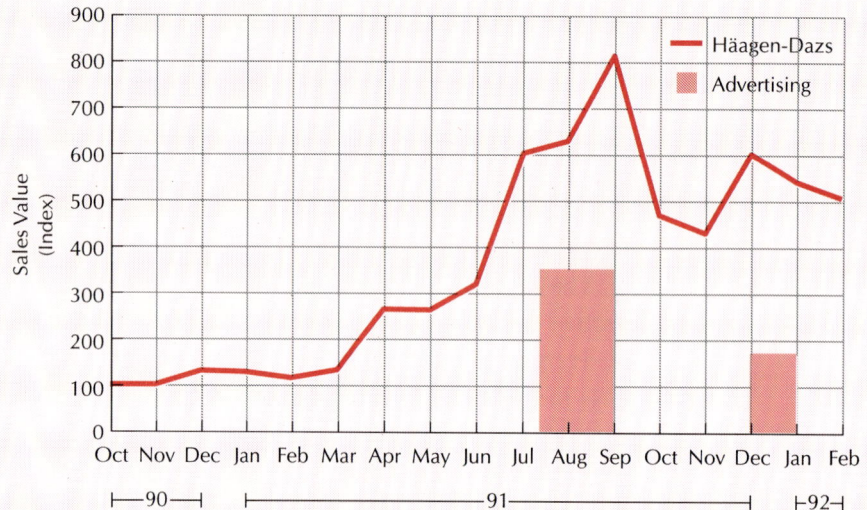

Häagen-Dazs sales growth compared with advertising

This achievement relied not only upon the advertising, but also on offering millions of product samples. Also crucial was the distribution drive started up by the Häagen-Dazs sales team. In April 1991 Häagen-Dazs was stocked in shops selling less than 20% of London's ice cream; by July this distribution level had risen to over 40%.

An innovative feature of the distribution strategy came from the earlier group discussions. Mentions of sharing Häagen-Dazs in front of a favourite film encouraged the sales team to supply refrigerated cabinets to Blockbuster Video. This proved so successful that, during one week, Häagen-Dazs was second only to *Terminator 1* as Blockbuster's biggest money-spinner. During the sales drive, some supermarket chains had turned Häagen-Dazs down, refusing to believe that their customers would buy such an expensive product. Once the advertising campaign had started, however, the same stores phoned up asking for the product. Clearly the distribution growth was both a cause and an effect of the rising demand.

Most important of all, in judging the effectiveness of the launch marketing strategy, was that sales and distribution not only went up but stayed up. Many products are highly sensitive to changes in marketing spending, with sales jumping up but then falling back once the advertising campaign or special offer has ended.

The marketing triumph of Häagen-Dazs was that customer loyalty built up so quickly. In America it had taken twenty years to achieve what Häagen-Dazs UK managed in two.

The Marketing Society voted Häagen-Dazs the 'New Product of the Year'.

Sources: *Biss Lancaster; Häagen-Dazs Report by Nick Kendall at BBH; Häagen-Dazs UK.*

Questions

1 What different methods of market research did the advertising agency use to find the strengths and opportunities of the Häagen-Dazs brand? **(5)**

2 What specific aspects of the marketing mix were used to launch the new product? **(4)**

3 How would you describe the characteristics of typical Häagen-Dazs consumers? **(3)**

4 What authorities exist to try to ensure that advertising is ethical? **(2)**

Do you feel that it is ethical to promote an ice cream through sexy advertising? **(6)**

5 Interpret the information provided by the graph within the text. **(4)**

6 The graph compares sales with advertising. Explain what other factors should be taken into account before drawing conclusions about the effect of the advertising on sales. **(6)**

Further work

1 What share of the ice cream market was held by Häagen-Dazs in

a October 1990

b October 1991?

(State your answers as a percentage)

To help you obtain core skills in Information Technology, use a suitable computer package to draw a graph showing the increase in market share. Plot a five-year market share forecast onto the same graph. Use a suitable key to show that some of your figures are estimated. Explain the basis of your forecast, and demonstrate that you can merge a chart with text by placing your text under the graph. If there are any mistakes go back and correct them, and then print a final copy. Your evidence will be a printout of a hard copy showing the skills used.

Elements: **3.1** *PC 345* **3.2** *PC 1234* **3.3** *PC 14*
               C **3.2** *PC 1234* IT **3.3** *PC 12345*

Key concepts: Consumer characteristics, Marketing objectives,
Economic information, Consumption patterns

In 1981 a London entrepreneur called Sheldon Grainer opened two 'wine warehouses'. They sold wine by the case at wholesale prices from no-frills outlets away from the high street. Despite high sales, the founder of 'Majestic Wine Warehouses' could not overcome the **cash flow problems** inherent to new, fast-growing firms and the business went into receivership. Two admirers of this innovative way of retailing wine (Esme Johnstone and Giles Clarke) bought Majestic from the Receiver and put their energies and capital into making it expand profitably.

Johnstone and Clarke's **marketing strategy** was to fill the gap they believed to exist between the supermarket wine department and the – perhaps intimidating – specialist wine merchant. As Johnstone put it: 'Once he's bored with the limited range at the supermarkets, the customer moves up to Majestic'. As their alcohol licence only allowed them to sell complete cases (12 bottles) of wine, a key element in the choice of sites was, and is, to provide free car parking. It also made it desirable to offer free tastings, which they built into a vital promotional tool.

Perhaps the most distinctive element in their strategy, however, was in the managerial and personnel policy. Most store chains aim for a high degree of uniformity between branches, which is achieved by training managers to implement head office policy rigidly. Majestic's approach was to give managers considerable freedom to run their own outlet in their own style. So if the Battersea store manager had a special love of Australian wines, he could run special tasting sessions for customers in those products alone. 'We motivate them to think of it as their own small business' said Johnstone. Nevertheless, buying was always done centrally – often direct from the growers – in order to keep unit costs down.

This approach, together with the strong growth of wine consumption in the United Kingdom, enabled Majestic to open new outlets steadily, so that by 1987 there were twenty-one generating annual sales of £7 million. Although there were, by this time, many chains imitating the Majestic formula, free publicity from journalists praising Majestic's range and service ensured that growth could continue.

Then came an extraordinary opportunity. Safeway Stores was looking for a buyer for its 104-strong chain of cut price liquor stores in California. Its sales turnover of $300 million dwarfed that of Majestic, yet investors with confidence in the Johnstone-Clarke team were willing to back their managerial skills.

The Liquor Barn chain was bought for $110 million in the summer of 1987, and although Majestic put up only $5 million of that, the deal gave the Englishmen a controlling share. Of the remainder of the finance, $10 million was share capital and the rest was bank loans. Johnstone later explained:

> *'We were presented with the opportunity to buy the world's biggest drinks retailer. Had it worked we would have made an enormous amount of money.'*

However, it did not work. Both men moved out to California and began to implement a policy of shifting Liquor Barn towards a Majestic-style trading policy. Forty percent of the U.S. chain's sales had been of spirits, but they wanted to put far more emphasis on wine. In effect, they tried to change the image from downmarket **discount store** to a more upmarket store for choosier customers. Regular customers began to drift away faster than new ones arrived, so sales turnover slid.

Two other problems hit the Liquor Barn enterprise. First, Johnstone and Clarke under-estimated the impact upon suppliers of the chain ceasing to be part of the Safeway group. Not only were bulk discounts less than before, but also suppliers were unwilling to deliver direct to the stores. When the Englishmen tried to overcome the higher supply prices by dealing direct with producers, their normal distributors became angry and disruptive. The second problem was the need to finance the huge borrowings made at the time of purchase. A U.S. trade magazine estimated that monthly repayments were about one million dollars. The combination of rising direct costs, high interest payments, and falling revenues drained Liquor Barn's cash very rapidly. By summer 1988 suppliers' bills were being paid later and later. By the autumn distributors put the stores on a cash-on-delivery basis, which meant that as there was insufficient cash to refill the shelves, the company was forced to file for bankruptcy. Clarke left both Liquor Barn and Majestic, while Johnstone returned to England as joint managing director of Majestic (which Clarke and Johnstone still controlled through a majority shareholding). He made clear his intention of expanding Majestic into a major, national wine store chain.

Johnstone later blamed his U.S. failure on paying too much for the store chain. However, his successor at Liquor Barn said:

> *'The British owners let expenses get out of hand and pushed for an upscale merchandise programme that alienated many of the discount chain's traditional customers.'*

In other words, Johnstone's expert knowledge of British drinks marketing proved inadequate in the States.

The Johnstone-Clarke era finally ended when, in August 1989, they sold Majestic for £15.5 million cash. Much of this purchase price was for the Majestic name, for despite the U.S. failure, British wine buyers regarded the company as a winner.

Sources: Management Today, May 1989; The Financial Times, August 1989.

Questions

1 What is meant by cash flow problems, marketing strategy, discount store? (3)

2 What were the marketing objectives when the original wine stores were established? (2)

3 What is the marketing mix? Use examples to show which elements of the mix were most important in marketing Majestic. (6)

4 Why was it difficult to change the image of a down-market discount store to a more upmarket store for choosier customers? (2)

5 What market research should they have done before paying $110 million for Liquor Barn? Explain how it might have prevented the problems that occurred. (7)

Further work

1 In order to cover the range for element 3.2 you have to make a short-term prediction of consumer demand based on identified consumer trends.

The drinks market can be divided into several market segments: spirits, wines, beers and soft drinks. What are the characteristics of the consumers in these markets? Look at income, age, gender, and lifestyle for each market.

Take any two of these types of drinks, and look at social and economic trends which may influence their consumption. Obtain statistics from *Social Trends* or the *Drinks Pocket Book* (published by NTC*), and predict consumer demand and sales forecasts over the next five years. Draw a line graph to show the trend lines for each drink. If you are using a word processor this is an opportunity to produce a report where text and graph are merged. Produce a hard copy as evidence of your ability to use this skill.

2 How would you research the potential market of a low alcohol spirit, for instance vodka? Devise a questionnaire, and ask an appropriate sample of potential consumers how they would feel about such a product. Taking into account any secondary informa-tion that may be relevant, write a report to your company recommending or rejecting the new product's introduction.

*Drinks Pocket Book, produced by the Advertising Association in association with NTC Publications Ltd, Farm Road, Henley on Thames, Oxfordshire, RG9 1EG.

29 AVOIDING A PRICE WAR

Elements: **3.1** *PC 12345* **3.2** *PC 4* **3.3** *PC 124*
C **3.2** *PC 1234* *AN* **3.2** *PC 124567*

Key concepts: Forecasting sales, Promotions, Numeracy, Solving problems, Making calculations

The Altrincham Petrol Company Limited (APC) has a prime site on a junction on the main road to Manchester. It is expensive to rent (£1,400 a week), but the Managing Director has no doubts about the site's value. At a retail price of £1.70 per gallon, this one outlet has averaged a customer every two minutes of its 18 hour day. The average customer buys eight gallons of petrol, and spends 60 pence on other goods. The garage is open for 350 days a year.

The firm buys its petrol from Shell on the following terms:

Up to 1 million gallons per annum	**£1,550 per 1000** gallons
1 to 1.25 million gallons per annum	**£1,520 per 1000** gallons
1.25 to 1.5 million gallons per annum	**£1,500 per 1000** gallons
Over 1.5 million gallons per annum	**£1,480 per 1000** gallons

Other goods sold in the garage shop have an average unit cost of 45 pence.

Of course, the firm has other overhead costs to pay for. Salaries and wages amount to £800 per week, maintenance costs £300 per week, and other bills (including electricity and rates) to £700 per week. (Assume a fifty week year.) The only other cost is that of marketing. The various promotions that Shell run cost the firm about six pence per gallon.

Now the firm faces a real dilemma. A new, very modern Jet station has opened up on the other side of the junction, and it is offering its petrol at £1.60 per gallon. In the week since it opened, trade at APC has fallen by 30%, and the Managing Director suspects that APC has traded at a loss during this week. It had been APC's intention to use the profits generated by the Altrincham garage to finance the start-up costs of a second site on the other side of Manchester. The firm already had £100,000 saved for this – and only needed another £60,000. Now, the Managing Director thought gloomily, it would never happen.

So what should they do? One option was to carry on as they were. The second was to cut their price to £1.64, which the Managing Director believed would restrict their volume loss to 10%. Or, more radically, keep their price at £1.70, and use their savings to refit the shop to turn it into an 8-till-late Spar outlet. That,

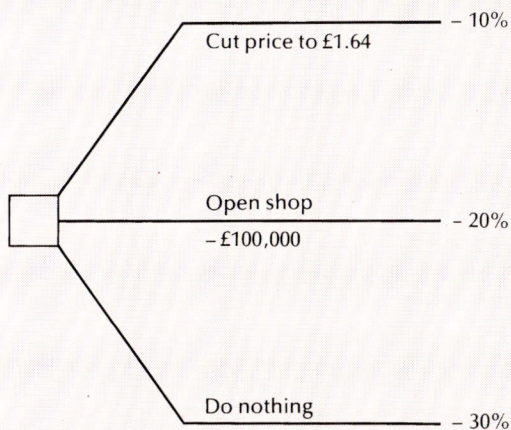

Cut price to £1.64 – 10%

Open shop – £100,000 – 20%

Do nothing – 30%

Decision tree showing the three options

he hoped, would cut the reduction in customers to 20%, and would also boost non-petrol sales to £2.00 per customer (at a unit cost of £1.50).

Questions

1 What is a promotion? Give two examples. Why do garages frequently use promotions? **(5)**

2 How many customers visited the site per day before the Jet garage opened? **(4)**

3 Calculate the number of gallons of petrol sold per day before the change in competition. Use this figure to work out the bulk purchase price of petrol per gallon from Shell. **(4)**

4 How much did the firm spend on petrol before the Jet station opened? How much gross profit did the company make on petrol sales? **(4)**

5 Calculate the annual gross profit made on goods other than petrol. **(3)**

6 Calculate the three alternative strategies. Assume that all costs must be accounted for fully within the first year. Which strategy appears most profitable? **(10)**

Further work

1 Garages do not make as much profit on their petrol as they do from selling other items. Write a report to a new owner of a garage, suggesting how the garage could be organised to increase sales of other items. You need to look at the forecourt, shop, repairs. Try to visit a local garage to conduct preliminary research before writing up your report . You may wish to video the visit as part of your evidence.

30

BODY SHOP INTERNATIONAL

Elements: **3.2** *PC 1* **3.3** *PC 145*
AN **3.1** *PC 12456* **3.2** *PC 4* *IT* **2.1** *PC 1234*
2.3 *PC 1234*

Key concepts: Marketing activities, Marketing objectives, Marketing mix, Consumer characteristics, Ethical considerations

When Anita Roddick launched her first Body Shop in a small street in Brighton in 1976, she devised a publicity stunt: a phone call to the local paper protesting at alleged attempts by neighbouring funeral parlours to block the shop and its name. That flair for publicity was to remain a theme throughout the following, dazzling years of growth.

Anita and her husband Gordon had hit upon a real commercial rarity – a trendy concept with staying power. Although 1976 was long before 'green' issues became prominent, there were already notable movements against animal experimentation, and towards healthy, natural products. The Roddicks' success was to encapsulate this into a genuine niche in the retail market – a shop providing a range of natural cosmetics and toiletries that had not been tested on animals, and that came in refillable containers. Bright window displays and prominent locations ensured high sales without advertising. As the biggest costs in the production of most cosmetics were the packaging and the advertising, Body Shop was able to charge relatively low prices, yet enjoy very high profit margins.

With the Brighton shop proving an instant success, the Roddicks decided to expand by the then unusual means of franchising. This would allow their brand name to become established quickly, thereby making sure that customers thought of Body Shop as the originator of this idea.

By 1981, twenty-two outlets had been established in Britain, and seventeen overseas. Company profits of just £31,000 reflected the experimentation that was still taking place under the Body Shop banner. To a great extent, Anita and Gordon were still teaching themselves how to handle a successful business. Finding suppliers to make their ever-widening range of products, screening franchise applicants, and organising distribution had all to be delegated to new, salaried managers. It also took them some time to realise just how high they could push the prices of their unique, highly fashionable products.

With the early 1980s seeing a rapid rise in the firm's fortunes, Gordon felt that the company was ready for a stock market listing. As its short life-history made it unsuitable for a full stock market launch, its shares were offered for sale on the Unlisted Securities Market (USM) in April 1984. Gordon has since said that:

'We were attracted by the advantages of a high profile, especially because of our High Street image. It also improved our credibility. We became contenders for prime retailing positions with people who would have shown us the door a year before.'

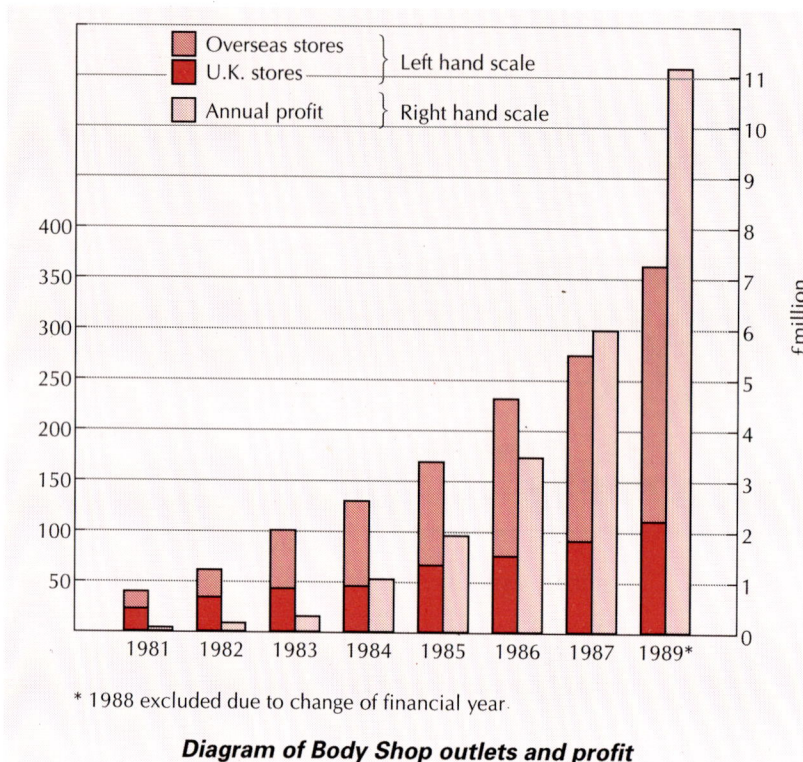

Diagram of Body Shop outlets and profit

Deciding what price to charge for shares in a unique company is always difficult. Body Shop's stockbrokers decided on a price of 95 pence – valuing the company at 25 times its forecast earnings (profit) for 1984. This seemed high, as most retail shares stood at a Price/Earnings ratio of 12. Yet the firm's growth record and potential ensured that investors clamoured for the stock. The share price doubled in the first week of trading, and within eighteen months had risen above 800 pence. As the Roddicks had sold less than a quarter of the shares in the company, their remaining holdings were worth over £50 million by the end of 1985. Early in 1986, Body Shop International plc left the USM and became fully listed on the stock market.

The company's continued growth moved increasingly towards overseas markets. By 1986, Body Shop was Britain's biggest retail exporter by far. The once esteemed Mothercare chain had suffered badly in its attempt to break into the United States; even Marks and Spencer had achieved little in its years of dabbling in France, Canada and Belgium. Body Shop's unique niche made it far better able to succeed. Yet the Roddicks also showed great sense in waiting until their formula had worked in other countries before tackling the huge US market in 1988.

One aspect of the formula that they began to rethink, though, was their early practice of granting franchisees monopoly rights to a city or area. This gave the franchisee the choice of how many outlets to open, plus freedom from competition. In 1989 they went against this by buying out some of their own franchisees. The Edinburgh franchise was bought for £1.3 million, giving its holder a capital gain of perhaps 1300%. Then the company that owned the monopoly rights to all outlets in Leeds, Liverpool, and Manchester was bought for £4.5 million. This firm had been making a £925,000 annual profit on net assets of £350,000.

More importantly, the end of the 1980s saw a shift in the public and political mood that gave the business yet more impetus. In 1988, the growing environmentalism forced Mrs. Thatcher to make a speech that set the Conservatives' claim to be seen as the 'green' party. In 1989, the real Green Party had great success at the polls. At the heart of this trend was Anita Roddick, who had (in May 1987) signed a two year agreement with the pressure group Friends Of The Earth. She agreed to display environmentalist publicity in Body Shop windows, and to encourage franchisees to campaign locally on pollution issues.

As concern mounted about the impact upon the ozone layer of the destruction of the Brazilian rainforests, Anita Roddick was to be seen not only talking about it, but also acting. Under the slogan 'trade not aid' she set about creating a range of rainforest-based cosmetics, such as a cleansing cream based upon Brazil nut oil. Creating a demand for raw materials from the forests would, she hoped, give the Brazilian government and landowners an incentive to keep the forests intact.

Within Britain, the Roddicks' social zeal found outlet in the establishment of a soap factory in Easterhouse, Glasgow. Its origins were in a visit made by Anita in 1988. A community leader pointed out that while her company was helping less developed countries, it was ignoring 'Britain's own Third World': the inner cities. As Body Shop needed extra supplies of soap, it was decided to set up a factory in Easterhouse rather than in the affluent area surrounding the firm's Sussex headquarters. It opened in April 1989 with 29 employees. Body Shop received widespread publicity for going, in Mrs. Roddick's words, 'where angels fear to tread'. A sceptical reporter from *The Financial Times* found locals who were irritated by 'her patronising attitude'; but none could doubt that the company had a magical way of combining social and environmental initiatives with self-publicity and therefore profitability.

By 1989, the Roddicks' family holdings in Body Shop were worth more than £200 million. Those who had bought shares in 1984 had seen their investment rise tenfold in five years. Staff and franchisees were encouraged to share in the Roddicks' nutritional and environmental concerns, and received a high standard of training at Body Shop's purpose-built centre. Customers received attractive, effective and environmentally-friendly products that they felt good about buying and using. In these early years of its life, Body Shop seemed to achieve the ideal mix of commercial success and social responsibility.

Sources: *Body Shop Prospectus and Annual Reports; The Financial Times; The Guardian; The Investors' Chronicle.*

APPENDIX A: Body Shop International – Financial record (1983-89)

	1983	1984	1985	1986	1987	*1989
					All figures in £000s	
Sales turnover	2,143	4,910	9,362	17,394	28,476	73,007
Pre-tax profit	202	1,044	1,929	3,451	5,998	15,243
Shareholders funds	374	812	1,683	3,445	6,587	23,477
Capital employed	450	1,132	1,941	3,692	6,865	24,236

1989 is the 17 months to 28th February, as the financial year was changed.

Questions

1 What is meant by a niche market? What was the niche that the Body Shop filled? **(3)**

2 How would you describe the type of customers who buy Body Shop products? **(2)**

3 What new products were identified by the Body Shop? **(2)**

4 Using Appendix A, for each of the years from 1984–1989, make an estimate of pre-tax profit as a percentage of sales turnover. Then calculate the actual percentages. **(9)**

5 What is meant by being ethical? Give examples from the text to demonstrate the Body Shop's high ethical standards. **(4)**

Further work

1 How would you react to the success of the Body Shop if you were the Director of a large chain of stores like Boots? How easy would it be to imitate the Body Shop image? What problems and constraints would there be?

2 Use Appendix A to help you achieve core skills in Information Technology. Enter the data for sales turnover, pre-tax profits and capital employed onto a spreadsheet. Use the wordwrap facility to present your row headings. Use a suitable file name to save the work. The file name might include your initials and the page number. From the spreadsheet information, produce a graph with labelled axes and a title showing the information. To fulfil the range for element 2.3, demonstrate that you can switch between portrait and landscape paper orientation, and make your printed version appropriate to page size. Print out a hard copy of your graph.

31

THE PRODUCT PORTFOLIO PROBLEM

Elements: **3.2** *PC 1234* **3.3** *PC 1234*
AN **3.3** *PC 123456*

Key concepts: Marketing mix, Product range development, Consumption patterns

Streamer has dominated the British cider market for over fifty years. Its Sparrowhawk and Target brands have been national best-sellers for decades. The company benefited from customer loyalty, plus the inertia of the pubs, clubs and off-licences that kept on buying Streamer brands because they always had done. Up until last year Streamer held over 50% of the cider market.

The big change began two years ago, when the Chancellor of the Exchequer reduced the tax rate for cider in the Budget. With beer tax levels held constant, customers started to switch to cider. Streamer passed the tax reduction on to customers by cutting its prices, in order to boost sales volumes. A smaller rival used a different strategy, however. Devon Cider chose to develop extra strength ciders with a distinctive image, priced at the same level as equivalent beers. The extra profit margin (from the lower tax rates) was used to pay for extensive advertising. So 'Silver Light' and 'Red Streak' became household names through a blaze of television commercials. With gross profit margins four times higher than Streamer's brands, Devon Cider became a highly profitable company.

Streamer's first response had been to dismiss Devon's new brands as a minor irrelevance. However, both products appealed to the young women who had always been the main consumers of Sparrowhawk, so Streamer had to act. To the surprise of outsiders, the company's first action was to dismiss its Marketing Director. The successor immediately set to work developing a distinctive, bottled cider called 'Clear Rain' and also a more modern product to launch on draught in pubs and clubs. The latter would make the most of Streamer's distribution strengths.

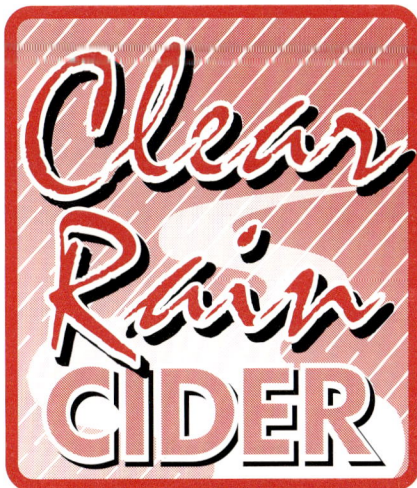

Launched six months later, the draught 'Scrumpy Star' proved a great success. Its stylish advertising and fresh taste made it fashionable, and its higher price made it more profitable than Streamer's older products. The bottled product started equally well, but faltered after a large amount of product trial failed to be converted into repeat purchase. Streamer put more advertising money behind it, to try to strengthen its image, but once the campaign stopped sales fell back disappointingly.

This problem was becoming increasingly evident just as the time was looming for Streamer's annual marketing strategy review. This year, the Board decided to trim the marketing budget to £3.8 million. This would not be enough to support each of the four brands adequately, so the strategy team would have to decide how best to split up the money.

APPENDIX: *Quarterly figures for average cider sales per month (thousand barrels, seasonally adjusted)*

| Period | Streamer's Brands | | | | Devon Cider Total | Total Cider Market |
	Sparrowhawk	Target	Scrumpy Star	Clear Rain		
1st Quarter 2 years ago	120	170	–	–	130	560
2nd Quarter 2 years ago	126	175	–	–	130	574
3rd Quarter 2 years ago	135	183	–	–	131	596
4th Quarter 2 years ago	137	186	–	–	138	613
1st Quarter 1 year ago	131	188	–	–	154	640
2nd Quarter 1 year ago	129	189	–	8	168	655
3rd Quarter 1 year ago	124	189	–	17	168	661
4th Quarter 1 year ago	110	182	22	24	171	670
1st Quarter this year	106	180	38	19	177	686

Questions

1 Give two examples of brand names mentioned in the text. What advantages does a company gain by using successful brand names? **(4)**

2 Which elements of the marketing mix were used to sell cider? **(4)**

3 Draw a line graph to plot the sales of the Streamer brands plus the Devon Cider company for the last five quarters. Describe the main trends in sales. **(12)**

4 What is meant by the Boston Matrix? Decide where to place each of Streamer's brands on a Boston Matrix grid. Justify your decisions. **(10)**

5 How do the two cider companies market their products? **(5)**

Further work

1 How would you describe the characteristics of consumers of cider compared with consumers of other drink products like wine and beer? What type of economic information would you like to obtain to help you to interpret the increase in the total market for cider over the nine quarters of the table? Use information from the text, and information from the *Drinks Pocket Book*, referred to at the end of case study 28, to help you to forecast sales. Your forecast should include a graph with a projection through to the year 2000.

32 MARLBORO AND MARKET POWER

Elements: **3.3** *PC 2345*
          AN **3.2** *PC 1235*   *IT* **3.3** *PC 1234*

Key concepts: Brand names, Marketing activities, Ethical issues

Within seconds of the announcement, its shares had plunged in value by $13.5 billion, and those of its rivals by even more. The whole US stock market suffered its biggest one-day fall for over a year. Within days newspapers were questioning the billion dollar value placed upon brands throughout the world. The cause was the decision by Philip Morris, the world's most profitable cigarette company, to slash the price of the world's most valuable brand – Marlboro cigarettes. The American media soon dubbed April 2nd 1993 as 'Marlboro Friday'.

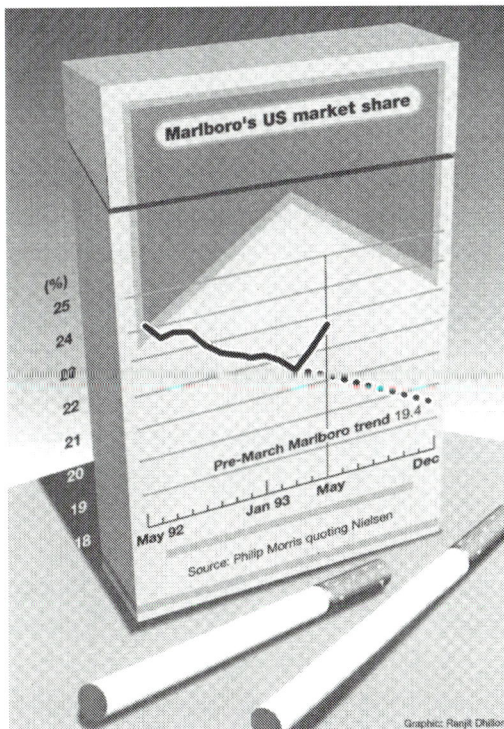

Marlboro's US market share

(%)
25
24
23
22
21
20
19
18

Pre-March Marlboro trend 19.4

May 92   Jan 93   May   Dec

Source: Philip Morris quoting Nielsen

Graphic: Ranjit Dhillon

The price cut of a full 20% applied only to the American market, but since Marlboro accounted for over 100 billion of the 500 billion cigarettes sold per year in the US, the profit implications were huge. Philip Morris acted to try to reverse the erosion of Marlboro's US market share, from 25.8% in 1991 to 24.5% in 1992. Recession-hit consumers were switching to cheaper branded cigarettes and to own-label varieties with no brand image. Discount cigarettes had grown from a 7% market share in 1985 to 19% by 1990 and up to 36% in 1992. Philip Morris, the industry's price leader with its best-selling Marlboro brand, felt it had to respond. As a Wall Street analyst put it:

'This is not a new price war. It's the latest blast in a price war which has already been going on. Philip Morris has come down with both feet on the market. It's going to destroy the discount brands.'

(Roy Burry, Kidder Peabody,
Financial Times April 5th 1993).

William Campbell, the tobacco president of Philip Morris laid himself open to potentially fierce criticism for a decision that was expected to cut 1993 and 1994 profits by over $2 billion dollars per annum. The image-building of the brand had been so successful that by the 1980s Marlboro outsold its nearest rival more than four times. With annual marketing spending of over $100 million in the US, Marlboro had been able to impose a series of price increases that rival brands had to follow. Otherwise their image might have become devalued.

Leading brands in 1991 (by volume)

Marlboro	25.8%
Winston	7.5%
Salem	5.4%
Newport	4.7%

Source: Tobacco Reporter/Euromonitor

Between 1980 and 1991, the price of 20 Marlboro trebled while prices generally (and government taxes) only doubled. This created an opportunity for the companies whose minor brands had been squeezed by the Marlboro marketing machine. For although Philip Morris had pushed the price of the main brands up to $2.20 by early 1993, the economics of cigarette production pointed to lower rather than higher prices. Raw tobacco prices were falling in real terms, and modern machinery could produce 15,000 cigarettes per minute – more than twice the speed and productivity of a decade before. It was now possible to manufacture and distribute a pack of 20 cigarettes for 30 cents. Even with 40 cents of tax and a retail mark up of 20% a profit could be made by selling at one half of Marlboro's price.

As Philip Morris pushed prices up, small producers were able to offer supermarket chains an own-label product that could sell below the psychological price barrier of $1 per pack. As discount sales shot ahead during the 1980s, the large manufacturers moved into the cut-price market. The second largest manufacturer, RJ Reynolds, made a key move in 1987 when it set up the Forsyth Tobacco Company to make a $1 house brand of cigarettes for the huge K-Mart store chain. The cigarettes were made at the same factories that produced the $2.20 Winston and Salem brands. RJ Reynolds hoped that the use of the invented company name 'Forsyth' would minimise the cannibalisation of their own brands. Its success, however, merely forced Philip Morris to pursue the same discount market.

By early 1993, the cigarette market had split into three price segments. The established brands at $2.20, second ranking brands at $1.50, and discount or own label products at $0.99. When it cut the price of Marlboro, Philip Morris also tried to merge the two bottom segments into one. Philip Morris pushed the prices of its mid-range brands down to around $1.30, and raised its cheapest products up towards that same figure. The tobacco giant wanted to change the market's structure as indicated below.

Price segments pre-April 1993		Segments post-April 1993
$2.20	Established brands	
$1.80		Established brands
$1.40	Second-rank brands	
$1.20		Second-rank and discount products
$1.00	Discount products	

Within a month RJ Reynolds announced that it was following Marlboro's lead. It cut the price of its Winston brand. By September it was forecasting that its 1993 US tobacco operating profits would be 43% lower than the previous year – a fall of $900 million.

Philip Morris, meanwhile, was putting a brave face on its announcement of a 53% fall in US tobacco profits for the three months to June. It declared that its price cut had been successful, reversing an eight month decline in Marlboro's market share. From a low of 21.5% in March, Marlboro's share was said to have risen to 24% in July. This would do little to restore the brand's short-term profitability, but that was not the point of the strategy. William Campbell was attempting to regain the initiative in the American cigarette market, to ensure the long term success of Marlboro and Philip Morris.

Although the Marlboro move made sense strategically, it led analysts to question the brand valuations that many companies were placing on their balance sheets. If the world's most valuable brand could not hold its desired price premium, could it be that consumers had learned to see beyond the packaging and the image to the product inside? In which case should companies such as Guinness drop the brand valuations from their balance sheets?

Whereas the financial analysts were worried, marketing professionals showed less concern. They felt consumers were still fully prepared to pay a price premium for a reputable brand, but that Marlboro had pushed that premium too far. Their only doubt was that Philip Morris may have overreacted to a problem made worse by recession. If the market share of discount brands stabilised at 35–40% of the market, Marlboro could still have traded very profitably at $2.20. No-one doubted, however, that Marlboro's action was one of the boldest decisions in marketing history.

Sources: The *Financial Times, The Independent, Wall Street Journal.*

Questions

1 How many billion cigarettes were discount brands selling in the US in 1985, 1990
   and 1992? Assume that the total American market is constant at 500 billion.
   Draw a graph to show your answer. If you are using a computer, print out
   a hard copy to generate your graph.   **(8)**

2 Suggest three reasons for the growth of the discount cigarette market.   **(3)**

3 What profit could be made per pack from a discount brand selling at 99 cents? **(4)**

4 What is psychological pricing? Give two examples from the case study.   **(3)**

5 In the 1980s Marlboro created a tremendously successful brand. Why were some
   of the executives, who were responsible for this, being criticised now?   **(3)**

6 What is meant by brand loyalty? Why does this case study lead to fears about
   the future of brands?   **(4)**

Further work

1 American doctors are worried that the Marlboro price cut might lead to an increase in
   the demand for cigarettes, and therefore an increase in the health problems caused by
   smoking.

   Discuss the ethics of sales and marketing activities involved in the cigarette industry.
   Write a summary to follow up the main issues and arguments.

33 MONEY AND MOTIVATION

Elements: **4.1** *PC 123456* **5.3** *PC 12*
  C **3.2** *PC 1234*

Key concepts: Human resourcing, Employee relations,
  Business performance, Incentive systems

The Walton Furniture Company is a long established, highly profitable business. Its sales turnover averages £15,000 per week. Given that it operates on a 200% **mark-up** (quite normal in furniture retailing), its £7,500 of weekly overheads are covered with ease. The owners have always believed that much of their success has been due to the incentive scheme they operate; the 2% commission on all sales provides a carrot of about £300 per week for the staff.

Recently, however, the owner/managers (Mr and Mrs Vine) have seen takings hit, following the departure of the only two full-time staff. Over the past eight weeks, sales have only averaged £10,500. Mr Vine believes it is just a temporary problem, as the two new full-timers find their feet. Mrs Vine decides to talk to each of the six staff members find out their views.

Joyce, a 55 year-old part-timer, has no doubts:

> *'It's the **commission system** that's causing the problem. Both the full-timers left because of it, and I'm totally fed up with it as well ... The problem is that you pay commission only to the person who writes out the customer's bill. So no-one wants to do any of the other jobs such as checking deliveries, chasing up special orders, or pricing new stock. You keep asking me to do these jobs because you know I'm reliable; but that prevents me from getting commission.'*

Eileen, a 22 year-old part-timer, is even more forceful:

> *'I can't stand Grace (another part-timer), because she's always robbing me of my commission. Yesterday morning, I spent two hours discussing sofas with a customer. After she'd settled on two £1,100 leather ones, she felt she should bring her husband along for a second opinion in the afternoon. And what happens? When I come back after my afternoon break I see them just leaving, and Grace has written out the bill for £2,200. So she makes £44 for doing damn all, while I do the work and get nothing. I'm still fuming, and I refuse to work with her again.'*

Questions

1 What is meant by: mark-up, commission system? (2)

2 How much commission would be earned in the eight weeks when sales only averaged £10,500? (3)

3 Give two reasons why some firms give commission. (2)

4 Outline three problems with the commission system operated by the Vines. (3)

5 How could the commission system be altered to satisfy more of the workforce? (4)

6 The case study shows a lack of consultation and employee involvement in decision making. What problems does this lack of communication lead to? (4)

7 What are two problems associated with having part-time staff in an organisation? (2)

Further work

1 In the organisation in the case study there is a problem of labour turnover. What is meant by labour turnover? How can it be measured? What is the cost of a high labour turnover? How could an organisation find out the cause of labour turnover? Having established the cause, how would you reduce labour turnover?

In order to answer these questions you could organise a local visit to a major employer and combine this aspect with the general requirements for unit 4. (Investigate human resources.)

During your visit you could ask about employee relations, training and development and legal requirements.

2 To help towards element 5.3, use secondary sources to study other incentive systems. What are some of the different payment by results methods used? Write about different profit sharing schemes. What other incentives are given to employees? To obtain a merit or a distinction for this part of the element, the grading criteria state that the candidate should independently identify, access and collect principal sources of relevant information.

3 One of the core skills in Communications involves writing a letter on a sensitive issue. Imagine that you are Mrs Vine. Write a letter to Eileen, Margherita or Grace, suggesting ways of sorting out their grievances, and helping to improve the general workplace atmosphere.

34 A SMALL BUSINESS START-UP

Elements: **4.3** *PC 12345*
AN 3.2 *PC 12345* **IT 2.1** *PC 123456*

Key concepts: Interviews, CVs, Letters of application

'He'll never give it to us,' said Michael glumly. Jane agreed that 17-year-olds could hardly expect to get a £1,000 bank loan, but she was determined to try. They sat nervously in the bank manager's waiting room, avoiding looking at each other.

Since leaving school, they had both put so much work into their business plan that it was impossible to believe they might have to abandon it. Both had worked to save £750 in a year, so £1,000 from the bank would give them the £2,500 they needed as start-up capital.

From their home in Surbiton they planned on serving the wealthy homes of Weybridge and Esher with a 'Dewfresh Flower Delivery', door-to-door service. Mike knew the routines of the Covent Garden wholesale market, and realised that he could buy boxes of Grade one daffodils for £20 per 100 bunches, which could be sold to customers for 90 pence per bunch.

They had worked out their fixed costs at £1,000 per month, and had conducted a survey of one hundred adults in Esher and Weybridge. From this they estimated that they would get 2,000 orders per month, with an average value of £5 per order. As the variable costs should only amount to £2 per order, this seemed promising.

As part of their preparations for their visit to the bank, Jane had worked out a cash flow forecast. This showed that they would have used up all the £2,500 by month two, but profits should bring money in after then. Jane's main worry was that customers would want to receive some credit.

Then a door opened and they were ushered in…

Questions

1 Interviews are used as a selection process for employment. What are two advantages and disadvantages of the interview method? **(4)**

2 If disappointing sales brought only 1,000 orders per month, what profit or loss would be made? **(4)**

3 How would an interview for a job compare with an interview for a bank loan? **(4)**

4 How should the interviewer prepare to make sure that the right person is chosen? **(3)**

5 Referring to the case study, write down five questions that the bank manager might ask before deciding whether to give a loan. **(5)**

Further work

1 Put yourself in the position of Michael or Jane and write a letter to the bank manager, requesting a meeting to discuss the £1,000 you wish to borrow. Include a summary of your business start-up scheme.

2 Draft a CV and enclose this with your letter. Make the CV appropriate to the business in the case study. When you have produced draft versions get someone to assess your documents for clarity, presentation and content. Make sure you save your CV with an appropriate filename, and secure it against accidental deletion or tampering.

3 Set up a role play between Michael, Jane, and the bank manager. An observer should make notes assessing the performance of the interviewer and interviewee.

PERSONNEL MANAGEMENT

Elements: **4.1** *PC 126* **B** **15.1** *PC 23*

Key concepts: Retention, Performance, Representation and consultation,
Trade unions

The ABC Company was proud of its reputation as a no-nonsense employer. The T.G.W.U. had once organised a six week strike over union recognition but the strikers had eventually given up. 'We want to make money, unions want to take money,' ABC's Chairman had once said.

The factory was organised with very high division of labour, in order to ensure that relatively unskilled workers could be used, yet output would be high. For the same reasons the factory was highly automated.

Now the Directors were having to admit that things were not working properly. **Absenteeism** (at 15%) and **labour turnover** (at 40% a year) were nearly three times the national averages, and were making it impossible for production to keep up with the demand for their products. Even more alarming was that the local Job Centre had told them that job-seekers were refusing to go for interviews at ABC because of its poor reputation.

The Board of Directors met to discuss the situation. The Production Director said:

> *'It's simple; we need much greater financial incentives. An extra £5 for every full week of attendance, a £500 bonus for each year of completed employment, and a £50 signing on fee.'*

The Marketing Director disagreed:

> *'I think we need a new approach. Our products are pretty poor quality, and my customers complain that if they phone the factory to check on deliveries, our people are very off-hand with them. It's not just a matter of money, we need to give our workers the job satisfaction that will lead to a more responsible attitude by them'.*

The Managing Director had a different solution:

> *'If we moved to the Northeast, the level of unemployment would mean people really want to get jobs and keep them. We could sell this factory, and with the proceeds could buy a factory in Newcastle plus management offices here in Bristol. So only Production need move.'*

Questions

1 What is meant by the terms absenteeism and labour turnover?

How do you measure each of them? **(4)**

2 Give two possible reasons why the ABC company was unable to retain staff. **(2)**

3 Labour turnover was high. What are two major costs involved in such a high turnover? **(4)**

4 What would be two advantages and two disadvantages of the Production Director's proposals? **(4)**

5 State and explain three personnel-based considerations in the decision whether to move to Newcastle. **(6)**

6 Job satisfaction is mentioned towards the end of the case study. What is it? Give two reasons why it might be difficult to increase job satisfaction for all the workforce. **(5)**

7 An employer has stated: 'We want to make money. Unions want to take money.' Is this an accurate summary of trade union objectives? Justify your answer. **(5)**

Further work

1 Human resources are often said to be the most important asset to an organisation. The human resources manager is responsible for all aspects of managing these resources. Research the different aspects involved using secondary material. The range requirement includes recruitment, retention, termination, Health and Safety, training and professional development.

2 Use the *Annual Abstract of Statistics* (HMSO) to identify the level of trade union membership since 1980. Represent this data in a diagram or in table format. Describe the main trends in membership. What may have been the main reasons for any changes in trade union membership?

36 BRINGING IN QUALITY CIRCLES

Elements: **5.3** *PC 1234*
              C 3.1 *PC 1234*

Key concepts: Quality circles. Japanese working practices

'But we don't have a quality problem!' exclaimed the Chairman, evidently put out by Sarah's suggestion. He pointed to the very low rates of customer guarantee claim (just 1%); and to the advanced electronic testing system operated by the seven quality control inspectors. But Sarah continued to press her case for the introduction of quality circles:

> 'There's more to quality than having fault-free products. Quality
> circles look at every aspect of a product's design and manufacture,
> with a view to providing a product the customer will be more satisfied
> with. Plus, of course, there are other vital areas such as delivery
> times. Quality means good service as well as good products.'

After some more, quite heated, discussion the Chairman agreed to provide Sarah with a £20,000 budget for a one year trial of quality circles within her own department. If her hedgetrimmer production line benefited, then perhaps the main lawnmower plant would follow. She would have to report to the Board on progress in six months, and give a final assessment at the end of the year.

She began by calling a meeting of all her staff, to explain the test that was to take place, and the reasons why she had pushed for it. They were used to – and quite liked – her meetings, which often involved open criticism of her management of their section, so most were receptive to what she had to say. Some had moaned before about 'the waste of the skills and brains of the shopfloor workers' so they responded positively to a proposal to use those very attributes. The only groans came when Sarah explained that the group would meet after work, and would be unpaid. Her reasoning was that to offer to pay people would attract many who did not really want to participate, so it needed to be truly voluntary work.

By talking individually to all of her eighty-five staff over the following weeks, Sarah was able to construct a list of eight volunteers. Before their first meeting, she and they went on a weekend management training course on 'Setting up successful quality circles'. This had the desired effect of making them feel far more confident and far more motivated towards the scheme, and helped to knit them together as a team. All were especially impressed by the potential of the 'fishbone' diagram as a way of tackling problems (see overleaf).

THE FISHBONE DIAGRAM FOR PROBLEM-SOLVING

Men : Methods : Machines : Materials

M   M

Name of problem

M   M

5 'W's and an 'H'

The problem (or effect) is identified in the rectangular box (right).
The four 'M's signify possible causes of the problem
(Men, Methods, Machines, Materials).
A problem-solving discussion then follows, based on the five 'W's and an 'H'
(Why, When, Where, Who, What and How).

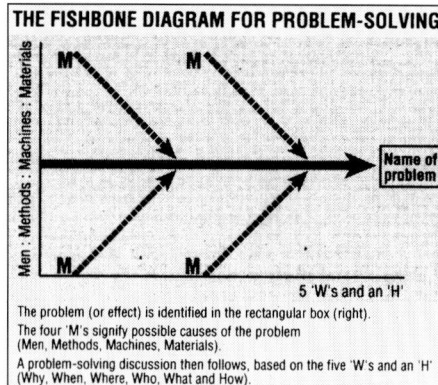

This invention of the Japanese management expert Ishikawa seemed easy to use. The problem to be solved is written in a box on the right hand side of a large piece of paper. An arrow is drawn across the sheet pointing towards the box, then the members of the circle suggest possible causes – which are put into one of the 'four M' categories: Men, Methods, Machines, Materials. Having agreed on the causes, a problem-solving discussion follows, based on the 'five Ws and an H' (Why, When, Where, Who, What and How). They were told that this technique is the one used most commonly by the two million quality circles operating in Japan.

The first week's quality circle proved a disappointment, as the topic they chose to look at (late deliveries) was so wide that they became swamped by the number of different factors. In subsequent weeks they corrected this, and then began to generate some useful ideas. The first triumph was when their idea for braking the hedge-cutting blades at the instant the user switches off was designed, tested, and then incorporated into all the firm's output. This was completed by the time the six month review took place, so Sarah felt very confident that the Board would congratulate her. In fact, she found that many Board members were worried about the implication of her work. The Production Director suggested that:

> 'The workers are already showing signs of believing that they know
> best. Two managers have reported insolence, and one has told me
> that some of his staff actually started changing the production process
> without his permission. I'd like this experiment abandoned.'

Fortunately for Sarah, the Marketing Director and the Chairman were so impressed by the improvement in the hedgetrimmer that they backed her for the other six months. She went away determined to overcome the resistance to change among the middle management, though not yet sure how to achieve this.

Source: *The Independent*

Questions

1   What is a quality circle?   (2)

2   State two advantages of quality circles for
    a   the organisation
    b   the individual worker.   (4)

3   Suggest a reason, not stated in the text, why Sarah had only eight staff joining
    her voluntary scheme.   (2)

4   How could the company Chairman measure the effectiveness of quality circles?   (2)

5   What management problems resulted from the workforce making decisions about
    the way in which they worked?   (5)

Further work

1   You could fulfil part of your communication skills criteria by giving a presentation on
    one or two of the following types of Japanese management practices:

    Kaizen and Kanban
    Just-in-time
    Total quality
    Approaches to trade unions and workforce – single status and single union deals.

    For each practice you should state how it might lead to an improvement in workplace
    performance.

2   In groups, discuss the use the fishbone technique to tackle a problem on your GNVQ
    course, for example, the problem of passing the unit tests or the difficulty of 'action
    planning' units. Group the causes of the problem under the 'four M' headings, and
    thoughts on solutions within the categories 'five Ws and an H'.

37 TEAMWORKING – THEORY AND PRACTICE

Elements: **4.1** *PC 2 3 6* **4.2** *PC 3 4* **4.3** *PC 2 3 4 5* *BTEC* **15.2** *PC 1 2 3 4*
C **3.1** *PC 1 2 3 4*

*Key concepts: Recruitment, Employee relations, Teamwork, Discrimination/equal
opportunities, CVs, Interviews*

'I'm Ronnie Stannard, very pleased to meet you.'

Ronnie sat down and looked carefully at Yeisho's three-man interview panel. They
all looked friendly, but very formal. Earlier that day she had undergone three hours
of aptitude and attitude tests; she felt tired, but now had to be at her best.

'Ronnie is, um, unusual. Is it your full Christian name?', asked one of the men
in suits. She assured them that it was hers from birth. Later, one asked suspiciously
about 'the reference on your form to Fulham Ladies' Football Club'. He needed
reassurance that women's football was increasingly widely accepted. Despite these
concerns about whether Ronnie would fit in with the other staff members, the
interviewers soon decided that she was an ideal recruit. Her astute answers to
questions about her commitment, ambitions and attitude to work came across very
well. She impressed them with her explanation of how she had become Fulham's
coach as well as player. To her great delight she was offered the supervisor job on
the spot.

That night she ran the training session for her football team. It was, as usual, a
quick-fire mixture of hard exercise, skills training, short five-a-side matches and
banter. After 90 minutes all the team were laughing and sweating in equal measure.
After a shower they pulled on their Fulham tracksuits and went out for their
customary curry.

During the meal, talk turned to their previous coach, Terry. He had been tough
on discipline, but the harder he tried to teach them a new skill, the less confident
they felt in their own abilities. He made them feel that their only role was to get the

ball to the team's star player – and she never passed it to anyone. Their season had been tense and unsuccessful. Ronnie had changed all that. The star had relaxed into being a proper team member, and the exact same players as last year's relegation contenders were now third in the National Women's League.

The following Monday Ronnie started work at Yeisho Electronics. She was to be the supervisor of the finished assembly production cell, though her first week would consist of induction training. She listened with amusement about the company's teamwork philosophy, its morning exercises, the company uniform and its continuous improvement (kaizen) groups. Yet whereas Ronnie looked happier and happier as the week progressed, the other staff on the induction course looked less and less so. When, on the Friday, they had to come in fifteen minutes early for a team briefing and exercises, most had surly faces. Ronnie positively glowed.

The next Monday would be her first day on the production line. She arrived at 7.30 to prepare herself for the 7.45 team briefing session. To her surprise the first worker strolled in at 7.55 and most came in together at precisely 7.59. All Ronnie could do was to insist that they arrive promptly tomorrow and then hurry them onto the production line for the start of the 8.00 shift.

That week proved the most stressful of Ronnie's life. She was being ignored by the men she was supposed to be supervising. Gradually, though, she pieced together what had happened. The previous supervisor had been promoted from the shopfloor and had built up a team spirit based upon contempt for the 'Japanese gimmicks'. The unit had worked effectively until quality problems emerged. Then an audit of the cell's methods of working revealed how far it was from the Yeisho approach. Foolishly, though, the factory manager had not told the personnel department about the problem before going on holiday. So Ronnie had been totally unprepared for the inevitable hardships of taking over such a team.

Saturday's fixture against Doncaster was a great relief for Ronnie. Her teammates realised that she was tense and, on the coach journey up the M1, dragged the story out of her. They felt that she should dump the problem on the factory manager's lap, but they also worried that people might see the situation as a woman unable to manage a group of men. Over coffee at a service station they agreed that she should:

1 explain the situation to the factory manager on his return from holiday the following Monday;
2 call each person, in turn, off the production line for a private chat about the situation, warning each that without cooperation she would have to issue formal warnings about insubordination;
3 keep the factory manager fully informed at every stage.

Coming to this conclusion was a great weight off Ronnie's mind. She was able to play a full part in the afternoon's 2 – 2 draw and slept more deeply on the coach home than she had done for days.

At 7.40 that Monday Ronnie went to see the factory manager. She was astonished to find two of her production line workers there already. The manager asked her to wait outside 'for a few minutes'. A quarter of an hour later she was called in to be asked how she had managed 'to upset the men so much in such a short time'. Although furious, she controlled her temper enough to put her side of the case and to state her three-point plan. The manager listened coldly to what she had to say, and just said 'leave it with me'.

Ronnie went to the personnel manager who had been on the selection panel and had inducted her. She explained the whole story but he seemed embarrassed to hear it. All he said was: 'Graham's the factory manager and what he says goes, I'm afraid.' She left in a daze, with her mind swirling with thoughts of teamwork and team management. Where should she go from here?

Questions

1   State two different selection methods by which Ronnie was chosen at Yeisho. Why were these methods suitable in this case study? Give two other methods that firms can use to choose employees.   **(4)**

2   Explain what is meant by induction training. Give two advantages of such training.   **(4)**

3   Describe the Japanese management methods used at Yeisho. Give three reasons why organisations use them.   **(6)**

4   Explain why Ronnie was more successful running her football team than the production line at Yeisho.   **(6)**

5   What signs, in the case study, point to a weak organisation with weak management?   **(5)**

Further work

1   Discuss with your classmates:

    a   the extent to which Ronnie was discriminated against at Yeisho;

    b   the legal and ethical requirements of an employer; did Ronnie's managers meet these?

    c   what you think happened next.

2   Research the meaning of a job description and a job specification. Write each of these for Ronnie's two roles as

    a   football coach at a ladies club

    b   a supervisor on the factory floor.

3   As part of the requirement for element 4.3, you are required to describe and explain the purpose of curriculum vitae as well as evaluate the effectiveness of letters of application.

Write two letters of application for a job, one copy to be written by hand and the other using a wordprocessing system. Apply for either of Ronnie's jobs, i.e. at the football club or at the factory. Enclose an appropriate CV.

You could then follow through the procedure and arrange an interview for one of these jobs. Preparation would be very important. You would need to design suitable questions. An interview situation would have at least one interviewer (who would need to design suitable questions), an interviewee and an observer.

4   To help you fulfil BTEC unit 15.2, you can use this case study to analyse the nature of group behaviour at work. Explain the behaviour of the group of workers at the factory. Using desk research, look at theoretical explanations of group behaviour.

38 MANAGEMENT STRUCTURE

Elements: *4.2 PC 12*
           *IT **3.3** PC 12345*

*Key concepts: Organisational structures, Types of business organisation,
            Job roles*

The new Chief Executive of British Aircraft Technologies (BAT) was a straightforward man. He thought it was his job to know how all the **divisions of the business** were doing. 'But how can I', he complained, 'when there are twelve divisions – each answerable to me?' He intended to set a **corporate objective** of cutting costs by 30% over the next three years, but was concerned about his own ability to monitor progress. As the objective was fundamental to BAT's survival in the competitive environment for high technology products, he decided a complete organisational restructuring was needed.

After several months of discussion with divisional senior management, it became clear that eight of the twelve could be merged into four new divisions – each headed by a Chairman. Of the remaining four, the managers in three were implacably opposed to any loss of independence. Yet the involvement of all three in military production suggested the solution that a Chairman be appointed to oversee the three independent divisions. The twelfth division fitted poorly with any of the others, so it was kept separate; it, too, was to be run by a new Chairman.

Within this new hierarchy, the divisional Chairman would be answerable to the Chief Executive, who would in turn be accountable to the Board of Directors. The Chief Executive would agree corporate objectives with the Board, then decide divisional goals and budgets in consultation with each Chairman before the start of each year. The Chairman would then have complete autonomy to work within the agreed constraint, and each division would be a **profit centre**.

The new structure proved highly successful. The Civil Aircraft division set its own priority as the reduction of production time, in order to speed up deliveries to customers. This, they reasoned, would increase demand and thereby enable existing capacity to be utilised more effectively.

Within two years the assembly time on their executive jet had been cut from twenty-six weeks to twelve. This was achieved by reorganising the factory layout, automating the more repetitive tasks, and retraining staff to use existing equipment more efficiently. These changes were only implemented after very full consultation with the workforce; indeed some of the most valuable ideas came directly from the shop floor. It was clear that the division would achieve its cost reduction target, and at higher output levels than many had thought possible.

Four of the other divisions adopted more conventional cost-cutting measures, which also looked likely to achieve the 30% cut the Chief Executive demanded.

The Military Products division, though, struggled badly. Its Thames Valley production site for Guided Weapons was losing many high quality, technologically educated staff to local computer firms. Labour turnover was averaging 35% a year on its 2,000 employees. Given that new employees were costing an average of £4,000 to recruit and train, the annual cost was enormous.

The Chairman of the Military Products division argued that the site should be moved to Derby, where the larger pool of skilled labour should ensure longer term employment. The Director of Guided Weapons refused to allow this, however, and reminded the Chairman that he had delegated to him the details of the restructuring. Six months after this, a reorganisation was announced for the Military Products division, in which the post of Director of Guided Weapons became redundant.

Questions

1 What is meant by these terms: division of the business, corporate objective, profit centre? **(3)**

2 A hierarchy is a common organisational structure. Draw a diagram to demonstrate the management hierarchy of British Aircraft Technologies before the changes. **(4)**

3 How would the reduction of the number of divisions from twelve to eight lead to a saving in cost? **(3)**

4 Draw a chart to show the new hierarchy after the first restructuring. **(4)**

5 What does span of control mean? How did the Chief Executive's span of control change after reorganisation? **(4)**

6 What was the annual cost to BAT of the high labour turnover on the Thames Valley site? **(2)**

Further work

1 A franchise is a good example of a 'flat' organisational structure. Try to arrange a visit to a local franchise and find out how it is organised. What does the franchisee obtain from the franchisor in the way of support? What does the franchisor gain from the relationship? Compare the organisational structure of the franchise you investigate with the structure of Brtish Aircraft Technologies.

2 To achieve Information Technology core skills you are required to use different formats. Using a software package such as Corel Draw or Clipart, draw a simple hierarchical relationship at your school or college.

Include in your drawing a span of control, and add text to give titles where appropriate. Import a suitable picture to illustrate your work. Arrange your text, drawing and illustration in a suitable format before printing out a hard copy.

39

WORKFORCE PERFORMANCE AND THE SKODA SUPPLIER

Elements: **4.1** *PC 12346*   **5.2** *PC 12*   **5.3** *PC 1*
              C **3.1** *PC 1234*   **3.2** *PC 1234*   **3.3** *PC 1234*
              AN **3.3** *PC 1246*

Key concepts: Training, Workplace performance, Absenteeism, Systems for improving employee relations, Calculating averages

Sadiq could hardly believe it. Only fifteen months out of university and he had landed this plum project. His employer Lincoln McGee, Management Consultants, hired him straight from college in preference to eighteen other shortlisted candidates. Three months of induction training were followed by a series of assistant roles in projects run by senior partners. Now Sadiq was being sent to Liberec, 50 miles northeast of Prague. His task was to advise Floc, a supplier to Skoda cars, on the modernisation of its factory working methods and practices.

Lincoln McGee had been hired because of Skoda's threat to withdraw orders from Floc if the supplier could not guarantee performance improvements within four months. The specification laid down by Skoda is shown in Table 1.

Table 1

Problem	Measurement	Current rate	Target rate
Quality	Rejects per thousand	24.5	9.9
Lead times	Time from order to delivery	18 days	6 days
Delivery reliability	% of occasions delivery is late	23.5%	2.5%

Over the following month he came to know the Floc components factory intimately. Sadiq's excellent German made it easy to communicate with the Czech managers and supervisors, and his youthful appearance encouraged people to talk openly.

The Works Director told him that the whole assembly section of the plant had, until the late 1980s, been staffed by political prisoners. To minimise sabotage risks, production was reduced to many simple operations. The winding mechanism for a car window, for example, involved eighteen different people, each recruited and trained to complete a task as quickly as possible. Such was the specialisation that workers who could carry out their own task in nine seconds per unit might take five times longer if switched to someone else's. This mattered little in the past, as the prisoners were not allowed to be absent. Now, with paid employees carrying out these tedious tasks, absenteeism had become a major worry.

Floc did not have conveyor-belt production lines, so to ensure high output rates the payment structure was through piece rate. As each stage of production took a slightly different time and skill, a staff of fourteen salaried clerical workers was employed to set, measure and calculate the piece work payments. Recently the factory workers had elected their own representative to negotiate the sums involved. There was even talk of joining the National Engineering Union. There were two main grievances: the piece rate wage loss caused to an individual by being forced to switch from their own post to that of another, absent colleague; plus the poor health and safety position within the plant.

The Floc factory was a huge, drab site with three corrugated iron buildings linked by pot-holed roadways. The machinery in most of the plant was 30 years old and revealed little concern for health and safety. There was no extraction system for the dust and fumes caused by the mechanical and chemical processes used. Not all the machines were guarded to protect workers from moving parts. Sadiq learned that the average accident rate was 9.5 per week, with serious injuries occurring at least once a month.

Sadiq spent the fourth week of his investigations visiting Floc's suppliers and customers. He wanted to find out their opinion of the company. The suppliers were understandably hesitant about criticising their customer, but Sadiq was able to learn that the Floc production staff had never met or even spoken to the supplier factory management. The only contact was through Floc's purchasing department. Skoda, the main customer, was complimentary about Floc's helpful customer service, agreeing to replace defective parts without a quibble. Nevertheless it did criticise the erratic deliveries and unreliable quality standards.

Lincoln McGee had a four week consultancy contract, so it was now time for Sadiq to present his findings to Floc's thirteen Directors, and to make his recommendations for change. There would be one other participant at the meeting, as Mr Fraser McGee was flying out especially. So Sadiq spent a whole day preparing the slides for his presentation.

For a full two hours, Sadiq was on his feet going through a detailed account of Floc's strengths and many weaknesses. As lunchtime approached, he summarised his argument:

Main strengths:
- effective control of output and costs
- good recruitment and training procedures for the manufacturing system being used.

Main weaknesses:
- absenteeism levels running at:

Monday	11.4%
Tuesday	9.1%
Wednesday	6.9%
Thursday (payday)	2.7%
Friday	10.1%

- ratio of direct (factory) labour to indirect (staff) of 1 : 1.6 compared with 1 : 0.6 in equivalent British plants, thereby generating a very high staff overhead cost

- a prevailing attitude (culture) of interest in high volume production at the expense of product quality, delivery schedules or customer satisfaction
- a climate of fear of detection; no-one wants to be held accountable for mistakes, so errors are hidden and decisions delayed: 'There is always a bunch of signatures on every document,' says Sadiq.

With Sadiq's report over, they all went off to lunch. He felt delighted by how well the morning had gone, but knew that the hardest part had yet to come: the recommendations for action.

Questions

1 What is meant by induction training? Give two reasons why it proved cost effective in this case. **(4)**

2 What is Floc's average absentee level over one week? Explain the weekly pattern of absenteeism. **(4)**

3 What other evidence is there that the workplace performance is unsatisfactory? **(4)**

4 What could be done to improve the situation? Make suggestions that would involve:

  a little or no money **(3)**

  b a sum of money. **(3)**

5 Why do businesses set targets? What are the problems involved with setting targets which are:

  a too easy to achieve

  b too difficult to achieve? **(5)**

6 What systems for employee relations are beginning to be established at Floc? **(2)**

7 To what extent does the past history of Floc help to explain present day performance and attitudes? **(5)**

Further work

1 To help reinforce the Communications core skills in elements 3.2 and 3.3, prepare a suitable document for the directors of Floc. Your format could be a short report using bullet point indicators for easy reference. The report format should include a title, date, terms of reference and recommendations.

Use an 'image' in the form of a sketch, diagram or chart to support your report at an appropriate point.

2 Absenteeism is highlighted towards the end of the case study. What are some reasons for absenteeism from work? What are the costs of unauthorised absence?

Explain one of the following patterns of absence, in the form of a short memo from a human resources manager to the Managing Director of a small firm.

  a Young people are more frequently away for short periods of sick absence, whereas older people have less frequent but longer periods of absence.

  b Manual workers have higher levels of absence than office workers.

  c New starters are absent more often than longer serving employees.

3 Lateness and poor timekeeping are also a problem. A college Business Studies lesson is due to start at 9.00, but students are still wandering in at 9.20–9.25. How could this problem be tackled with a solution which would satisfy both the teacher and the student body? Discuss, with your classmates, recommendations for action.

40

RACE DISCRIMINATION AT WORK

Elements: **4.1** *PC 3456*
             C **3.2** *PC 1234*

Key concepts: Discrimination, Training, Industrial tribunal

Despite one awful year of being bullied, Conrad's school career had not been too bad. It had been his good fortune that a huge Jamaican boy joined his class in the third year which stopped the racial taunts. Progress through university was smoother, with nothing getting in the way of his good honours degree.

Then came the task of getting a job. For his first 40 job applications he was able to put the rejections down to the economic climate. Then an aunt advised him to use her address instead of his home in Liverpool 8. 'Employers think that everyone from Toxteth is a dosser' she explained.

There was no doubt that when his letters were sent out from Birkenhead there was a much better response. He started getting interviews and after several months got a job as a trainee in a large insurance company.

Conrad always had a flair for maths, so the early training proved easy; he also got on very well with his immediate colleagues and best of all with his boss. Some departments within the firm were offhand, almost hostile to him, but he was too mature to get upset by people he rarely dealt with.

The years passed and Conrad's career seemed to be progressing well. He was disappointed never to have been given an opportunity to work in the sales department, if only because of the high commissions the sales representatives could earn. Nevertheless, in five years he had moved up to the level of Section Manager, which was impressively fast progress.

As Section Manager, he was responsible for a budget of £200,000 and for the training and appraisal of six staff. Every year his section increased its profitability until it was the best in the company. So when his boss took early retirement, Conrad felt very confident in applying for his job. The interview panel included, to his surprise, the company's Divisional Director, a man who Conrad had hardly met in eight years at the firm. When Conrad was answering questions, it was the Director's sceptical tone of voice that unsettled him. The man appointed to the job was the same age as Conrad, though he had been at the company longer as he had joined straight from school; his section was only averagely successful. Although Conrad suspected race discrimination, there was no clear evidence.

Over the next two years Conrad struggled to work effectively with his new boss. The man adopted a superior stance that irritated all the Section Managers. He kept hold of information that used to be passed down the hierarchy, and interfered with the most petty decisions. Conrad found himself making decisions that proved quite wrong, simply because his boss had not given the right information. After one occasion, he went to complain to the Divisional Director. All he received was a lecture about trust and authority.

A series of problems in other sections forced the firm to shuffle the incompetent boss into a different, less important job. So the post was vacant again. Although Conrad had not given up hope, he was less confident this time that he would get the job. Nevertheless, he impressed the panel with his newly awarded Open University Masters Degree in Business Administration (MBA). A result of four years of part-time study, it made him far better qualified than his rival candidates. It was a bitter blow, therefore, to find that a younger Section Head got the job.

Fired up by his aunt, Conrad decided to fight the discrimination that he believed was in force. He phoned the Commission for Racial Equality and read with care a booklet called 'Race Discrimination and Employment' produced by Thompson & Partners, a firm of solicitors. This explained that only 19% of race discrimination complaints are successful, because of the difficulty of establishing proof. Nevertheless he took heart from the fact that compensation of up to £10,000 can be awarded, and from the statement that:

> *'An Industrial Tribunal is allowed to infer racial discrimination in the absence of an adequate or satisfactory explanation by the employer for the discrimination.'*

Three weeks later Conrad brought his case to an Industrial Tribunal under the Race Relations Act 1976.

Questions

1 Outline the events of Conrad's working life in which discrimination may have been involved. **(5)**

2 What professional qualifications did Conrad obtain? Why does the attainment of such qualifications not necessarily result in promotion in the workplace? **(5)**

3 Use secondary sources to explain briefly the workings of an industrial tribunal. **(5)**

4 On what grounds should employers see it as in their own interest to eliminate discrimination? **(4)**

5 How might employers try to eliminate discrimination in the workplace? **(6)**

Further work

1 a Imagine you are a member of the tribunal. Write a short report, weighing up the evidence for and against the case of racial discrimination against Conrad.

 b Discuss what you suppose was the industrial tribunal's actual finding.

41 A BMW AT TWENTY-THREE

Elements: **5.3** *PC 1* BTEC **15.1** *PC 1 2 3* **15.3** *PC 1 2*
CGLI **10.1** *PC 1 2*

*Key concepts: Features of workplace performance, Motivation,
Human relations theory*

Yin Fan had a wonderful time at the school reunion. It started as soon as she turned up in her BMW. She happily told all the inquirers that it was her company car. 'A BMW at twenty-three!' gasped one. Throughout the evening she was grilled about her career, with many of her former classmates eager to know where she was working and at how high a salary. Several others had made good starts to their working lives, but none as glitteringly as Yin Fan.

When asked for details, Yin Fan explained that her advertising agency job involved planning and buying multi-million pound media campaigns for the agency's clients. She had to liaise with the marketing managers of advertisers such as Cadbury, Heinz and Dixons to find out the target market they were aiming for and then decide which media to use – TV or newspapers? If TV, how much on Channel 3 or Channel 4 or on satellite? How much in each ITV region? And so on. Yin Fan's working life was one of meetings, business lunches and a frantic social life revolving around an advertising agency staffed by young, well-paid people.

Back at her desk the following Monday, Yin Fan found herself enjoying the work more than ever. She smiled at the thought of her school friends' amazement that she had a PA (personal assistant) and a trainee working for her. The day's work revolved around an important negotiation for Cadbury with Channel 4. She met her boss, the Media Director, for twenty minutes to discuss tactics.

Tony was an unusual boss; from the day he hired Yin Fan two years ago, he had hardly ever told her what to do. On that day he gave her the Cadbury and Heinz business to run, and since then had done little more than to offer her the huge Dixons account as well. At first she had been daunted by her total responsibility for decisions involving millions of pounds. She knew that her predecessor had been fired, reputedly because one of the clients had talked about him unenthusiastically to Tony. Yet as the weeks passed she felt liberated by the freedom to make instant decisions. At her previous agency the Media Director had fussed over every aspect of the job, frustrating Yin Fan by interventions that seemed to cause more mistakes than they cured. Occasionally she and Tony talked over work at lunch, but otherwise he focused on his own clients and his Board responsibilities.

So her visit to talk things over with Tony was unusual. She wanted advice because the Sales Manager she would be dealing with at Channel 4 was an old friend of Tony's. With a planned budget of £500,000 for Channel 4, a discount of as little as 10% would represent a lot of money to hand back to Cadbury. So she wanted to establish the right approach to the negotiations.

Despite the pressures of the day, Tony found the time not only to advise Yin Fan, but also to ask her generally about how things were going. She took the opportunity to tell him how she had struck a deal giving Heinz £150,000 of extra, free TV airtime in Scotland, and about a costly mistake on a new business presentation. After 50 minutes she left Tony's office feeling invigorated. By mid-afternoon she had a 16.5% discount rate from Channel 4 and a rather smug smile.

Questions

1 Give three reasons why company cars are given to employees. **(3)**

2 Why did Yin Fan enjoy her work? **(4)**

3 Describe Tony's style of management. **(4)**

4 Why do you think that Alison was able to negotiate such a good deal with Channel 4? **(4)**

5 Referring to any major text book, read what Abraham Maslow and Elton Mayo revealed about motivating the workforce. Write a short report on Yin Fan's working life in relation to Maslow's hierarchy of needs and Elton Mayo's Hawthorne Effect. **(10)**

Further work

1 It is very easy to motivate executive workers like Yin Fan, but how can factory workers be motivated or those stacking shelves at a supermarket? Arrange a visit to a local company and ask about workplace motivation. You should prepare a questionnaire beforehand. Some aspects which could be covered include: wages, benefits and conditions of work, training policy, equal opportunities policy.

2 To help you in the attainment of unit 15, a study of leadership styles should be undertaken. Research the main types: autocratic, democratic and laissez-faire. Describe these types. You should also state the tasks of a leader, and what qualities make a good leader. There is an opportunity to use desk and primary research. Think of good leaders who have influenced you and list their qualities, or interview a successful leader.

42 THE WORK OF ACAS

Elements: **5.1** *PC 1 2 3*   **5.2** *PC 1 2 3*

Key concepts: External influences, Trade unions, Government,
Demand for labour, Employment trends, Flexible working practices

In September 1986, 870 employees at a Midlands-based manufacturing company, took strike action over the company's proposals to transfer surplus **indirect workers** to '**direct**' jobs. This led to the laying-off of a further 1,200 employees.

The independent Advisory **Conciliation** and Arbitration Service (ACAS) initiated regular contact with the parties during the strike, but neither side was prepared to ask for its involvement. After five weeks of strike action, however, both sides accepted an invitation to a conciliation meeting.

Management argued that a declining world market, cut-throat pricing policies and successive years of loss-making had made it necessary to reduce overheads sharply, in order to keep the company competitive. Surplus indirect labour had been identified and these workers were to be transferred to direct factory work after appropriate training.

The unions AEU, TGWU, and TASS did not accept some of the company's arguments, and were aggrieved that management were continuing with their policy of **sub contracting** some work. This, they contended was one of the causes of the surplus labour. There was also concern over management's selection criteria for transferees, and for those skilled or white-collar workers who would suffer a pay cut. While prepared to cooperate with **voluntary job transfers**, the unions were not prepared to accept compulsion of any kind, be it transfer or redundancy.

After heated talks covering four days, agreement was reached that compulsory transfers would be withdrawn to allow full discussion and consultation with the unions on selection. This discussion would be subject to a strict timetable at the end of which, failing agreement, management would make the selection. A timetable for future transfers was also agreed, and assurances given by management on their sub-contracting policy. Agreement was also reached on longer training and trial periods.

The agreement was put to a mass meeting resulting in a 2:1 acceptance and a return to work.

Source: ACAS Annual Report 1986

Questions

1   What is meant by: direct workers, indirect workers, conciliation, subcontracting and voluntary job transfers?   **(5)**

2   Why might indirect workers resent being transferred to direct jobs?   **(2)**

3   Outline the role of ACAS in the dispute, taking care to distinguish between arbitration and conciliation.   **(3)**

4   Why might an independent body like ACAS succeed in resolving a dispute?   **(3)**

5   Explain why each of these events would cause a decline in profits for the company:

   a   a declining world market

   b   cut-throat pricing policies.   **(4)**

6   Give three reasons why the workers may have been keen to return to work, despite not getting all their demands.   **(3)**

7   Disputes are often settled by making sure no-one loses face. Analyse the settlement terms here. Do you feel that either side won?   **(5)**

Further work

1   ACAS offers guidance and advice on a wide range of employment issues. Find out the changing features of employment in the UK using a variety of sources, for example textbooks, business dictionaries and Social Trends. You could also write to ACAS (address and telephone number on page 253) asking for a copy of their annual report. Areas which should be covered include the trend towards more flexible working practices; the increase in part-timers, jobsharers and employees on fixed term contracts. Why do firms seek increasing flexibility? What are the consequences for the workforce? A visit to a local company or an interview with a human resources manager would cover the range.

2   Employment is a contractual arrangement. What is a contract? Draw up a contract between yourself and your Business Studies department; include what is expected of you and what the department should provide for you. Research an employment contract; what legal rights do employees have? Refer to pay, training, unfair dismissal, and employee representation.

THE TRENCH

Elements: **5.2** *PC 1* **5.3** *PC 1234*
AN **3.1** *PC 12456* **3.2** *PC 1245678* *IT* **3.3** *PC 1234*

Key concepts: Features of workplace performance, Health and safety, External influences, Law, Government, Trade unions

'Gary Wilson was very lucky. He suffered a collapsed lung and a broken pelvis, but others have died in similar circumstances…' began the Magistrate as he summed up the evidence he had heard.

It began with Gary's decision to have a year off between A-levels and college. He wanted to earn money quickly so that he could spend the spring in America. As the local builder (Lancashire Houses) offered the highest wages, he started there as a general navvy earning £5 an hour.

Lancashire Houses had been enjoying a local housing boom caused by the arrival of a large Japanese electronics factory. From a two man business, the firm had taken on forty-five employees on three different sites – each building eight houses. The two directors were finding it very had to keep control over the sites as they had to spend so much time sorting out the problems of financing the £500,000 investment. To get round this problem, they hired site managers for each development and offered each one a £10,000 bonus if they could complete the work by a specified target date. (One week late would mean £8,000, two weeks late £6,000 and so on.)

Gary was shocked from the start at how hard the foreman worked him. In his first week he had shifted mounds of bricks, dug drainage holes, put up hundreds of feet of security wire fencing and cut dozens of metal pipes to length with a fearful metal-cutting saw. Shattered at the end of the week, he looked upon the weekend's driving rain with some optimism, hoping that the site would be too wet to work on Monday. Such illusions were soon dispelled by the foreman's orders, and Gary's day was spent carrying supplies to the bricklayers who were building up the walls in the rain.

The following day a JCB dug an eleven foot trench for laying drains. The foreman called Gary over to help him. Gary saw that water was running into the hole, but the foreman assured him that it was 'as safe as houses'. Both went down into the hole to lay the pipe. Gary was unaware that the correct procedure is to drive strong timbers into the ground at the sides of the hole, to create a wall. The foreman knew, but had not been supplied with the right type of wood, and felt that it was not worth hours of delay for what he considered to be the tiny risk of earth slippage.

Without warning, one of the sides collapsed. The foreman just managed to scramble out, but Gary was trapped. As another side gave way, it looked as though Gary would be buried alive. Miraculously, the wet mud kept just below his neck. After an hour he was freed and taken to an intensive care unit in hospital. He was only fit to be released after three weeks, and then needed two months in a nursing home. The collapsed lung would be a permanent disability.

Lancashire Houses were prosecuted by the Health and Safety Executive under the 1974 Health and Safety at Work Act. By failing to support the trench sides they had committed an offence under the construction regulations. They had also failed to notify the safety inspectors of the start of any of their three construction projects, and had no written safety policy as required by the law. The Burnley Magistrates Court found the company guilty on all charges. The company director in the dock apologised to the court, and explained that since the accident, they had sent their foremen on safety courses. A fine of £2,250 was imposed, plus costs of £56.50. During the hearing it emerged that the company had not had a visit from a factory inspector for three years.

Gary's friends urged him to sue the company for negligence, but when he went to a solicitor he realised that his father earned too much to be able to get legal aid, but far too little to afford the legal costs. The solicitor also made it clear that such cases can take years to come to court, by which time the company might have gone into voluntary liquidation. It was no help to be told by a friend that he should have joined a trade union, which would have taken up his case for him.

Although his accident caused some delays, better weather helped two of the sites to be completed within the bonus deadline. One of the two was the site where Gary's accident took pace.

Source: *Legal reports in 'Health and Safety at Work' magazine.*

Questions

1 What were the physical causes of Gary's accident? **(2)**

2 What were the underlying causes of the accident? **(5)**

3 The site managers were being paid by results. State two advantages and two disadvantages of such a system to Lancashire Houses. **(4)**

4 Why were Lancashire Houses negligent under the Health and Safety at Work Act, 1974? **(3)**

5 Statistics show that young people suffer from more accidents at work than any other group. What might be the reasons for this? **(5)**

6 What research or checking might Gary have done before taking the job? **(3)**

7 a How might a recognised trade union have helped:

- Lancashire Houses

- the employees? **(4)**

  b Given these advantages, why may there have been no union representation? **(4)**

Further work

1 The following statistics relate to safety performance in the workplace.

Accident statistics

The total numbers of accidents at work in 1992, for all employees (does not include self-employed) were:

Deaths	346
Major injuries	19 896
Over three days' time lost	160 811
TOTAL	181 053

In respect of the building and construction industry only, the figures were:

Deaths	96
Major injuries	2 907
Over three days' time lost	16 689
TOTAL	19 692

Source: *Employment Gazette* and CITB Research department

To help with your core skills in Application of Number and Information Technology, and to complete element 5.3, make estimates of the percentage of all accidents, deaths, major injuries, and cases of over three days lost, which are attributable to the construction industry. Check your estimates with a calculator to get accurate figures.

Write a memo to explain the link between age and accidents. How could all these figures be used by the industry to improve workplace performance?

2 New health and safety at work regulations came into force at the beginning of 1993. They are needed to implement European Union directives on health and safety at work. The new regulations cover areas which include:

- appointing a competent person to devise and apply measures needed
- ensuring that employees have adequate health and safety training
- ensuring that equipment conforms with EU product safety directives
- putting warning notices in appropriate places
- providing adequate lighting, heating and ventilation.

Assess all the implications of the new directive for a typical organisation. Look at the impact on costs, training, personnel, premises and insurance.

You could research your own college, or visit a local organisation and talk to a health and safety representative.

44 PUTTING HERZBERG INTO PRACTICE

Elements: **5.2** *PC 1 2 3* **5.3** *PC 1 2 3* *BTEC* **15.1** *PC 1 2 3*
CGLI **10.1** *PC 1 2 3*

Key concepts: Wages, Benefits and conditions of work, Motivation, Specialisation,
External influences on business

Although Professor Herzberg's researches date back to the late 1950s, it was still unusual in the mid-1970s for British businessmen to have heard of him. So Frazer Park was a rare managing director to not only have studied Herzberg, but also to be determined to implement his recommendations. His target was the semi-skilled workers producing his firm's main product: plastic-coated wire bindings. He knew he was taking a risk, because Herzberg's researches into job satisfaction were conducted on white collar and engineering jobs. There had always been dispute, therefore, about whether the theories could be applied to semi-skilled and unskilled factory work.

At the time Frazer Park became Managing Director of Russell Gray Holdings (RGH), the production of the wire bindings (the kind used on calendars and computer manuals) was divided into five tasks (see below). He saw his first task as the combining of these functions into one. In that way, each worker would have a complete unit of work; they could follow an order through from its arrival to its despatch. All the operatives would be trained to check the quality of the wire on arrival from suppliers, and the quality of their own finished products. Any sub-standard goods sent out would be traceable, because every box sent out was to be signed by the worker. This began as a sensible monitoring process, but quite soon clients started to ask for specific operators by name, which provided recognition for achievement.

This reversal of the classic process of division of labour did cause a short-term reduction in output, especially from those workers whose previous, specialised jobs had higher status than that of machine operator. To counter this, Park knew that he

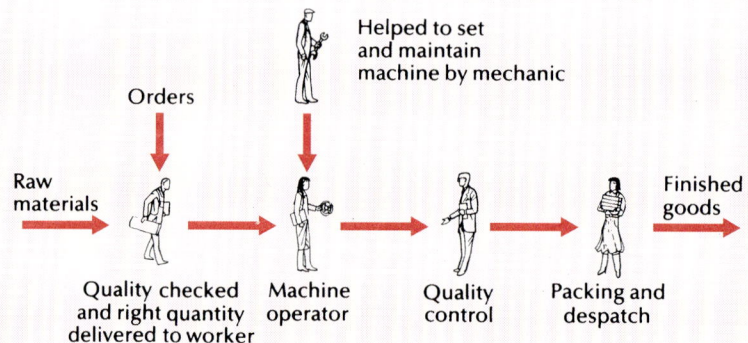

Orders

Helped to set
and maintain
machine by mechanic

Raw
materials

Quality checked
and right quantity
delivered to worker

Machine
operator

Quality
control

Packing and
despatch

Finished
goods

**The 5-person production system, prior to the change to a
complete unit of work**

would need to enlist the help of the employees to improve working practices and methods. So problem-solving groups were established. Typically, they would consist of two operators, an engineer, and one person from each of Purchasing and Sales. Problems tackled and solved included strengthening the packaging, designing a new wire-pressing machine, and tackling the problem of late deliveries caused when workers were ill or on holiday. Russell Gray Holdings (RGH) had this system in place long before quality circles became trendy.

When asked about the value of these groups, the Works Manager said:

> *'The more angles and options you can get to make the decision from, the nearer you are to a correct solution...and involving the people in the factory creates interest – a break from the normal routine – a chance to think...One of the biggest problems a manager has is getting people to change their ways of working. Involving people in making decisions helps to overcome resistance to change.'*

Having addressed the higher order needs of the workforce, Park tackled the 'hygiene/maintenance' needs. Productivity bonus schemes were phased out, so that factory workers could be put on the same salaried basis as office and managerial staff. The foremen were very apprehensive about this, as they imagined it would be much tougher driving a workforce that no longer had a financial incentive to work hard. In fact, this problem arose with a mere handful of the sixty workers, and most of those chose to leave within a month.

In the longer term, RGH found that moving people from piece rate to time rate helped focus on the need to raise productivity by better machinery or methods, rather than by 'harder work'. Furthermore, Park made it clear that he intended his workforce to be paid at the top end of the local pay ranges, and for a share of any productivity gains to be used to increase real earnings further. These policies helped to bring about an atmosphere in which raising productivity could be viewed as a common aim.

By 1979 Park felt the confidence to remove a standard complaint among industrial workers – the differences in conditions of service between them and 'staff'. So the shopfloor workers were given pension rights and sick pay, while for the first time clocking-in was stopped for all employees (though new white and blue collar staff had to clock in for their first 12 months until they had earned the right to staff status).

As Herzberg's study highlighted, for many employees the major source of dissatisfaction is not related to status or pay, but is due to a feeling of being over-supervised. Frazer Park's own trust in his workforce, and his establishment of enlarged jobs with self-checking, both pointed to the need for a streamlined management structure. So, in consultation with staff, he cut the layers of hierarchy from five to three over a number of years.

This led to a wide span of control, which forced supervisors to delegate more, and check up less on their subordinates. Throughout the organisation, people were expected to take responsibility for their own decisions.

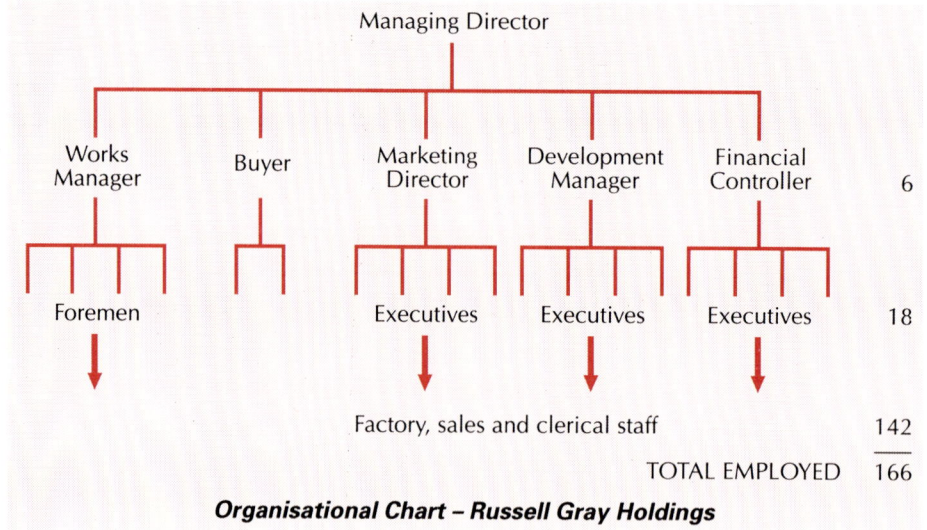

Organisational Chart – Russell Gray Holdings

Works Manager	Buyer	Marketing Director	Development Manager	Financial Controller	6
Foremen		Executives	Executives	Executives	18
		Factory, sales and clerical staff			142
				TOTAL EMPLOYED	166

A further benefit of the new management structure was the reduced number of intermediaries between shopfloor and boardroom. This helped Park to achieve what he felt certain was a key piece in the jigsaw – the achievement of good communications. He wanted the workforce to understand fully not only what was going on currently (and why), but also what was planned for the future. Monthly briefing meetings were established, and a company newsletter was distributed every week.

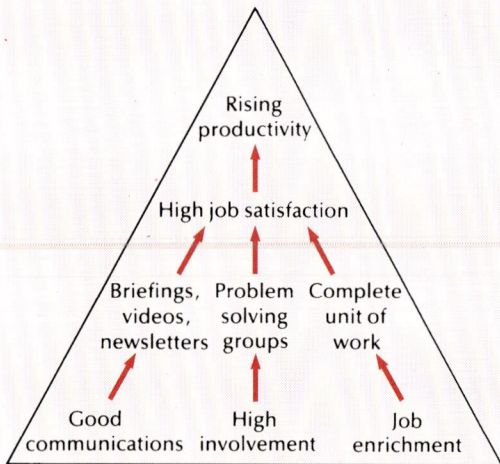

The Russell Gray Method

He felt particularly strongly that staff (even managers) tended to misunderstand the nature of 'profit'. By now, in the early 1980s, RGH's profit was approaching £750,000 per annum on a turnover of £5 million, so there was a lot of scope for employees to feel that someone was getting very rich from their efforts. So Park bought a video camera, and made – each year – a film to explain where the profit had come from and how it was going to be ploughed back into the business. All employees were given an hour off work to see the film and to talk about it.

RGH's style of management proved highly successful. After initial teething problems, product quality, delivery reliability and productivity all rose. Yet higher productivity can represent a threat to jobs, unless rising demand allows output to rise. This could have undermined Park's whole programme, as no-one would discuss labour-saving or cost-cutting measures if they were talking themselves out of a job. In RGH's case, the ending of long-standing patents during the 1970s meant that maintaining market share and output was a real struggle. So a strategy was needed to absorb the extra labour time being generated.

At first, RGH retrained staff to work in-house on processes that had previously been subcontracted. When there were no more jobs that could be done internally, the managers looked for new product opportunities. One such was the Snakey toy (the rings that walk downstairs), which was produced in a variety of bright colours for firms such as Habitat and Hamley's. For the management, Snakey represented a business opportunity; for the workforce it represented an outlet for their extra productivity – in other words, job security.

By 1985, with sales of over £7 million and profits topping £1 million for the first time (a better profit margin than ICI), it appeared that RGH's model management was set for long term success. Then to the complete shock of the workforce, Frazer Park 'resigned'. The reasons for this remain unclear. Probably either RGH's American owner decided that Park was becoming overly absorbed in his design of a perfect employee-centred company, or they demanded that he generate higher short-term profits than he thought wise. Visiting the factory soon afterwards, it was clear that the workforce was deeply sad to lose him. The Personnel Manageress, who had helped implement many of his ideas, left soon afterwards. The new Managing Director had a tough act to follow.

Source: *from visits to the firm, the name of which has been changed.*

Questions

1   What is meant by white collar and blue collar workers? **(2)**

2   Explain the term division of labour. State two advantages of this system of production. **(4)**

3   Given the advantages of the division of labour, why did Frazer Park dispense with it? **(3)**

4   The new system of production involved motivating the workforce. Describe and explain two methods that were adopted. **(6)**

5   Productivity was increasing; why did this lead to workforce insecurity? How did the Snakey toy lessen these fears? **(5)**

6   Describe and explain the reasons for the change in wages policy that took place as people were moved from piecerate to timerate. **(5)**

Further work

1   Progressive companies adopt a Quality of Working Life strategy, with the broad aim of bringing together and satisfying both the aims and development of the organisation and the aims and development of all their people. Describe and explain how each of the following would contribute to an increase in the quality of working life: a flat organisational structure, joint problem solving, performance appraisal.

2   Explain how the following changes would help to improve workforce performance at Russell Gray Holdings:

   a   The introduction of multi-skilling

   b   Warehouse staff to be issued with new anti-slip boots to comply with Health and Safety regulations.

How could improvements in workforce performance be recorded?

45 BRITISH MANAGEMENT TECHNIQUES UNDER FIRE

Elements: **5.2** *PC 1 2 3*   **5.3** *PC 1 2 3 4*   *BTEC* **15.1** *PC 1 2 3*

Key concepts: Features of workplace performance, External influences

A research study into British versus German management style and practices has highlighted many differences. It found that in Britain, attitudes to leadership and consultation showed a more personalised and one-way view which is more suited to a more traditionally authoritarian kind of organisation.

British attitudes to the workforce showed a stronger tendency to emphasise the 'Economic Man' approach associated with F.W. Taylor. There tended to be more **layers of hierarchy** in Britain and more **differentiated conditions**, e.g. in canteens, rest rooms, and employment contracts. Researchers found that engineers and production people had a lower status in the United Kingdom, and tended to occupy fewer of the top management positions than the marketing and finance professionals. Furthermore, there was less training and education among the workforce in the U.K. than in Germany.

To develop this analysis further, they decided to compare British and German management within the same company – a German manufacturing firm with a large British subsidiary. This would remove certain variables (such as different production processes) and therefore help to focus on factors such as management style, leadership, and consultation.

The company selected was a very forward-thinking one – much concerned with employee job satisfaction. It had already done away with high division of labour assembly lines, and provided exceptionally clean, neat factory conditions. The latter point struck one researcher most forcefully in Britain, 'where standards in factories are so much lower in general than in Germany'.

It emerged that the main contrast was between the British subsidiary and other local British firms, rather than between the British and German branches of the same firm. The company's British workers liked the absence of conveyor belt assembly lines and the payment by salary; one said: 'At other places it's a rat-race because of the **piecework**.' They also appreciated the more equal treatment: 'Usually office workers are better looked after than us; here the management are pretty decent.'

The comparison with Germany did yield some useful points though:

1   In the German branch, a **Works Council** had been operational for twenty years, with great success. It provided a regular meeting point between management and elected worker representatives to discuss future plans and any immediate problems. The workforce considered it much more valuable than the contact they have with the boardroom via their two **Worker Directors** (all German firms have elected Worker Directors – by law).

2   The relationship between Management and Trade Unions seemed much more mature in Germany, as was revealed in this quote from a German manager:

'Here, during the recession, the Unions were very reasonable. The company placed all their accounts and statistics before them – not only the annual accounts… it's no use to employers having dissatisfied workers.'

3   The firm's German managers seemed more aware of the psychology of management and of the need to delegate. The idea of German authoritarianism proved a myth.

Questions

1   What is meant by the following terms: layers of hierarchy, differentiated conditions, piecework, Works Council, Worker Directors?   (5)

2   Why may clean and neat factory conditions help improve workplace performance?   (3)

3   Identify 3 ways in which a firm could benefit from training its whole workforce.   (3)

4   Why may office workers be better looked after than assembly line workers? What may be the consequences for an organisation of treating different groups of staff unequally?   (6)

5   Why may a Works Council be more successful than having Worker Directors?   (4)

6   What is meant by an authoritarian type of organisation? What evidence was there that British managers were more inclined to an authoritarian management style?   (4)

Further work

1   To complete the criteria for element 5.3, you need to compare the workforce performance of two business sectors. You could compare the company in this case study with the Japanese company in case study 46 (Kaizen).

2   A claim was made by an ex-employee that some Nissan car workers were taking drugs to cope with the pressures of the production line. Research Japanese management methods, and the way workers in UK Japanese factories are treated. What type of pressures would be faced on a production line?

46 KAIZEN – CONTINUOUS IMPROVEMENT AT OKI

Elements: **5.1** *PC 1 2 3 4 5*   **5.2** *PC 1 2 3*   **5.3** *PC 1 2 3 4*
AN **3.2** *PC 1 2 5*

Key concepts: *Workplace performance, Data sources, Economic relationships, Training*

OKI

In 1992 a company only four years old won three prestigious awards. *Management Today* magazine named it the 'Best Electronics Factory in Britain'; ICL awarded it a total quality accolade; and it became one of the first companies to reach the government's standard as an 'Investor In People'. The management was delighted, but fearful that complacency might set in. So OKI (UK) Ltd redoubled its efforts to improve continuously.

The Japanese electronics company OKI had decided to establish a dot-matrix printer factory in Europe in 1987. After brief consideration of Germany and Spain, the project leader, Mr Kojima, decided on Britain. This was due to the success of other Japanese firms in the UK, plus the familiarity of OKI staff with (American) English. Mr Kojima settled upon Cumbernauld in Scotland for its air and sea transport and its closeness to numerous electronic component suppliers in the heart of 'Silicon Glen'.

Mr Kojima was appointed Managing Director of OKI (UK) Ltd and given the task of getting a new factory up and running within two months. Sixty experienced OKI staff were flown over to help commission a factory layout designed and developed in Japan. Meanwhile, Mr Kojima recruited new managers and supervisors and arranged for each one to spend at least a week in Japan. From the start, it was established that OKI would be a **single status employer**, with everyone paid on a straight salary basis.

By mid 1988 the Cumbernauld plant had 300 staff producing 2,400 printers per week. Twelve months later a doubled staff level made 6,000 printers weekly. Having coped with the pressures of rapid expansion, OKI's UK management team wanted time to think through the company's future. A series of discussions was held with managers and a hundred shopfloor representatives. All agreed that OKI should build its future around its staff rather than automation. Yet the highly competitive market for printers made it essential for costs to fall and for quality to rise each year. This pointed to the Japanese idea of '**kaizen**' (continuous improvement).

OKI management translated kaizen as follows:

改善

KAIZEN

> *'The establishment of a process for continued improvement involving everyone – managers and workers alike.'*

This became the unifying theme that ran through the company's production and personnel practices.

Ian Smith, the production manager, realised it would be hard for each individual among many to see how to contribute meaningfully to OKI's overall improvement. Therefore a system was needed to provide immediate, localised feedback on performance to each staff member. OKI now follow a two-stage process to achieve this.

1 **Cell production**. The factory operation is split into five cells, each with its own suppliers and 'customers' (internal and external). For instance, completed printed circuit boards (PCBs) are delivered to the final assembly line, so the assembly line is the customer. If the 'customer' finds any quality defects, these are reported back to the relevant PCB workers. An important side-effect of this system is that quality is checked several times over. In 1992, buyers of OKI's printers reported a defect rate of only 0.25% (one in 400).

2 Performance targets. Each section has a daily quality target (such as a maximum of eight reported defects per day). This is displayed on a large board to which is added, every hour, the 'customer's' report on quality performance (see the diagram below).

PCB Quality Performance Friday 24th

FAULT	MAXIMUM	ACHIEVEMENT			
		9.00	10.00	11.00	12.00 →
Loose fit	1	–	N O	1	–
Cracking	3	–	D F	–	–
Electrical fault	2	I	E E	–	–
Discolouring	2	–	C T	1	1

This system ensures that the PCB workers know within an hour if a fault has slipped through to the assembly line. The individual responsible can be traced and the cause discussed. This might lead directly to a suggestion that would improve the production process. For example, workers have suggested changing the height of work benches, criticised the quality of materials from certain suppliers and learnt to spot when machines are starting to go wrong.

Improvement need not only stem from mistakes, however, so it is important to find ways of discussing how good methods can be made better. OKI's approach to communications begins with a 5–10 minute meeting every morning. Problems concerning the previous day's production are discussed and possible improvements may emerge. Twice a year all employees have an appraisal interview with their immediate superior. This is not concerned with pay or bonus levels, but with any problems or ambitions the employee has. It is a form of more reflective communication.

Interlinked with OKI's approach to communications is its heavy expenditure on training. Within its £250,000 training area, OKI provides new recruits with full **induction** courses, including simulated conveyor belt production lines. Existing staff are encouraged to take between six and fifteen days of training per year, primarily focused upon learning new skills. This creates a more flexible workforce and provides the skills (such as public speaking) to foster the discussion and involvement that the management seeks. In addition to job training, the company is very proud that 126 staff are taking Further Education evening courses up to degree level – sponsored by OKI.

In 1993 OKI piloted its first suggestion scheme, among the **sub-assembly workers**. A rule set from the start was that suggestions would only be considered if they related to the person's own performance. Suggestions on how others could improve were not welcome. The management team – all with experience of suggestion schemes in British firms – had debated about what type of financial rewards to offer. When raised with the pilot staff, however, this was treated with surprise. The staff felt that suggestions to improve people's working life or performance were worthwhile in themselves. The scheme got off to a strong start and is to be extended to other sections of the plant.

The result of all this effort is measured in two ways within the factory: quality defects and productivity. In 1988, 75% of completed PCBs passed first time when tested. After a year an 80% target was set, which was extended to 85% in 1992. With that having been achieved, the 1993 pass rate was pushed to 89%. This progress not only reduces the chance of a faulty product slipping through to the customer, but also reduces production time and therefore cost. Instead of 25% of all PCBs needing extra work in 1988, the target for 1993 pointed to only 11% failing first time.

The factory manager likes to measure productivity in a slightly unusual way. He believes that 'the 1990s are about speed' so he concentrates on the time it takes for a printer to be produced. In 1988 it took 120 minutes from the start of the final assembly line until packing. This included 45 minutes of 'robust test printing in extreme temperature conditions'. In 1994 the assembly target will be 75 minutes, even though the test has not changed. This approach to improvement has enabled output per worker to rise to sixteen printers per week in 1993.

When asked about the company's management approach, Mr Kojima denies that it is purely Japanese. He makes it clear that he prefers the plain speaking of his Scots staff to the respectful language of the Japanese. Yet as he sits with his blue jacket on – the same jacket as on the shopfloor – there is no doubt that he has brought Japanese thinking to Scotland; and it seems a marriage of continuous improvement.

Questions

1 Explain what is meant by these terms: single status employer, kaizen, cell production, induction training, sub-assembly workers. **(5)**

2 Why have so many Japanese firms located in the UK since 1970? **(3)**

3 Use relevant figures from the case study to demonstrate that OKI's workplace performance has improved. **(4)**

4 What contribution did the following make to the improvement of workplace performance?

   a training **(3)**

   b management methods **(3)**

5 Calculate OKI's output per worker in 1988 and 1989. **(3)**

6 What determines the demand for printers? Is there a straightforward link with the demand for workers to make printers? **(4)**

Further work

1 In order to meet the criteria for element 5.3, it is necessary to compare the workforce performance of two business sectors. You could compare the performance of the workforce at OKI with the construction industry using case study 43 (The Trench).

2 An alternative approach for element 5.3 would be to visit one local firm and use that firm as a comparison with OKI. It is important to remember that workforce performance is a very sensitive issue, and there must be a thorough preparation of questions before the visit. Draw up an action plan to include the following:

   - aims of visit

   - best places to visit

   - alternative times for the visit

   - suitable questions on the background of the company

   - suitable questions to reveal the main factors which influence the performance of the workforce.

47 JUST-IN-TIME PRODUCTION – THE JAPANESE WAY

Elements: **5.1** *PC 1 2 3 4 5* **5.2** *PC 3*
C **3.2** *PC 1 2 3 4*

Key concepts: Features of workplace performance, Productivity, Specialisation, External influences, Technology, Competition

As Redlin's new Group Production Controller, Booth felt it important that he should make his intentions clear from the start. So he arranged a meeting with the seven senior and middle-managers answerable to him, to announce his commitment to Just-In-Time (J.I.T.) production systems. He put his case as follows:

'Given the low profitability of our products in recent years, plus the threat of increased competition when EU trade barriers really come down, we have to tackle our uncompetitiveness compared with the Germans and the Japanese. We have not got the demand to justify a fully automated flow production system, so we must ensure that we make the best use of our 500 staff and our financial resources by moving towards the Japanese Just-In-Time (J.I.T) method. In other words production that operates so smoothly that waste of time, labour and resources is minimised, as each part arrives just in time for the next stage of manufacture.'

Booth concentrated first on the suppliers, with three objectives in mind:
1 to minimise the need for raw material stocks;
2 to eliminate the need for goods-inward quality inspection;
3 good communications with suppliers to ensure their awareness of new product developments that may require them to redesign and retool.

To achieve the first objective, it was necessary to switch from the traditional system of infrequent deliveries of bulk orders, to very frequent – even daily – deliveries. To make that economic, one supplier had to be chosen to get the whole order instead of having competing suppliers. Before the J.I.T programme, Redlin had 330 suppliers with an average on-time delivery performance of 82%. As J.I.T. relies upon 100% reliability of supply (since virtually no buffer stock is held), Booth began discussions with the suppliers with a view to cutting their number to one hundred of the most reliable.

For the second objective, since 207 of the 330 had already achieved 100% quality, Booth could act decisively to ensure that suppliers took their materials straight to the production line, rather than through a quality control inspector. The latter could be switched to checking the quality of Redlin's finished goods.

To improve Redlin's communications with suppliers in order to meet the third objective, Booth began an education programme for each: a factory tour, conversation with the workers using those materials, and a discussion between the New Product Development engineers and the supplier. After several months of close contact, he persuaded the suppliers that if they delivered a faulty component, they would have to pay for all the costs generated. In other words, if a 25 pence switch was discovered to be faulty after it had been built into a Redlin RangeVan, and it cost £40 of labour time to replace it, the supplier would have to pay Redlin £40.25 compensation. Both sides could see that such a strong incentive to supply 100% reliability would be to everyone's long-term benefit.

Having completed the preparations for supplier reliability, Booth was in a stronger position to convince his managers of the opportunities provided. After all, if components could be relied upon totally, less labour would be needed to handle stocks because the suppliers could deliver straight to the factory floor. The Assembly Manager also spotted that: 'Less warehousing should be needed for stocks, so perhaps we could convert half the warehouse into the assembly line extension we need so badly'.

The Group Production Controller reminded them, though, that J.I.T. would require some fundamental changes. Meticulous production planning would be needed, so that suppliers could receive their orders four days before delivery was needed. No less importantly, it would be essential to ensure that work flow in every section of the factory was uninterrupted. Previously, a temporary breakdown in one section would not stop work elsewhere in the factory, because semi-finished products were stockpiled at every stage of manufacture and assembly. Now the approach would be what the Japanese term 'Kanban', whereby good communications between production sections enable each to produce the right quantity of the right components for the next section to use. As a result, no stockpiling of work-in-progress should be necessary.

One senior production manager looked at Booth with disbelief, and said:

'We're not dealing with Japanese machine-people out there, you know! On a Monday 15% of them will be "off sick", and we won't know which 15% until 8 o'clock that morning. What if they're mostly from one section, so we can't get any production of a vital component that day? Must we send the rest of the workforce home?'

This comment emboldened others to add:

'And what about machine breakdowns? The average one takes three hours to re-start and we get at least a couple a day. After all, we've a good 180 machines on each production line.'

'I'm more worried about the power it'll give to the shopfloor workers. We'll be so dependent on each one of them that they'll have us over a barrel.'

Booth listened as one after the other criticised his proposal, then he fished some sheets of paper out of his briefcase which, without speaking, he handed to each of them. They quietened down as they looked at the contents (see below). After five minutes of silence he asked them if they accepted his view that the situation was critical, and needed drastic action. Glumly, they nodded.

Key facts on Redlin's competitive position

Redlin's market share

	UK	Europe	Rest of World
Last month	19%	8%	5%
1 year ago	23%	10%	8%
5 years ago	31%	12%	11%

Output per worker (productivity)

	Redlin	Average European rival	Average Japanese rival
Last month	24*	31	45
1 year ago	24	29	40
5 years ago	19	23	26

*Units of output per month

Stockholding per worker*

	Redlin	Average European rival	Average Japanese rival
Latest year	£9,800	£6,500	£1,800
Previous year	£9,500	£6,600	£2,700
5 years ago	£7,100	£5,800	£4,900

* Stock value divided by no. of workers

Although that meeting had ended gloomily, over the following weeks Booth saw each manager individually to discuss how they should help move towards the Japanese J.I.T. production method. Each came to realise that full co-operation from the workforce was an essential element in the process. Some saw this as a marvellous opportunity to adopt a different management style from the authoritarian one they had used in the past. Others, though, dreaded the changes involved; two sought early retirement and one asked for time off to look for another job. Booth agreed, knowing that full commitment among the management was essential.

After three months of intensive training on J.I.T. the managers felt able to implement changes. One of the first was to negotiate a job flexibility deal with the trade unions. This would overcome the problem of individual absentees holding up production. If all workers could do each other's jobs, staff could be switched as necessary. After this change was achieved, Booth experimented by doing away with a component stockpile between the grinding and the plating departments. The plating team were made responsible for ensuring that the grinders had their 'orders' at the beginning of each day – so no overnight stocks were needed. When this process was running smoothly (after two months) it was introduced step by step through the factory. After two years, the improvements began to show through in dramatic productivity and financial gains.

Questions

1 What was wrong at Redlin when Booth arrived? **(3)**

2 Explain how Just-in-time (JIT) works. **(4)**

3 What is meant by productivity? How would it be improved by the introduction of JIT? **(3)**

4 What is meant by specialisation? Give two examples of specialist jobs at Redlin. **(3)**

5 Give three examples of changes that Just-in-time would bring to Redlin. **(3)**

6 State how the following would be affected under a JIT system: wages, training, productivity, motivation. **(8)**

7 With Just-in-time, the key to success would be to change workplace attitudes. What attitudes were prevalent at Redlin? How did Booth attempt to overcome them? **(6)**

Further work

1 Just-in-time's success was dependent on job flexibility and multi-skilling (meaning that all workers would do all jobs on the shopfloor).

Research other ways in which flexible working takes place, for example, the rise of part-time workers, more flexible hours, and the increase in temporary workers. What are the potential advantages and disadvantages for the firm and for the individual workers involved? If possible, visit organisations in two different sectors to obtain your information, for example, retail and manufacturing.

2 Obtain statistics from the latest copy of *Social Trends*, on the trend towards more flexible working. Is there any evidence that women are becoming more important in the workforce? Write your answer in the form of a short report to your teacher.

48 WHIZZ KIDS

Elements: **4.1** *PC 3*   **5.1** *PC 1 2 3 4 5*   **5.2** *PC 1 2 3*
IT **3.3** *PC 1 2 3 4 5*

Key concepts: Employment trends, Technological and economic change, Training

He could not help feeling bitter. Twenty-three years as Production Director, yet they had dismissed his proposal in four minutes. Now they were on to a topic they really cared about - 'Treasury management'. No phrase irritated him as much. As his five fellow Directors proceeded with their discussion, Tony thought back.

His first Board meeting had been a great thrill, for he had worked his way up from the factory floor. Old Mr. Patterson was still in charge, and the sixty minute meeting had consisted largely of chat about engineering problems and production methods. Even the Sales Director was a chartered engineer, so the Finance Director was the only one who had little to say.

It was in the 1975 recession that the first great change came about. Mr. Patterson retired in the midst of a terrible financial crisis, to be replaced by an American whizz-kid. For the next ten years all he ever heard about was marketing. Although he had hated it at the time, he now realised that it had its good points. Even though they treated the process of production as if it was as easy as turning a tap on and off, at least they talked about products and customers.

Now, thought Tony, as he tuned back into the conversation, they might as well be a bank. The Director of Treasury Operations was just saying:

> *'We're taking a six month put option against the Deutschemark*
> *to hedge ourselves on the Dusseldorf deal'.*

All he understood of that was that it referred to the contract he had spent three months tying up with Thyssen of Germany. Now that contract was reduced to gobbledegook and the profits generated would probably be claimed by the Finance bunch as a tribute to their skills in the foreign exchange markets.

The last item on the agenda was the capital estimates for the coming financial year. Tony was keen to gain agreement to £4.2 million of fixed capital expenditure on a new, computer-controlled metal stamping and assembly unit. He had worked out that he would reallocate the seventeen staff replaced by the machine to a series of new quality control centres within the factory. This would make the pay-back on the investment rather slow, but would ensure rising customer satisfaction over coming years.

After Tony had finished, the Treasury Director put forward a plan for a new, £4 million computer system. This would make it possible to monitor the interest rates offered on every type of bank deposit or loan throughout the world, and to calculate the degree of foreign currency risk involved. As a result, the £380 million of cash that

passed through the firm per year would be able to generate an estimated £2 million of extra interest and therefore profit. Even this rapid payback would be speeded up by offering the service to other local firms, which should generate fees worth an extra £1 million a year. As the Managing Director believed that capital spending could be no more than £7 million in the coming year, a decision was needed. After some debate, Tony lost the argument.

Questions

1   What external factors made Tony's job much less satisfying?   (3)

2   State two technological changes mentioned in the case study.   (2)

3   What do financial orientated, production orientated and market orientated mean?   (3)

4   State three types of training relevant to a factory.   (3)

5   Nowadays it is normal for managers to be recruited from universities and channelled straight into a management training scheme. What are the advantages and disadvantages of this system?   (6)

6   What are the advantages and disadvantages of promoting someone from the factory floor to a management position?   (4)

7   Production engineering is not a popular education and career path in Britain. How might manufacturing firms set about tackling this problem?   (4)

Further work

1   Draw up an action plan stating how you would identify changing employment trends in manufacturing in the UK. In your action plan write down information that you require, and state how you would get hold of this information. You may wish to research terms like primary, secondary and tertiary sectors.

2   One employment trend within a specific sector is the decline of manufacturing. De-industrialisation is the name given to this decline. What is the extent of de-industrialisation and what are its causes? Is it something to be worried about within the UK economy?

    As part of your core skills in Information Technology, obtain statistics on the percentage of people employed in each of the primary, secondary and tertiary sectors. Convert these statistics into a chart and import the chart into the text on de-industrialisation. Ideally, you should gather statistics for three different years to identify trends, for example 1974, 1984 and 1994.

3   Choose any two business sectors, such as travel and tourism, leisure and recreation, construction, retail, catering, textiles, or energy. For each sector look at changing employment trends and economic trends. You may wish to look at the changing balance between skilled and unskilled workers and the impact of technological, demographic and social change on your chosen sectors. You can use the *Lifestyle* pocket book, issued by the Advertising Association, to help with statistics on travel and recreation.

49 THE FORD STRIKE

Elements: **5.1** *PC 345* **5.2** *PC 123*

Key concepts: Employment features and trends, Economic relationships, External factors affecting business

The U.K. market was booming in 1987, with sales rising 7% to two million cars for the first time. Ford took an increasing share of this growing market (up from 27% to 29%), with its Escort, Fiesta, and Sierra models in the top three places in the U.K. sales league. Ford U.K. annual profits were set to beat £350 million.

Encouraged by low inflation in Britain, and keen to match the three year pay deals signed by Ford's German, Spanish, and Belgian workers, Ford U.K. set out to agree a similar scheme with its unions. In October 1987, Ford offered a 4.25% per annum pay rise to its employees. This was rejected as 'insulting', and during the negotiations that followed, **unofficial industrial action** lost Ford production of 26,000 cars (worth over £200 million). On 7th December, the company announced its final offer:

1 6.5% in the first year of a three year deal.
2 Rises in line with inflation for the second and third years.
3 In return, Ford demanded radical **changes in working practices**, including the introduction of team-working, flexibility between skilled and unskilled workers, acceptance by skilled workers of semi-skilled workers as their supervisors, and acceptance of temporary workers to meet seasonal peaks in demand.

The unions arranged a secret ballot of all workers on this offer; they recommended its rejection. On 22nd January 1988 the results showed 90% of Ford's manual workers against the offer. Eighty-seven per cent of employees voted. Although surprised by the scale of their majority, the unions quickly declared that a national, all-out strike would start the following Monday, unless management improved on their 'final' offer. It was to be the first national strike at Ford since an eight week strike in 1978. Management hastily increased their offer to 7% in the first year, and 2% above inflation in the second and third years, but the union considered this an insufficient improvement.

As the deadline approached, the Ford unions became increasingly confident of their position. The leader of the Amalgamated Engineering Union (AEU) described management as 'desperate' for a settlement. There were two reasons for this confidence: first was the realisation that buoyant demand meant that Ford's stock levels were too low to keep the showrooms supplied for long. The other factor was more fundamental: that Ford's development since 1978 of a fully integrated European production system left them very vulnerable to strike action. For although Ford U.K.'s plants accounted for less than a third of Ford of Europe's 1.6 million cars a year, the United Kingdom was Ford's only supplier of certain key

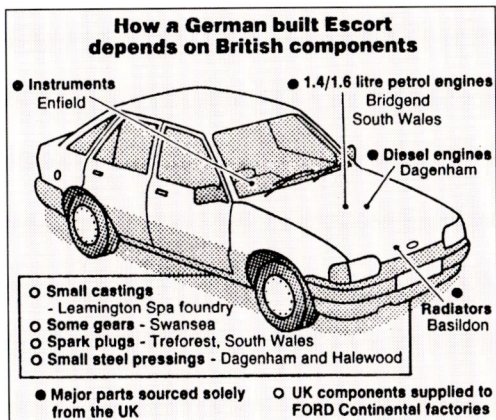

How a German built Escort depends on British components

- Instruments Enfield
- 1.4/1.6 litre petrol engines Bridgend South Wales
- Diesel engines Dagenham
- Small castings - Leamington Spa foundry
- Some gears - Swansea
- Spark plugs - Treforest, South Wales
- Small steel pressings - Dagenham and Halewood
- Radiators Basildon

● Major parts sourced solely from the UK   ○ UK components supplied to FORD Continental factories

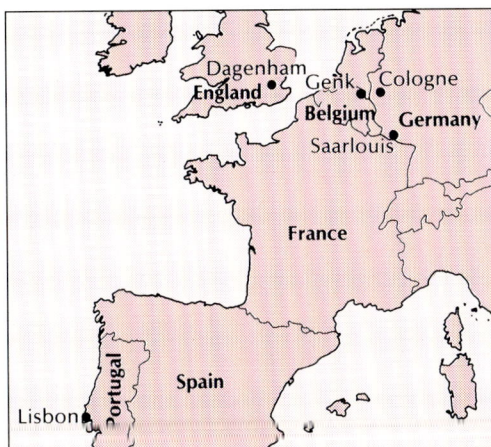

components. Ford's Dagenham plant, for instance, was the sole producer of the 1.6 diesel engine used in Sierra, Escort and Orion models throughout Europe.

As a multinational with major plants in Britain, Germany, Belgium, and Spain, Ford's strategy had been to maximise economies of scale by concentrating output of components on particular sites. This also enabled them to use local labour to its best advantage – hence the highly paid, highly skilled German workforce produced the gearboxes, a particularly complex item. The components would then be shipped to the assembly plants located in each of the major production sites. As far as possible, Ford aimed to transport components from one country to another, rather than finished cars.

At the same time, Japanese competition was forcing Ford to review existing practices. The start of production at Nissan's highly efficient Sunderland factory in mid-1986 hastened this review. There were two key areas Ford wanted to improve:

1. the rigid job demarcations between skilled and unskilled workers, and between one skill and another;
2. excessive stock levels; the company wanted to move towards the Kanban (Just-In-Time) system used increasingly in Japan; increasing reliance on prompt, frequent delivery instead of **buffer stocks** would cut Ford's working capital requirements significantly.

Surprisingly, an emergency meeting of both sides on Sunday 31st January led to the announcement that the strike was to be called off. Ford had further improved their offer, and the unions believed that the new package should be recommended to their members in a new ballot. At the local, shop-floor level, Ford's **shop stewards** were furious at the acceptance of the new offer, and criticised their union leaders openly. The new ballot produced a 60% vote to reject the offer, and the strike was on again.

The all-out strike started on Monday 8th February 1988, and was unanimously supported – even at plants which had voted to accept the offer. The *Financial Times* reported that the Labour Party spokesman 'maintained that the 7% increase…did not represent a fair share of the company's rising prosperity when compared with the increased payments made to directors and shareholders'. The Conservative Minister for Employment warned that 'strikes destroy jobs'.

On the hastily formed picket lines, discussion was of the £350 million profit made by Ford U.K. in 1987. One striker said:

'It's a question of whether we get a bit of the cake, and how we get treated. But it isn't all about money. Some people have to ask

permission to go to the toilet ... (and) they're taking away the incentives for trained people like me'.

The Ford management emphasised that the key issue was whether their U.K. factories would be profitable enough to warrant continued investment.

Within one day of its start, the strike forced Ford to lay off 2,500 workers at Genk, Belgium. Not even the plant's management had realised before that they were totally dependent upon daily deliveries of sheet metal parts from Dagenham. By Friday, the Genk factory's 7,200 workers producing 1,400 Sierras a day were told they would be laid off due to non-availability of body panel reinforcement brackets from Dagenham. Similar cut-backs were reported at the massive Saarlouis plant in West Germany, and at Cologne and in Portugal. Ford's management had to face up to the fact that even one minor item missing on a vast assembly line could halt all production.

On Tuesday 16th February, management offered to drop the three year pay deal in favour of a two year one in which the second year rise would be 7% or 2.5% above inflation, whichever was the greater. Other elements of the package included a 9% improvement in pensions, better sick pay, and 100% lay-off pay. The company also agreed that the changes to working practices would not be imposed against local opposition – an important concession to the shop stewards.

On the union side, there was acceptance of quality circles (discussion groups), and of the principle of reorganising the factories so that shop-floor workers could work in teams, instead of being individual cogs in a large wheel. Ford's Personnel Director denied that the revised offer was a climb down, though he acknowledged that both sides in the collective bargaining process had misread the strength of shopfloor opposition to the original deal.

On Monday 22nd February, the Ford workers returned to work after 70% voted to accept the new offer. Ford declared that they had lost about £200 million of output during the strike, in addition to the £300 million lost through unofficial action between October and February. The workforce considered themselves victorious, but one year later Ford announced that Sierra production was to be transferred from Dagenham to Genk, and that redundancies would be inevitable.

Sources: *The Financial Times; The Guardian; The Times*

Questions

1 Explain the meaning of the following: unofficial industrial action, changes in working practices, buffer stocks, shop stewards. **(4)**

2 Explain why Ford tried to implement changes in its working practices, such as team working, temporary workers, flexibility between skilled and semi-skilled workers. **(6)**

3 Name two external influences which had an effect on Ford's employment structure. For each influence explain how it affected employment. **(4)**

4 To what extent were the workers on strike because of wages or because of the way in which they were treated? Explain your answer. **(6)**

5 Referring to both the short and the long run, what effect did union activity have on wages and job security? **(5)**

Further work

1 Many firms have undergone radical changes in their employment structure and working practices. Using resource material from newspapers, annual reports and accounts, *Business Studies* magazine, or any other secondary source, choose a company and analyse how its employment structure and working practices have changed in recent years.

Elements   **6.3** *PC 23456*   **7.4** *PC 6*   *AN* **3.1** *PC 123456*
              IT **3.1** *PC 12345*   **3.4** *PC 2*

Key concepts: Calculation and explanation of ratios, Use of accounts to secure a bank loan

Sadaf bought the shares after seeing the company featured on *The Clothes Show*. She had wanted to invest part of the £4,000 inherited from her grandfather, and this company seemed just right. Brilliant clothes designers with shops in all the major high streets, Sting plc was now expanding into Europe. At only 40p each, Sadaf considered the shares a bargain; she bought 2,000.

As the economies of Europe picked up during the spring, Sadaf felt increasingly confident about her investment. When the share price hit 56p in July, she was tempted to sell and enjoy a 40% profit.

Then in August the share price dropped back unexpectedly. Two days later the Chairman issued the following profit warning:

> '*Poorer than expected trading in Britain plus a disappointing first season in Europe has led to a profit downturn. I remain convinced that our move into Europe will be in the long term interests of your company. Full details will be available in the interim accounts, to be published within two weeks.*'

By the time the accounts arrived in the post, Sting shares were quoted at just 18p. Sadaf wondered whether to sell while her investment still had some value. So she looked at the accounts with great interest. Did the company's finances look strong enough to survive a period of poor trading, while still expanding into Europe?

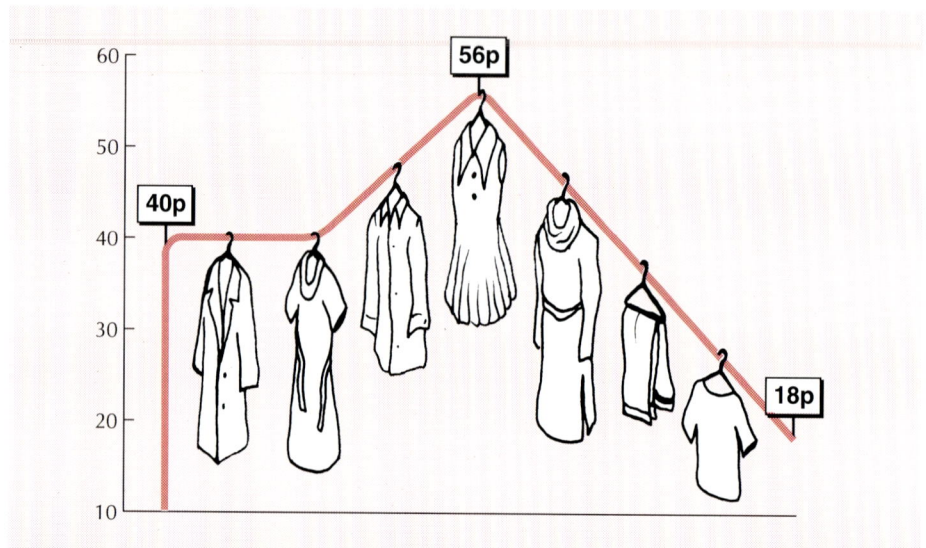

Interim Accounts for Sting PLC, Jan – Jun (unaudited)

Profit and loss account

	£m
Sales turnover	34
Cost of sales	26
GROSS PROFIT	8
Overheads	10
TRADING PROFIT	(2)
Taxation	3
NET PROFIT	(5)
Dividends	1
RETAINED PROFIT	(6)

Note: Issued share capital of 50 million 10p shares

Balance sheet (June 30th)

	£m
Property	16
Machinery	4
Vehicles	4
Stock	6.5
Debtors	4.5
Cash	1
Current liabilities	11
Working capital	1
ASSETS EMPLOYED	25
Loans	15
Shareholders funds	10
CAPITAL EMPLOYED	25

Questions

1 a How much did Sadaf pay for her 2,000 shares? **(2)**

   b If Sadaf's stockbroker charged a 1.5% commission, what was the final price paid? **(2)**

2 How much were the shares worth at their lowest and highest points? **(4)**

3 State three factors Sadaf should take into account before selling her shares at 18 pence. **(3)**

4 What is a ratio? Work out the current ratio, acid test ratio and gross profit margin for Sting plc. **(5)**

5 Show, by using a formula, that working capital equals £1 million. **(2)**

6 Why may Sting plc be paying a dividend even though it is making operating losses? **(2)**

Further work

1 Sting plc decides that it needs more finance to continue its expansion into Europe. Imagine that you are the bank manager meeting the Finance Directors. What questions would you ask after looking at the accounts? What would you take into consideration before deciding whether to grant a request for further funds?

2 Using an appropriate spreadsheet package, produce an amended balance sheet after the following happens: the bank agrees to a loan of £5m and this is used to fund property in Europe (£2m), vehicles (£0.2m), machinery (£1.1m), stocks (£0.7m), cash (£1m). Print out a hard copy of the balance sheet with a new title, and call the new file Sting plc. Keep a back-up version in case of difficulty. Underneath the balance sheet, explain what you think may happen to the share price after this £5m loan is granted.

51

CREDIT FACTORING

Elements: **6.1** *PC 123456* **6.2** *PC 12345*

Key concepts: Financial transactions, Purposes and types of security checks,
Correct and incorrect completion

SiteCo is a site investigation company. It is hired by property developers to test the soil structure on a site, to see if it is suitable to build on.

The firm started five years ago with two directors/ engineers working from one of their houses. They now employ six staff and have acquired an office and a laboratory. Their development can be seen from the following record:

	Sales Turnover £	Profit £
Year 1	16,835	174
Year 2	27,348	5,336
Year 3	82,488	1,536
Year 4	142,540	16,102
Year 5	251,310	44,531

Although delighted with their recent progress, the Directors were frustrated that they could not generate enough cash to buy the equipment they needed to cope with their expansion. So, for example, they had to subcontract sulphate testing, which was expensive and time-consuming, as an average of four trips were needed per week to the outside lab. At present the testing was costing them £175 per week. This would be cut to £25 per week if they could find the £6,000 needed to buy the machine. However, this was just one among many pieces of **capital expenditure** that seem pressing, and it had to join the queue.

All rapidly growing firms have a strained cash flow position, but the particular cause of SiteCo's difficulties was the Directors' inefficiency with paperwork. Both enjoyed the testing work, and the relationship with their customers, but neither liked dealing with administration or the job of chasing late payers. So the busier they were, the more reasons they found for not processing the paperwork. As a result, the last time they checked they were owed £60,000 by customers.

Now, rather than going to their bank manager to ask for their **overdraft limit** to be increased, they called in a management consultant. After a few days of investigation, she concluded that there was no point in looking for a solution that would have to be implemented by the current staff. Nor could she believe that the appointment of a Credit Controller would be worth the expense, as it would still be essential for the Directors to cooperate fully with the administrative system. Hence her recommendation that SiteCo should use the **credit factoring** service of one of the major banks. She suggested that they should use the full service, including 80% of invoiced amounts paid within 24 hours; sales invoice management and analysis; debt collection; and insurance against bad debts. This service would result in a charge amounting to 5% of sales turnover.

Both Directors loved the idea of someone else being responsible for debt collection, especially as their business was so dependent on good relationships with clients. Yet the cost did concern them, so they needed to be convinced that the cash flow benefit would be large enough to enable them to make several of the cost-saving investments they had planned.

Based on their sales forecast of £360,000 in the coming year, and on their current three month lag between invoicing and receiving payment, the consultant made a back-of-the-envelope calculation. She estimated an immediate cash benefit of £72,000, being whittled down to £54,000 in the following twelve months. That reassured the Directors fully, so after the bank had made the necessary checks into SiteCo and its customers, the new system became operational. Within a month both Directors were convinced that it was a great success.

Questions

1 Explain the meaning of the following: capital expenditure, overdraft limit, credit factoring. (3)

2 One of the problems highlighted by the case study was the Directors' inefficiency with paperwork. Give two reasons why documents like receipts and invoices are needed in business. (2)

3 Companies have a legal obligation regarding their accounting information. What legal requirements do companies have to fulfil? (2)

4 The management of SiteCo certainly knew about simple documentation, but did not administer it properly. Describe the main purchase and sales documents, and why they are used. (4)

5 What steps can be taken to make sure invoices are paid before a specialist factoring service is called in? (3)

6 State two advantages and two disadvantages of having a three-month lag between invoicing and receiving payment. (4)

7 What would be the effect on a firm's cash flow if it stopped using the services of a factor? (3)

8 Work out the management consultant's 'back-of-the-envelope' calculations of the cash generated by factoring. (4)

Further work

1 Arrange a local visit, in small groups, to a newsagent or other suitable small business where there is a delay between receiving goods/services and payment. Your purpose is to find out how the system of financial transactions and documents works.

   ■ How does the business document its sales to the public?

   ■ How does the business organise payments and receipts?

   ■ What security checks does the business have for payment documents?

   ■ What would be the consequences of incorrect completion of documents? When and how would errors be picked up?

   If possible, arrange to see a completed example of a purchase document, sales document, payment document and receipt.

2 SiteCo was burdened with chasing up payments by customers who were late payers. Research the steps which can be taken to collect money and encourage more prompt payment.

52

FASHION GOES WEST

Elements: *6.3 PC 123467   IT **3.1** PC 12345*

Key concepts: Users of accounts, Explanation of simple balance sheet terminology

'The Americans are crying out for clothes like these,' said Hazell, the fashion journalist. Lucy and Ted looked pleased, but not totally convinced. They still remembered the £40,000 they lost when they tried to market products in the United States last time. Those losses had almost forced their company into receivership. Ted, who was responsible for production and finance, recalled this episode with particular horror.

Hazell saw their scepticism and so went into further detail. 'Nothing has hit the young scene over there since punk. High fashion womenswear is worth £850 million in the United States, and any new craze can easily pick up 1% of that.'

Lucy explained that the real problem was financing such a venture. 'At present,' she said, 'our monthly cash inflow is balanced by outflows, and we've only got £50,000 on deposit at the bank.' Lucy then jotted down some estimates:

> *Start-up costs:*
> *£100,000 (incurred in month one)*
> *Running costs:*
> *Cost of stock – £16,000 per month*
> *Transport costs – £4 per item*
> *(Both these costs would affect the*
> *month before sale)*
> *U.S. overheads – £10,000 per month*

'From day one we'd start incurring those overheads', said Lucy, 'but I think we would only start selling clothes from the start of month four. So even if we managed sales of 1,000 garments a month at £40 each, it'd take us over a year to get back into the black. And that is assuming we can get away without giving our customers any credit.'

Ted decided to look more closely at the U.S. fashion market. He found a distribution pattern dominated by big, staid firms.

He wondered if New York would be a good starting point, and so checked on the regional sales pattern. He found that although New Yorkers are only 8% of all Americans, they buy 12% of all new fashionwear. A research report stated that: 'Fashion clothing in New York is price inelastic, but has an income elasticity as high as four.'

As the weeks went by, Hazell convinced Lucy that they should try America. This was potentially decisive, as Lucy owned 51% of the company's shares to

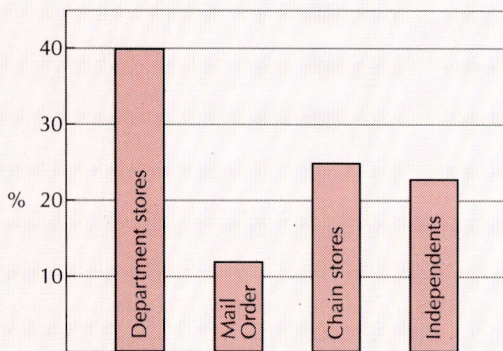

Percentage share of fashion wear for 16–24 year old women. (Total US market)

Ted's 49%. She used this lever to persuade Ted that they must have a go.

Ted prepared a business plan, including a cash flow forecast and a thorough investment appraisal, which they took to their accountant. Having looked at the balance sheet (see Appendix A) the accountant expressed concern: 'Borrowing all the extra funds would put you in a very difficult position if the United States move fails. Can you increase the equity capital?' Neither Lucy nor Ted wished to.

Taking this constraint into account, the accountant modified Ted's business plan to make it seem as professional as possible to the bank. When Ted and Lucy went there, they were delighted to find the manager happy about the financial side, though he seemed concerned about the protectionist climate in America since the U.S. trade deficit was so high. Happily, within a few days a loan was agreed and the expansion could begin.

APPENDIX A: Balance Sheet (as of yesterday)

	£000	£000
Fixed Assets		
Machinery [1]	45	
Property	95	140
Current Assets		
Stocks [2]	40	
Debtors	10	
Cash	50	
Current Liabilities		
Creditors	65	
Overdraft	10	
Net Current Assets		25
Net Assets Employed		165
Shareholders Funds		
Share Capital	50	
Reserves	60	110
Long term loans	55	55
Capital Employed		165

Notes: (1) Assuming ten year straight line depreciation.
(2) Including £20,000 of stock written down by 10% for being over twelve months old.

APPENDIX B: Discount factors

At 10%:

end of year 1	–	0.91
end of year 2	–	0.83
end of year 3	–	0.75

Questions

1   Name three organisations or groups of people who might be interested in the accounts of Ted and Lucy's business.   **(3)**

2   Explain the meaning of the major components of a balance sheet: fixed assets, current assets, current liabilities, shareholders funds, reserves, capital employed.   **(6)**

3   What is meant by equity capital? Why do you think that Lucy and Ted were not keen to increase their equity capital?   **(3)**

4   What is meant by the liquidity of a business? How can liquidity be measured? Use two liquidity measurements to assess Lucy and Ted's business.   **(4)**

5   What is depreciation? Explain Note 1 in Appendix A. How much would the machinery depreciate per annum if it originally cost £45,000?   **(4)**

Further work

1   In order to fulfil most of element 6.3, you need to explain why businesses need monitoring. Using a spreadsheet package, set out a cash flow forecast for Lucy and Ted's business for the first six months, assuming that they start their American expansion today. What aspects of the cash flow need monitoring the most? Explain why.

2   If you feel happy with the terms listed in the balance sheet, attempt an analysis of Lucy and Ted's business. What parts of the balance sheet may have worried the accountant, and which parts were more positive?

    What non-financial factors would the manager have to take into account before making a decision?

53

THE SOFABED SAGA

Elements: **6.3** *PC 4567*
AN **3.2** *PC 1235*

Key concepts: Monitoring a business to improve performance, Use of ratio analysis,
Calculating percentages

The Sofabed Company Chief Executive was examining her firm's accounts in comparison with those of her nearest rival, SofaSogood. She found that margins were similar, but her **return on capital** (ROC) was markedly worse: 21% compared with 30%.

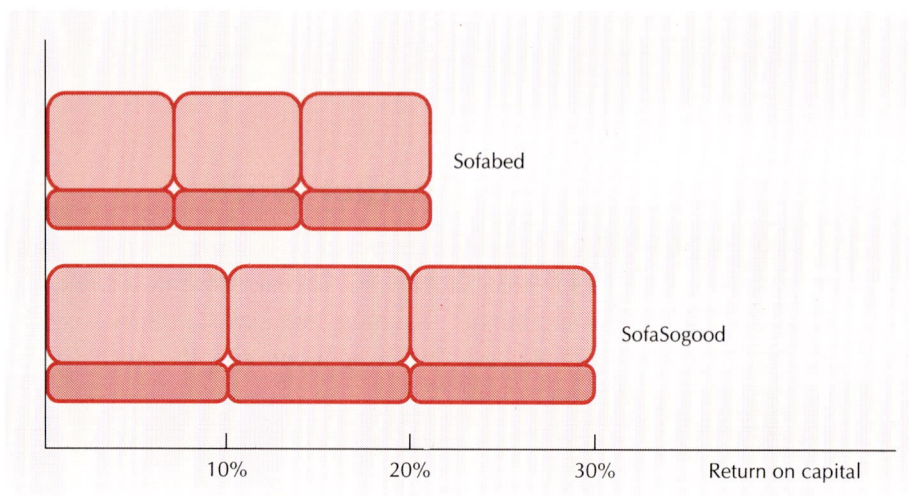

This was a worry because the current economic downturn made it likely that future trading conditions would be poor, so the weaker of the two might be forced out of business. The subject came up at the next Board meeting, where the Finance Director and the Sales Director put forward alternative methods for boosting the ROC.

The Finance Director spoke first: 'At present our net margins are 14%, which is only 1% below those of SofaSogood. So our real problem is **asset turnover**. I propose that we negotiate a **sale and leaseback** on our head office. That will bring in £400,000 that we can use to pay off some of our long term loans. Our assets employed will be cut by 25%, boosting our asset turnover and therefore our ROC.'

The Sales Director replied: 'Paying off our debts may be sensible, but I am more concerned about our margins. Two years ago they were 17%, last year 14%. What of the coming year, given the recession? Our sales staff are under constant pressure to give bigger discounts to customers. If they give an extra 7% discount our margins will be halved! So my proposal is that we should boost our advertising spending with a highly distinctive campaign, in order to make demand for our products less price sensitive. That should protect our share of this falling market.'

The Finance Director was unimpressed with this argument from Sales, as it: 'Just holds gross margins up at the expense of net margins.'

Eventually the Chief Executive decided on a third option: to open up a sixth outlet in rented premises in a different town. It would use stock from existing outlets, the same distribution lorries, advertising budget and office staff. Therefore 'our assets can be made to work much harder'.

Questions

1 What is meant by: return on capital, asset turnover, sale and leaseback? **(3)**

2 If a sofabed was sold for £300 and the profit margin was 17%, how much profit would the company make? **(2)**

3 In the case study, the profit margin fell to 14% and there was a threat that it might plummet to 7%. Calculate profits for the £300 sofabed on the basis of these figures. **(4)**

4 Explain why it was so important to raise the £400,000 from the sale and leaseback of the head office. **(3)**

5 State the advantages and disadvantages of the three options facing Sofabed. **(6)**

6 **a** What is meant by an accounting ratio? **(2)**

   b Why may it be unfair to compare Sofabed and Sofasogood just on the basis of return on capital, asset turnover and their profit margins? **(5)**

Further work

1 Using an Accountancy or Business Studies textbook, identify some of the main ratios under the headings: performance ratios, liquidity ratios and shareholder measures. What is the purpose of ratios and why are there problems in using them?

2 Asset turnover measures sales turnover in relation to the assets held by the business. A successful firm would hope to 'make the assets sweat' by generating a high sales level from their asset base. In this case, discuss how well the Sofabed Chairman is using the concept of asset turnover.

54

LIQUIDITY CRISIS

Elements: **6.3** *PC 1234567*

Key concepts: Users of accounts, Key components of accounting information,
Reasons for monitoring the performance of business

All through the 1980s commentators had stressed the problems of an ageing population. Annabelle was one of the first to realise that this trend would also throw up business opportunites. Her family electrical manufacturing business (Raysun) had been struggling for years and she looked forward to the wider, competitive market of 1992 with horror. She knew that their small output from a 30-year-old factory was no basis for matching the economies of scale of the major producers like Philips and Electrolux. Even worse, her father's decision five years before to stop producing branded goods left them at the mercy of the price conscious own-label buying managers at the store chains. So, appreciating that her firm could not compete in the mass market, Annabelle decided to aim her products at the only segment that was both growing and uncatered for – the elderly.

Her father took some convincing, but eventually he conceded that 'Since I retired last year, you're the boss, so your decisions count.' The next problem was how to organise and finance the required Research and Development (R & D) and market research programmes. A constraint was that years of poor trading had led to a run down of Raysun's capital stock. That meant the firm's machinery and vehicles had been allowed to get older and older, as operating losses made it impossible to finance the purchase of new fixed assets. Such actions had helped the firm survive, but now there was little of value left on the balance sheet to give a bank manager the confidence to provide a long term loan. This can be seen in the following balance sheet.

Raysun Ltd. Balance Sheet 31st December

	£000	£000
Fixed Assets		
Property leases	25	
Machinery	12	
Vehicles	15	52
Working Capital		
Stocks	60	
Debtors	88	
Cash	7	155
Creditors	55	
Overdraft	10	65
Net current assets		90
Assets employed		142
Share capital	10	
Reserves	82	
Bank loans	50	
Capital Employed		142

After discussion with her Engineering Director and Sales Manager, Annabelle decided that she would need to budget £180,000 for development spending on a vacuum cleaner for the elderly over the next twelve months. She anticipated an operating profit on her existing business of just £12,000 in that period, after deducting £8,000 of depreciation. Her father had given his agreement to a Rights Issue in which shareholders would subscribe for three new shares for each one held currently. Therefore, the remaining £130,000 would have to be squeezed out of working capital. This would have a severe impact on Raysun's liquidity position, but she felt that the firm's long standing relationship with its suppliers should make them willing to accept some temporary delays.

For nine months both strands of the policy went well. The Sales department found out that the over-70s wanted cleaners that were very light, easy to manoeuvre, and with extra long leads so that the user need bend down only once to plug it in. The Engineering department went ahead with this brief, experimenting with new, lighter plastics and with power-assisted wheels that enable the user to push the cleaner along effortlessly. By month ten, however, it was becoming clear that technical problems would delay the launch by six months, and cost a further £50,000.

Annabelle carefully worked out a cash flow forecast for the coming two years, and converted it into the graph shown left. She used it (plus the market research findings included as **Appendix A**) to attempt to persuade her bank manager to increase Raysun's overdraft facility. This proved fruitless.

A frantic week followed in which Annabelle visited a series of different banks – all with the same depressing result. At the same time she had to fend off creditors who complained that they had not been paid for goods supplied 20 weeks ago.

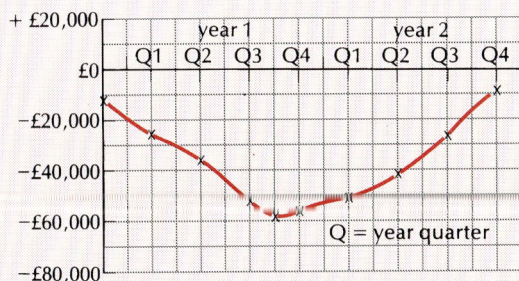

Raysun cashflow forecast for the coming two years

Despite her pleadings, two suppliers refused to supply any more goods on credit and one said he would instruct his solicitor to take her to court to retrieve his £2,800 debt. As she had no cash, and the week's cash inflow was only going to be sufficient to pay her wage bill, she felt powerless.

It was while she waited to see a sixth and final bank manager, nervously flicking through a local newspaper, that she noticed an article about the Regional Enterprise Board. A local politician was complaining about the 'waste of public funds involved in using Council money to prop up firms that the banks consider a bad risk.' Annabelle apologised to a puzzled secretary, and sped to the Enterprise Board's offices. They sent a business advisor over to see her factory, the R & D work, and her finances. He was impressed with the enthusiasm of all the staff he met, and with the clarity of her marketing strategy. They agreed that the financial package needed would be £20,000 of equity capital and £40,000 of loan capital.

Annabelle felt awkward about telling her father that she had to dilute his shareholding by a third, but she knew that the risks the Board was taking deserved the chance of a share in the profits of success.

To avoid being taken to court in the ten days before the Enterprise Board's committee met to approve the finance, Annabelle had to sell her VW Golf to raise the £2,800. After the successful launch of the 'Ageless' vacuum cleaner, though, she was able to look back on the struggles of the liquidity crisis with some relief and much pride.

APPENDIX A Summary Of Market Research Findings

	Age of respondents		
	60–69	70–79	80+
Q1 Last bought a vacuum			
Up to 5 years ago	34%	22%	8%
5–10 years ago	42%	39%	31%
11+ years ago	24%	39%	61%
Q2 Think vacuums are poorly designed for elderly			
Agree very strongly	20%	39%	64%
Agree strongly	24%	32%	31%
Agree	32%	23%	5%
Disagree	24%	6%	–
Q3 Would buy a vacuum designed for older people			
Yes, definitely	36%	61%	42%
Yes, very probably	31%	28%	22%
Yes, quite probably	11%	7%	12%
Probably not	22%	4%	24%

Questions

1   Research all the potential users of accountancy information.   (5)

2   Name three users who would be particularly interested in Raysun's accounts.   (3)

3   Give two reasons for monitoring Annabelle's business.   (2)

4   What is a ratio? Why do firms use them?   (3)

5   From the balance sheet, work out the company's current ratio and acid test ratio.   (4)

6   Give two reasons why the balance sheet was not strong enough for Annabelle to be given a long-term loan.   (2)

7   Why did the banks turn down her application for an increased overdraft facility?   (3)

8   How could Annabelle 'squeeze' £130,000 out of working capital? When you have an answer, work out liquidity ratios for your revised figures.   (8)

Further work

1   As bank manager, what questions would you ask Annabelle about the evidence she produced in support of her loan application? What non-financial factors would you have to take into account when deciding whether to give a loan?

2   Arrange a visit to a local bank and look at its services to small firms. How does a bank monitor the small businesses to which it has lent money? Do they use ratio analysis? What sort of performance do they expect from businesses that have been granted loans?

55

INVESTMENT WITHIN FINANCIAL CONSTRAINTS

Elements: **6.3** *PC 3 4 6 7*
AN **3.3** *PC 1 2 3 4* *IT* **3.2** *PC 4 5* **3.3** *PC 1 2 3 4 5*

Key concepts: Forecast profits and cash flow, Calculating future profits

ScanCo is a medium sized producer of X-ray machines. Last year its sales were £4.5 million at a **gross margin** of 60%. It expects sales growth of £0.5 million per year for the coming five years, with gross and net margins staying constant.

ScanCo's Research and Development manager has just come up with a new product idea for a portable scanner that will require an investment outlay of £400,000. Each machine will cost £4,000 to make and will be priced at a 100% **mark-up** on direct costs. It will be ready for launch at the start of next year. Forecast sales and **overheads** are given below:

Year	Sales forecast (units)	Forecast overheads (£000s)
Next year	150	600
1 year later	250	700
2 years later	250	750
3 years later	250	750

The target market for the new X-ray scanner is the oil industry, to check the accuracy of pipeline welds. The Research and Development manager decided on the sales forecast after discussion with an expert on North Sea oil technology.

ScanCo's Directors must decide whether to approve the £400,000 investment at their next Board meeting.

APPENDIX A

ScanCo balance Sheet Dec 31st

	£000
Fixed assets	1,900
Stock	450
Debtors & cash	150
Current liabilities	700
Net current assets	(100)
ASSETS EMPLOYED	1,800
Loans	720
Shareholders' funds	1,080
CAPITAL EMPLOYED	1,800

Questions

1 What is meant by: gross margin, mark-up, overheads, shareholders funds, fixed assets? **(5)**

2 Calculate ScanCo's gross profit for last year, and the projected gross profit at the end of Year 5. **(5)**

3 When you calculated the projected gross profit, state one assumption that you made. **(2)**

4 Calculate the net cash inflow/outflow on the new portable scanner each year, assuming that the investment outlay takes place next year. **(4)**

5 Using the balance sheet, explain the possible source of the £400,000 investment capital. **(4)**

Further work

1 Using your data from question 4, draw up a spreadsheet to show the forecast cash flows on the portable scanner. Edit the forecast for years 1, 2 and 3 if actual sales are 200, 220 and 225 units. Use the tool bar facility to make your calculations. Produce a hard copy of your spreadsheet.

56 THE RISE AND FALL OF LAKER AIRWAYS

Elements: **6.3** *PC 234567* **7.1** *PC 1234*

Key concepts: Legal requirements, Monitoring business performance,
Sources of finance for a business plan, Balance sheets

Freddie Laker started his freight airline in 1948 with £38,000 of borrowed money. It soon received a huge boost from the 1949 Berlin Airlift, for which his aircraft were hired round the clock to fly in food supplies. By the 1960s, it was a well enough established airline to be able to **diversify** by starting up a fleet of aircraft for the packaged holiday market – Laker Airways. The success of this move led Laker to announce in 1971 his intention to challenge the major transatlantic carriers by forming a no-frills, low price, London-New York 'Skytrain'.

At that time no passenger airline was allowed to operate on any route without government approval. The convention was that on major routes such as London-New York, each country was allowed to have two carriers. This was considered to be sufficient to provide competition, yet with enough control to ensure that competitive pressures did not force the companies to cut back on costly safety measures. So TWA and Pan-Am battled with British Airways and British Caledonian for market share. Alone of the four, British Airways was state owned.

During the 1970s Freddie Laker became a well known figure as he battled to get Skytrain accepted by the British and U.S. governments. To do this, he had to take out expensive court action to prove that the existing arrangement was a **cartel** that acted against the public interest. Only in 1977 did the first Skytrain fly from Gatwick, in a blaze of publicity in Britain and America. Prices were half those of the other carriers, and customers liked the fact that no reservations were possible; you just turned up on the day you wanted to fly, and bought a ticket as you would when travelling by train. Such was Laker's popularity that the Labour government that had fought him in the courts knighted him in the 1978 Honours List. Sir Freddie was born.

The demand for Skytrain was such that travellers in the summer months found that they had to wait for days to get a seat. As Laker's base airport (Gatwick) was not yet fully developed, this could be uncomfortable. The cramped conditions did not seem to put people off, however, as the prices were so low.

By 1980, Sir Freddie had a 17% market share on the London-New York route, plus 23% and 30% respectively on his new London-Miami and London-Los Angeles flights. This success led him to order ten Airbuses, with a view to using these European-built planes to break open the highly regulated, high fare European airline market.

The purchase was financed by a £130 million loan (in America, in dollars). The first Airbus was delivered in 1981, but no European government would agree to let him fly to their airports.

In the early 1980s, three factors affected the transatlantic airline business:

1   Whereas the initial impact of Skytrain had been to increase the number of people who wished to travel across the Atlantic, by 1980 an economic recession halted that growth in market size.

2   Having allowed Sir Freddie to break the cartel, the United States government then deregulated all air travel in 1978. This allowed many new, low fare U.S. airlines to start a London-New York service.

3   Between 1978 and 1980 the cost of fuel oil doubled in the wake of the supply shortages that accompanied the Iranian Revolution.

As a consequence of these factors, all the original four transatlantic carriers were trading unprofitably. Pan-Am, which had plunged into heavy losses, decided to fight back in the summer of 1981 by offering a stand-by ticket priced at just one pound above Skytrain's. The other three followed, so now Laker had competition that offered better comfort and a Heathrow base, for only one pound more. Laker cut prices further to try to restore its advantage, but the rivals followed Laker's prices down in a classic price war situation. This would damage the profits of all the carriers in the short term, but the major airlines knew that their revenue from First and Business classes would make it easier for them to survive than it would be for Laker.

Major Airlines – Fare Structure Winter 1981/2

Single	London–NY	London–LA
First Class	£917	£1268
Business Class	£315	£684
Economy	£124	£169
Stand-By	£90	£131
Laker Skytrain	**£89**	**£130**

Sir Freddie continued to make confident pronouncements about how loyal his customers were proving, but the increasing volume of traffic on the other airlines suggested differently. It was also significant that he introduced the option of booking reservations in advance, perhaps to assist cash flow. By the Autumn of 1981, rumours spread in the financial markets that Laker Airways was unable to meet the interest payments on its loans. As these leaked out, passengers became more reluctant to book onto Laker flights. By January 1982 it was public knowledge that the banks that had lent Laker £220 million were desperately looking for a solution.

On 3rd February, however, a beaming Sir Freddie announced that his cash crisis had been saved by £60 million of fresh loans. He said:

THE STANDARD CITY PRICES
Friday, February 5, 1982. 15p. Incorporating the Evening News

**Breakfast-time crisis meeting
—then Laker calls in Receiver**

SIR FREDDIE GOES BUST

by Roger Bray and Andrew Hogg

'I couldn't be more confident about the future.'

Within thirty-six hours, though, the banks had forced him to call in the Receiver to supervise the **liquidation** of the company's assets. Six thousand Laker passengers were stranded with worthless tickets as Laker aeroplanes leaving from Gatwick were recalled in mid-flight. At Gatwick, the British Airports Authority impounded a DC10 aircraft to cover the company's unpaid bills for landing and parking fees.

Journalists rushing to Companies House to look up Laker Airway's company accounts were shocked to find that despite the legal requirement that up-to-date accounts should be filed there for all limited companies, the most recent for Laker Airways was from March 1980. These showed just £23 million of shareholders funds, and that the firm was 90% owned by Sir Freddie and 10% owned by his (former) wife.

They also revealed that on March 31st 1980, Laker forecast that it must make forty-one million dollars of loan repayments and hire purchase instalments during the coming twelve months – a tall order for a firm that had never made an operating profit of more than £2.5 million (about $5 million) in a year. Appendix A shows a summary of Laker's five year financial record up to March 1980.

The Times reported that:

> *'Bankers said Laker's losses were running at £15 to £20 million a year. It owes banks £230 million, with a further £40 million owed to unsecured creditors. Assets were estimated at about £250 million*…*
>
> *…New figures showing worse than expected ticket sales, combined with disappointing forecasts for cash flow in the months ahead were the final straw. No-one could be confident that Laker would pay the bills…By any standards the company was extraordinarily highly geared…the banks showed a considerable lack of banking prudence.'*

* *This proved a considerable over-estimate, as the second-hand value of aircraft during a recession can fall sharply.*

Newspapers contrasted the losses of his ticket-holders with his 1,000-acre farm in Surrey and 85-ton yacht. Yet Sir Freddie's earlier successes ensured that he kept the respect of many people. Two years later, his work in breaking the transatlantic cartel was to receive praise from Richard Branson when setting up Virgin Atlantic.

Sources: *Companies House; The Financial Times; The Times.*

APPENDIX A: *Summary of the Laker Airways Balance Sheets (1976–1980)*

| | £000s (as at March 31st) | | | | |
	1976	1977	1978	1979	1980
Fixed Assets	29,700	27,800	44,900	82,900	146,300
+ Net Current Assets	−1,100	−1,800	−1,800	−7,800	−11,700
= Assets Employed	28,600	26,000	43,100	75,100	134,600
Shareholders Funds	3,500	4,300	5,800	13,900*	23,200*
+ Loans and HP debts	25,100	21,700	37,300	61,200	111,400
= Capital Employed	28,600	26,000	43,100	75,100	134,600

* including £3.3 million of unrealised foreign currency gains in 1979; in 1980 this figure increased to £4.6 million (it proved an illusion as the value of the $ weakened in1981).

Questions

1 Explain the meaning of the following terms: diversify, cartel, liquidation. **(3)**

2 Give examples of how Freddie Laker financed his different activities. **(3)**

3 How did Freddie Laker get into a poor cash flow situation? **(2)**

4 Give examples of different fixed assets that Laker Airways held. Why did some of these assets lose value? **(4)**

5 Laker Airways were not fulfilling certain legal requirements. What were these and why are all companies required to fulfil them? **(4)**

6 What is meant by a gearing ratio? Using Appendix A, calculate the gearing ratios for 1980 and 1981. **(4)**

7 Using the financial information in the text, explain why Laker Airways eventually went into liquidation. **(5)**

Further work

1 Using the case study as the source of your material, draw up the financial part of a business plan for the start of Laker Airways. In your plan, state:

■ the asset and working capital requirements

■ how the finance will be obtained for the working capital and working assets.

You should research the different methods of finance available, and then state reasons for the methods you choose.

THE 3 IN 1 WASHING MACHINE

57

Elements: **7.1** *PC 1234* **7.2** *PC 1234567* **7.3** *PC 1234567*

*Key concepts: Direct and indirect costs, Sources of finance for a business plan,
Production of a projected cash flow*

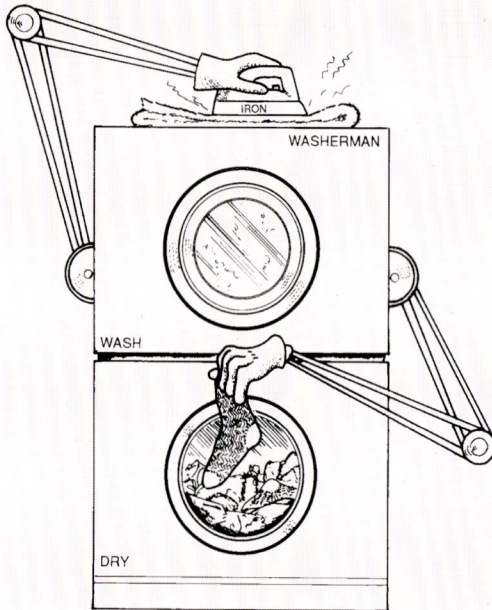

It was Jane's idea that had started it. She had been so fed up with her Mum's moaning that she snapped: 'You won't be happy till there's a machine that washes, dries, and irons all the clothes automatically.' When her boyfriend heard about it, he started messing about with electronics; ten months later the 'Washerman' 3 in 1 washing machine was a full, working prototype.

Now came the big decision; should they sell the idea to a big company, or try to manufacture it themselves? All Tim was sure of was that he should patent the idea as soon as possible.

They decided to visit a bank manager for advice. Before going, they tried to work out what kind of sums were involved. Much of the costs would come from bought-in components, so they felt fairly certain of the following estimates:

components	£280 per unit
materials	£60 per unit
factory labour	£10 per unit

(they had argued about whether labour is a direct or an indirect cost, but Jane's view prevailed – that as they intended to pay their workers per unit produced, they must treat factory labour as a direct cost).

They were less certain of the indirect costs, and so decided to work on both optimistic and pessimistic figures.

rent and rates	£6,000–12,000 per month
staff salaries	£14,000–24,000 per month
other overheads	£10,000–14,000 per month

After further arguing, they agreed that they could charge £500 per machine, and should sell their total output of 300 machines per month. Armed with this information, they went to the bank.

The manager worked out the best and worst profit position based upon their information, and frowned. He then said:

'You really need to do a lot more work before I can help. Have you thought about the likely length of life cycle of the Washerman? After all, your forecast of overheads assumes that the machinery you buy will have useful life of five years. But what if the product fades away after three? And what about a cash flow forecast? Surely you realise the importance of that.'

By the end of the meeting, though, the bank manager was becoming increasingly impressed with Tim's explanation of the mechanics and performance of the 3 in 1. So Jane and Tim went away feeling optimistic that the bank would help, once they had given their financial and marketing planning some more careful thought.

Questions

1   What are direct and indirect costs? Give two examples of each from the case study.   **(4)**

2   Why is it difficult to classify labour as either a direct or indirect cost?   **(2)**

3   Calculate total direct costs per washing machine.   **(2)**

4   Calculate total indirect costs per month, taking
   a   the optimistic forecast
   b   the pessimistic forecast.   **(2)**

5   Calculate profits if 300 machines were produced per month, taking:
   a   the optimistic view
   b   the pessimistic view.   **(4)**

6   Outline two reasons why it would be useful for this business to construct a cash flow forecast.   **(2)**

7   Taking the optimistic figures, what are the indirect costs per unit at sales of 300 units per month? Calculate their level if sales fall to 200 units. Comment on how this would affect the profitability of the 'Washerman'.   **(9)**

Further work

1   Calculate the amount of capital required in the first year of business on the basis of a pessimistic forecast; then produce the financial part of a business plan for a 3 in 1 washing machine.

Your financial input should include:

■   an assessment of the types of finance available, and a decision on the types of finance most suitable for your plan; actual amounts should be stated

■   a twelve-month cash flow forecast on the basis of income and expenditures mentioned in the text (use the fill row facility to replicate figures across rows)

■   an explanation of the purpose of such a forecast, and the significance of the timing of outflows and inflows.

58 BOMBAY PIZZA

Elements: **7.1** *PC 1234* **7.2** *PC 1234567* **7.3** *PC 1234567* **7.4** *PC 12*
AN **3.1** *PC 12345* **3.3** *PC 13456*

Key concepts: Cash inflow and cash outflow, Purposes of cash flow statements,
Direct and indirect costs, Sources of finance

It was when Sunil Tanna's daughter went out with a group of Indian friends for a pizza that it struck him. In his business trips to Bombay he had never seen a pizza outlet there. If Indian teenagers liked pizza in Birmingham, why not in Bombay?

Three weeks later, while making a January visit to India for his air conditioning company, he stayed on for an extra couple of days' 'holiday'. He quickly confirmed that there was no pizza outlet in the Bombay telephone directory and spent the rest of his time researching the prices of comparable fast foods, wage rates, locations and the availability of ingredients. Sunil considered the £400 it cost as money well spent.

The following month he identified a British supplier of pizza dough-making machines and conveyor-belt ovens (which cook the pizza in three minutes and ensure that the pizza cannot burn). In total this capital equipment would cost £12,800 on delivery in Bombay, though transport charges plus Indian import tariffs would push this up to £18,000. His month's expenses were £200.

In March Sunil paid a professional chef £2,400 to devise eight pizza recipes suitable for Bombay (four vegetarian). In each case the chef drew up cards that set out precisely the method of preparation and cooking. Sunil would have to hire a good manager to run the first outlet, but he did not want to have to find (or fly out) an experienced pizza cook.

Luck did not provide a further business trip to India, so he had to pay for his own flight to Bombay to acquire a site in a busy, middle class area of the city. His strategy was to pitch his pizza prices at around Western levels, making the decor Chicago/Italian-American, using the brand name Al Capone's Pizza. This would cash in on Indian awareness of Hollywood gangster films. The site he chose required an initial payment amounting to £800, plus £200 a month rent starting immediately. All in, Sunil's April travel expenses came to £1,600.

While in Bombay in April, Sunil arranged for the design and refitting of the site to turn it into a Chicago pizza restaurant. This was completed during May at a cost of £8,000. He also hired a manager whose salary of £600 per annum commenced at the start of June. The manager immediately hired staff at the following monthly rates:

$$
\begin{array}{rcl}
\text{cook} & : & £25* \\
\text{2 waitresses} & : & £15 \text{ each} \\
\text{delivery driver} & : & £10 \\
\text{cleaner} & : & £5
\end{array}
$$

Once a delivery motorbike had been bought for £200 in early June, everything was in place for the start of the staff training programme. Unfortunately a combination of supplier and Customs delays meant that the pizza machinery only turned up in July. It was installed, tested, and did not work. It emerged that it needed a power adaptor which was ordered from England. That added £400 to the cost of the machinery, which was now due to be paid.

At last, in August, everything was ready and with £500 spent on local advertising, Al Capone's Pizza opened to a large, curious crowd. The average customer spend proved to be £5 at a cost of sales of £2. This would need to cover the monthly overheads of £680 plus the rent and wages of £320 per month.

Monthly customer figures	
August	1,600
September	1,200
October	1,100
November	900
December	800
January	900
February	1,000
March	1,200
April and onwards, a monthly average of 1,200	

* Although the wage rates in this case seem incredibly low, they are exactly as researched by the real Mr Tanna.

Questions

1   Give three examples of cash outflows from the business.   (3)

2   Why is it useful to know about projected cash inflows and outflows?   (3)

3   What is the difference between a direct and an indirect cost? Give examples of direct and indirect costs in running a pizza business.   (4)

4   Why may the actual cash inflows and outflows vary from the forecast figures? Give three examples of possible variations.   (4)

5   What is meant by fixed assets and working capital? How much has the business spent on fixed assets before it has begun to trade?   (4)

6   Construct a cash flow forecast for the first twelve months of the business, that is from January to December. Your spreadsheet should be computer generated using a spreadsheet package (use formulae to enter figures where appropriate).   (12)

Further work

1   In order to meet the criteria for element 7.1, a financial plan could be produced from this case study. Investigate the alternative sources of finance that could be obtained to start the Bombay Pizza business. Choose appropriate methods of finance for fixed assets and working capital. Justify your choices from the alternatives available. You may wish to investigate loans, overdrafts, forming a private limited company, taking a partner, own funds.

The result of your investigation and your cash flow forecast would form your financial plan to be presented to a bank or alternative investor in your business. Produce your plan in report form for a potential creditor.

2   Depreciation involves spreading the costs of fixed assets over their expected lifetime. Assume that the machinery depreciates over five years on a straight line basis, and the decorations depreciate on a 50% declining balance. With this knowledge, calculate the profit before interest and tax during the first trading year, i.e. from August to July.

3   In order to achieve the core skills in Application of Number you are required to use two-dimensional representations of three-dimensional objects. Given the information from the text, and using your own research, make a two-dimensional plan with measurements of a hypothetical Bombay pizza house. The best form of research would be to visit a local restaurant. It is very important that your data are shown accurately and precisely.

59 WORKING CAPITAL

Elements: **7.1** *PC 1234* **7.2** *PC 1234567*

Key concepts: Asset and working capital requirements, Sources of finance for a business plan, Cash flow requirements

Tracey and Neil were sure they had a winning idea on their hands. A laptop computer linked by radio waves with a head office computer. Their prototype machine worked beautifully, and some preliminary market research showed that there were many keen buyers. They had also worked out how to mass produce it cost-effectively.

The next stage was to get the finance to set up production and to launch the product. Tracey had calculated that £1.8 million would be needed for **fixed capital** (i.e. money used to buy fixed and long term assets such as machinery). More problematic was calculating the **working capital** that would be needed. Eventually, profits would provide the source of working capital. Until sales began, however, raw material stocks, wages, and many other day-to-day expenses would have to be financed by borrowings of some kind.

Both went to visit their bank manager. She was very interested, and seemed very eager to help, until she found out more about the cost estimates in the start-up period. 'You say you want £500,000 of working capital on top of the £1.8 million of fixed capital. But are you sure it will be enough? More new businesses fail through under-estimating working capital needs than for any other reason.'

So Tracey explained her estimate:

> *'I think we will need £50,000 of raw material stocks – all paid for in cash – before production starts. Production will eventually be able to turn out finished products in four hours, but in this early period we must allow one month of slow, careful testing of each part of the production. So* **work-in-progress** *(including stocks and wages) will add £120,000. After that, production will be in full swing, but the two month credit period required by our clients means we will have to fund two months of our full production costs of £150,000 per month.'*

At that point, Neil butted in:

> *'In other words we expect to use £470,000 of working capital in the first few months (£50,000 plus £120,000 plus two lots of £150,000). In addition, we think we ought to have some spare resources in case something goes wrong, which is why we want an extra £30,000 of cash. So our total request is for £500,000 of working capital available, of which we plan to use £470,000.'*

The bank manager smiled. She said:

> *'I think that to allow yourselves the cushion of just £30,000 of spare capital is rather risky. I'll tell you what I'll do. I will get my assistant to look at your research results more fully, and to see the magic machine*

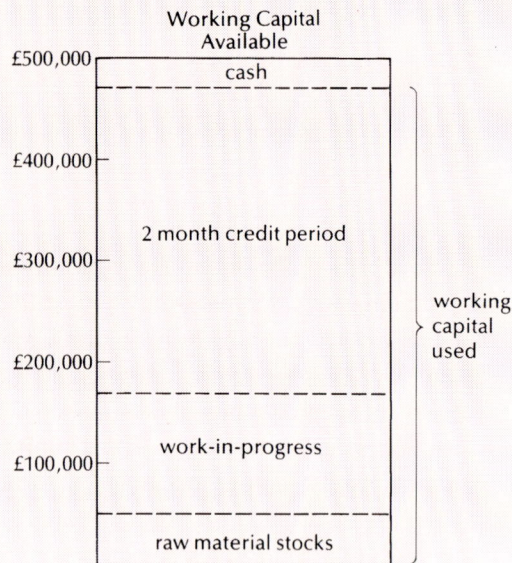

Working capital available

at work. If he's satisfied, we will put together a finance package consisting of share and loan capital to cover the £2.3 million you have asked for.

In addition, though, I will give you an overdraft facility of £150,000. This will not increase your own working capital available, but it will enable you to buy more materials if you need to. I know it sounds daft, but it will enable you to use up to £150,000 more than your balance sheet will tell you there is available. Your own resources would allow you to spend up to £500,000 on stocks and work in progress. With this overdraft you can actually spend another £150,000 on top. Of course, you should try your best to restrict the amount of working capital you use, because if you have to dip into the overdraft, the interest charges will eat into your profits.'

'And if we manage to keep our working capital usage below even the £470,000 mark?' asked Neil.

'Then you earn interest at the bank, and boost your profit.'

Tracey and Neil nodded at each other, thanked the manager and left.

Questions

1 What is meant by the terms fixed capital, working capital and work in progress? **(3)**

2 What sources of finance were used by Tracey and Neil for the £2.3 million needed? **(4)**

3 What is an overdraft facility? Why is it useful for a business to have one? What are two disadvantages of such a facility? **(5)**

4 Working capital was very important to this business. What were the main sources of working capital? **(4)**

5 What are the consequences of having too much working capital, or too little? **(4)**

Further work

1 In order to fulfil element 7.1, a business plan could be produced from this case study. You could investigate the production or sales of laptop computers, or the establishment of a shop selling computer accessories. Your financial part of the plan should identify:

- possible sources of finance and the decision you make
- fixed asset and working capital requirements.

60 THE MINI-MERGER

Elements: **7.1** *PC 1 2 3 4*   **7.3** *PC 1*   **7.4** *PC 1 2 3 4 5 6*

Key concepts: Sources of finance, Working capital, Fixed assets, Profit and loss accounts, Balance sheets, Trial balance

Jay Bhatt and Jason Alexander were, at one time, sole traders – both operating in sheet metal works. They had known each other for several years and worked at their similar trades at different locations. They eventually decided to pool their resources and knowledge, and work under one roof. They considered going into Partnership, but on advice from their accountants and bank managers decided to form a Private Limited Company instead.

As they had similar machines, they sold off the outdated and retained the modern. This enabled them to handle double the work for half the overheads per unit.

However, their situation proved to have its difficulties:

1 Mr. Bhatt had to move his business from South Norwood to Battersea. Many of his staff were unhappy with having to travel long distances in London traffic and decided to leave.

2 Personality clashes arose between Mr. Bhatt and the staff who used to work for Mr. Alexander. There was also a lack of co-operation between the staff from the two old businesses. This problem became very clear when Mr. Bhatt demanded that every effort should be made to squeeze more credit from suppliers and give less to customers; only after months of argument did he succeed in impressing this on all the staff.

3 It became evident that Bhatt and Alexander had different objectives for the company. Mr. Bhatt wanted to maximise profits because he still had a young family to cater for and a large mortgage to pay off. Mr. Alexander's main concerns, though, were to be able to share the decision-making, and to have regular holidays with his wife. All his children had left home, so his need for profit and income was far less.

4 At present, due to lack of time, both react to crisis rather than plan ahead. They have tried, unsuccessfully, to find a manager to take over the day-to-day problems.

On a brighter note, business is good and demand for their services and skills seems endless. The progress in this, the firm's second year, can be seen in the accompanying accounts.

APPENDIX A: Profit and Loss account

Last year			This year	
£	£		£	£
302,500		**Sales**		355,640
		Cost of sales		
	108,700	Purchases	128,900	
	15,380	Machine hire	14,520	
	61,450	Salaries	64,000	
	16,800	Vehicle running costs	19,800	
	39,200	Casual labour	34,720	
241,530				261,940
+7,800		Change in value of stock		+12,000
68,770		GROSS PROFIT		105,700
		LESS: **Overheads**		
	26,000	Directors' fees	36,200	
	21,400	Rent and rates	24,500	
	5,800	Depreciation	7,800	
	10,400	Promotion/sales	13,450	
	11,350	Other expenses	12,800	
74,950				94,750
− 6,180		NET PROFIT (Pre tax)		10,950

APPENDIX B: Balance sheet (as at year end):

Last year			This year	
£	£		£	£
27,870		**Fixed Assets**		38,200
		Current Assets		
	53,200	Debtors	41,800	
	35,500	Stock	47,500	
	250	Cash	6,400	
	88,950		95,700	
		LESS: C. Liabilities		
	31,400	Creditors	43,900	
	11,600	Overdraft	−	
	43,000		43,900	
45,950				51,800
73,820		ASSETS EMPLOYED		90,000
	−	Loans	4,800	
	80,000	Share Capital	80,000	
	− 6,180	Reserves	5,200	
73,820		CAPITAL EMPLOYED		90,000

Questions

1   Explain the difference between a profit and loss account and a balance sheet.   **(2)**

2   What are fixed assets? Identify two possible fixed assets owned by Bhatt and Alexander.   **(3)**

3   What is meant by working capital? What was the amount of working capital this year and last year?   **(3)**

4   Distinguish between direct and indirect costs. What other terms can be used for indirect costs? Give examples of indirect costs for Mr Bhatt and Mr Alexander's business.   **(5)**

5   **a**   What is the normal trading period for a profit and loss account?   **(1)**

   b   When is a balance sheet usually drawn up?   **(1)**

6   Using the accounts, identify the main reasons for the improved profit performance for this year.   **(5)**

Further work

1   Research the purpose of a ledger and what is meant by the double entry system of book-keeping. What is the purpose of a trial balance? Why should all trial balances correctly total zero? (Your information could be drawn from any accountancy textbook.)

61 GOOD MANAGEMENT PRACTICE IN RETAILING

Elements: **7.1** *PC 1234*
AN **3.2** *PC 1235*

Key concepts: Identification of sources of finance for a business plan, Costs

Marie started in the shop at nine years old, helping to fill shelves and occasionally serving customers. Later, she helped her mother deal with the buying side and with the accounts. So by the time she was twenty, her knowledge of the grocery trade was good enough for her parents to feel happy to hand the business over. Marie arranged a **mortgage** on the shop flat and premises, to provide the capital to buy them a Devon cottage, and then, one day, found herself on her own.

She had taken over a medium-sized, independent grocery shop of 2,000 square feet. Its weekly sales turnover was £24,000 at a gross profit margin of 15 per cent. This was sufficient to cover the £1,000 wage bill and £1,800 of other fixed costs, yet still leave a healthy profit. Marie had no intention, however, of allowing the business to just tick over. She wanted to prove that she could build it up into the biggest independent grocery chain in Derbyshire. To do this would require either a programme of store openings, or buying out rival owners. Whichever way she eventually chose, she knew that the starting point was the raising of finance.

Having already undertaken a large mortgage on the shop, she had neither the **collateral** nor the capital structure to borrow any more. For the business's shareholders funds were outweighed 2-1 by borrowings. She had no wish to bring new shareholders in, so the only option was to generate capital from the business itself. Could she squeeze cash out of her assets? Not from the premises or van; and as she offered no credit to customers, there was no kitty of **debtors**. So stocks were the only asset that might have some potential. Yet her parents had boasted when they handed the shop over that stock was being turned over fortnightly, so it was hard to imagine that much wastage existed there. If stock reductions had limited potential, that left profits as the sole remaining source.

Marie decided to undertake a detailed analysis of the profitability of the different sections of the store, to find out what to do next. She spent three weeks measuring up the shop and sifting through the stock books to produce the breakdown shown on the following page.

Before rushing to draw conclusions from this analysis, Marie decided to spend a fortnight chatting to customers about their usage of, and attitudes towards, the shop. They emphasised that convenience was the key – best achieved by offering a wide enough range of goods to ensure that they would not have to travel the nine miles to the nearest large supermarket.

Then she embarked on her new strategy. Fresh foods would be expanded by installing in-store bakery equipment. This would not only give more space over to a section that appeared to deserve it, but would also make the store smell inviting

Weekly Turnover and Profit Analysis

Product	Turnover £	Gross profit £	% of total gross profit	% of sq. ft.
Fresh food	2,800	580	16.5	14.0
Frozen food	1,500	200	5.5	4.5
Other food	6,500	820	22.5	33.0
Confectionery	3,800	810	22.5	8.5
Tobacco	2,400	200	5.5	4.0
Household items	3,500	590	16.5	23.0
Alcoholic drink	3,500	400	11.0	13.0
Total	24,000	3,600	100.0	100.0

and wholesome. Confectionery would be expanded by means of a high quality Pick-and-Mix counter, and by increasing the range of children's lines. It would be supplemented by installing two new counters that would each – she felt – attract more passing trade (and therefore confectionery impulse purchasing), newspapers, magazines and a video library. All these items would, between them, require 500 square feet of floor space. One hundred could come from converting a small office, while the remainder would have to come from the other departments.

The conversion cost £12,000 but soon proved a great success. Turnover rose to £30,000 per week and margins expanded to 17%. This meant a **pay-back period** of eight weeks – an astonishingly short time – and a greatly improved profit level thereafter. Marie followed this up by extending the video library into full children's and pop music ranges. For the first time, she advertised this development in the local paper, and featured an 'Opening Day Offer – 50p For Any Title'. Just as she hoped, video and confectionery sales grew still higher, reaching £35,000 a week. At this level of trading, £250 of extra staff costs were necessary, but weekly profit was still buoyant at £2,900 per week.

Within six months, the firm's bank balance was high enough to enable Marie to obtain a second outlet. Several weeks of careful looking revealed two interesting opportunities. One was shop premises in a new private housing estate on the outskirts of Mansfield. The other was a thriving grocers and delicatessen in the town centre of Chesterfield. The latter was much nearer to her original shop, so ease of transport and delivery persuaded her to concentrate on it. For she was certain that the next step in improving the profitability of her first store lay in direct purchasing from the manufacturer.

This would entail dropping the business's long association with Spar, but buying direct would boost margins by three per cent. The minimum delivery size imposed by the manufacturers would mean that all deliveries would go to the one site, and would then have to be shuttled from one to the other by a full-time delivery driver. It would also make it likely that higher average stock levels would have to be held. So Marie planned to install a computerised stock control system – efficient enough to counteract the upward pressure on stock levels. She realised that all these apparently high costs would be covered comfortably by the 3% margin improvement on her forecast revenue of £50,000 per week.

In the event, her purchase of the Chesterfield branch provided Marie with another benefit. The store manageress had many useful ideas on improving customer service, such as training staff to keep an eye on the checkouts and to open up an extra till if there was ever more than one customer waiting.

Five years later it was the manageress who was the Personnel Director of Derbyshire Supermarkets, a chain of fourteen stores employing over four hundred people. Marie, the Managing Director of the county's largest independent grocery chain, was starting to set her sights on national horizons.

Questions

1 Explain the meaning of the following: mortgage, collateral, debtors, pay back period. (4)

2 What is meant by fixed assets and current assets? Give two examples of each for Marie's business. (6)

3 How did Marie finance her initial asset requirements? (2)

4 Look at the different options Marie had for financing her expansion. Describe each one and explain why it was unsuitable. (3)

5 What are indirect costs? Give examples of such costs for Marie. (3)

6 Calculate the gross profit margin for each product. (3)

7 Give examples of how Marie monitored the performance of her business. (3)

8 Why was Marie able to remain solvent? Compare the fortunes of this business with Laker Airways in case study 56. (6)

Further work

1 Try to visit a small community store and arrange an interview with the owner. Find out whether budgeting and business planning takes place. What corrective action can a shopkeeper take if his/her sales are below budget? How can a business plan be amended, in the light of changes during the first year?

2 Demonstrate from the case study that:

a the payback period was eight weeks

b 'weekly profit was still buoyant at £2,900 per week'.

62 OVERTRADING IN JEWELLERY

Elements: **7.1** *PC 1 2 3 4* **7.3** *PC 1 2 3 4 5 6 7*

Key concepts: Sources of finance for a business plan, Direct and indirect costs

Claire had always loved jewellery and with the help of her grandfather could make rings and earrings before the age of thirteen. By the time she reached sixth form, her production sideline was generating a useful income from her fellow students. After a year's foundation course at art college, Claire decided to turn full time.

Although she could produce all types of jewellery, Claire's favourite items were rings and necklaces. She had experimented with high quality silver gemstone rings, but found these hard to sell. So she decided to concentrate on costume jewellery, using the flexibility of her one-woman business to respond quickly to changing fashions and musical tastes. When 'Take That' became the group girls screamed for, Claire's were the TT rings and Mark Owen chains.

Even though her business had been growing fast, she was in no way prepared for what hit her when 'Blade' arrived. The Blade twins' blond hair and good looks made them stars even without their great dancing and singing. Claire had chanced upon them just before their first Number 1 record, when it was still possible to meet them without bribing the bodyguards. They had loved her suggestion of sword-shaped 'Blade' earrings and a neckchain. She designed and made them just in time for their first appearance on *Top of The Pops*. As their single and album raced to number one, Blade's management signed a deal with Claire to provide the jewellery for sale as official merchandise on their hastily arranged British tour.

Occasionally in the past, Claire had needed to bring an old friend in to help meet a large order. Never before had she hired unknown staff to work with her in the small workshop. Overnight, everything had to change. The initial order for

Blade earrings and chains was for 40,000 of each – within three weeks. This was as much as she had produced in the whole of the previous year. Thank goodness, she told herself, that I negotiated such a profitable deal.

Each item would be bought by Blade Management Incorporated (BMI) for £1.25, but the materials cost was only 10p and she had always costed her labour time at 25p per unit. Other unit costs usually came to no more than 5p, so there was plenty of contribution for covering the overheads plus the fixed cost of designing and making the mould in which the jewellery was produced.

Through her tutor at art college, Claire quickly brought in three new workers. None had experience, but all they would need to do is pour powdered gunmetal into the moulding machine, take the finished rings out, then give them a vigorous polish. More of a constraint was the lack of machine capacity and physical space. After setting up her new staff at their posts, Claire scurried round commercial estate agents trying to find bigger premises. Within two days she found an adequately sized unit in a smart business park nearby. At £1,500 per month rent and rates, it was more expensive than she wanted, but impatience led her to accept it.

In the two days it took before succeeding, several problems had occurred in the workshop. The student workers had no idea what to do. For some time they carried on producing rings they knew to be sub-standard (all of which were later scrapped), then decided to wait for Claire's return.

Even with her greatest endeavours, it was ten days before the new workshop was operational, with its two new moulding machines – each costing £10,000. The machinery suppliers had given her two months' credit, but the materials for the 80,000 units had to be obtained with cash that Claire did not have. Fortunately the bank manager proved very helpful, extending the business overdraft to £10,000 without even asking to see her books (the loan was secured, however, on her parents' house).

The contract was completed only after Claire had switched to two-shift production at the new factory unit. This required higher pay for the night-shift workers and the recruitment of her old friend as the night supervisor. To find the funds to pay the wages, she had to go cap in hand to BMI for a 20% interim payment. Claire was, again, fortunate to get co-operation. Without it, lack of funds would have meant no wages and therefore no workforce.

When, three weeks late, she delivered the full order, she found BMI desperate for still more product. They paid her immediately and asked for a further 60,000 rings and 40,000 necklaces within two weeks. This caused still more feverish work, with each shift extended to ten hours and with weekend working as well. Again cash proved terribly tight, as the bill for the machines became due.

A visit to the bank manager led to a full discussion of how she was handling the finances and administration of the business. The manager was horrified to realise that Claire was operating without budgets or a cash flow forecast. He insisted that she should take time out from the production process to work out exactly what her cash inflows and outflows had been since the start of the 'Blade' boom, and then forecast the coming three months. He also wanted a full calculation of the actual profit generated by the first contract. Only then would he consider a loan or an overdraft extension. The bank manager said sternly: 'You are suffering the symptoms of overtrading: expanding too rapidly from a low capital base and with an inadequate management structure'. He recommended that Claire should hire a small firms consultant to come in for a couple of days and make recommendations on how to proceed.

Although her diversion into accounting held the completion of the job back by five days, it probably saved her business and her parents' home. It persuaded her to take on an office manager who would handle the administration and the finances, while she focused upon design, production and sales. Blade's success proved far more long-lasting than anyone had imagined, and when, three years later, the twins' popularity faded after a failed film production, Claire's business was well enough diversified to cope.

APPENDIX A: Actual production costs on first Blade contract

Wages and salaries	£48,000
Materials	£12,800
Other direct costs	£ 3,000
Fixed costs	£ 1,200
Overheads	£14,000

Questions

1 What were the actual costs per unit on the first Blade contract? **(3)**

2 What is meant by contribution? How much contribution did Claire expect, to cover overheads and the fixed cost of designing and making jewellery moulds? **(5)**

3 Why do businesses need to forecast their cash flows? **(3)**

4 Why did Claire's costs on labour and materials vary from those anticipated? **(4)**

5 What is meant by overtrading? Why did it occur in this case? **(4)**

6 Claire's business was profitable and she wanted to take new orders. How should she have arranged these new orders so that she would not incur cash flow problems? **(4)**

7 How did Claire obtain the initial finance for the machinery she had to buy? **(2)**

Further work

1 Write a report to Claire, as her small firm's consultant, making recommendations under the following headings:

1.1 How to benefit from the flexibility of small firms
1.2 Financial controls

63

THE COUNTRY HOUSE HOTEL

Elements: **7.2** *PC 1234567* **7.3** *PC 1234567*
IT 3.1 *PC 12345*

Key concepts: Direct and indirect costs, Cash flow forecast

Jenny had inherited the large country house from her father. It had been very run down, but the Loan Guarantee Scheme had helped fund its renovation and transformation into a smart hotel. Its site (just outside Edinburgh) made it ideal for the large foreign tourist market attracted up to see Scotland.

From the start, marketing activity had been concentrated on overseas travel agents, especially in America. Their initial direct mailing of a sumptuous, glossy brochure had certainly brought in a lot of custom, but with their second trading year just ending, Jenny was worried about the cash flow position. Following a two year interest rate 'holiday', from next month they would have to start paying for their loans, which looked difficult given the projected profits.

| | Year 1 | | Year 2 | |
	Revenue	Direct Costs	Revenue	Direct Costs
April	£30,000	£25,000	£27,000	£27,000
May	£36,000	£30,000	£34,000	£31,000
June	£46,000	£34,000	£43,000	£35,000
July	£74,000	£45,000	£73,000	£46,000
August	£79,000	£47,000	£76,000	£48,000
Sept	£57,000	£42,000	£52,000	£42,000
Oct	£48,000	£35,000	£45,000	£38,000
Nov	£30,000	£29,000	£30,000	£33,000
Dec	£32,000	£30,000	£32,000	£33,000
Jan	£22,000	£27,000	£19,000	£28,000
Feb	£17,000	£25,000	£13,000	£26,000
Mar	£34,000	£31,000	£31,000	£33,000

After opening in April, the first Summer season had been marvellous, with each of twenty rooms full at £100 each. She had known that things would quieten down in the winter, but was shocked at how bad takings actually were. In their first February, average room usage was just three per night; cash flowed out of the company bank account like red ink. Now, exactly two years after opening, the time had come for a review and perhaps a rethink of strategy. Jenny arranged a meeting with her fellow Directors: her chef husband Allan and their accountant Finance Director Chang-Wei.

Chang-Wei began with a presentation of raw data on monthly revenues and direct costs for the past two years. She emphasised that they were not profit figures since they did not take into account depreciation or the interest that had been accruing.

'What were those other costs you mentioned?' asked Allan.

'The depreciation was £40,000 each year, and the interest was 15% on our £200,000 loan,' came the reply.

After some pressing of calculator keys, Allan declared that the recent position was not at all bad. They had only made a loss in the second half of the financial year – as in their first year of trading. Chang-Wei's shake of the head signalled her disagreement with this analysis.

Allan felt it time to put forward his theory.:

'I read an article in The Sunday Times *about the effect of the pound's exchange rate against the dollar. It said that the pound being so strong against the dollar last year made it expensive for Americans to come here – so they stayed at home. That would explain why we did so disappointingly. After all, from the start half our revenue has come from Americans. Anyway, I found some figures on this from the library that seem to confirm* The Times' *view.' (See Appendix A.)*

'As the pound is now slipping against the dollar, I feel confident that business will pick up soon. So we don't need to change our strategy.'

Jenny was pleased to hear such optimism, but wanted to discuss her fears. She explained that she now doubted whether they could ever get enough business from the tourist market during the lean, November–April period. In which case perhaps they would have to aim for the business traveller. Unfortunately the leisurely, country house atmosphere that she knew the Americans loved would have to be compromised for the sake of the fast-moving modern executive. Would they lose their tourist trade as a result? And in any case, did they want to end up running the kind of impersonal hotel that business people seem to require?

'There is one other possibility,' continued Chang-Wei, 'which is that something has gone slightly wrong with the day-to-day management of the hotel. This might have led to costs creeping up, and even to customers going away feeling slightly disappointed. How much of our custom is repeat business, Jenny?'

'Very little; much more important for us is customer satisfaction leading to word of mouth recommendation. I ask every visitor how they heard about us and keep quarterly records of their answers. A higher and higher percentage of our clients have heard of us from friends. That must be good.'

After she had gone, Allan spoke bitterly about Chang-Wei's insulting reference to their management of the hotel. He then went off to phone their advertising agency. Allan was a great admirer of their tasteful designs, and felt sure that their appointment a year ago would prove a cornerstone of the hotel's future success.

APPENDIX A: *Quarterly data on the number of foreign visitors to the U.K.*
(all figures in thousands)

From:	America	Europe	Other
April–June Year 1:	938	2475	635
July–Sept Year 1:	1283	3200	1135
Oct–Dec Year 1:	672	1988	599
Jan–Mar Year 1:	519	1704	524
April–June Year 2:	846	2484	683
July–Sept Year 2:	1201	3301	1043
Oct–Dec Year 2:	710	2050	600
Jan–Mar Year 2:	552	1802	530

Questions

1   What is meant by the terms: raw data, loan guarantee scheme, depreciation, direct costs, contribution? **(5)**

2   Calculate the total contribution towards fixed costs for

   a   year 1

   b   year 2. **(2)**

3   Work out the effect on profits for year 1 and year 2 if you include depreciation. **(5)**

4   State three other indirect costs that the hotel would incur. **(3)**

5   How could the financial performance of the business be improved? (Look at revenues, direct costs, and indirect costs). Set two targets for year 3. **(5)**

6   What external constraints might affect the hotel achieving any targets mentioned in your answer to question 5? **(3)**

7   State two financial implications if the hotel was to be aimed at the business traveller. **(2)**

Further work

1   To help towards core skills in Information Technology, construct a suitable bar chart to show revenue against total costs for year 1 and year 2. Use a spreadsheet package if possible. Use the data and your graphs to comment on Allan's statement that: 'the recent trading position was not at all bad'. Print a draft version of your bar chart, and then amend it if necessary before printing a final version.

64

CONSTRUCTING A BUSINESS PLAN

Elements: **7.1** *PC 1234* **8.1** *PC 12345*
IT **3.2** *PC 2345* **3.3** *PC 1234*

Key concepts: Identify sources of finance for a business plan, Prepare work and collect data for a business plan

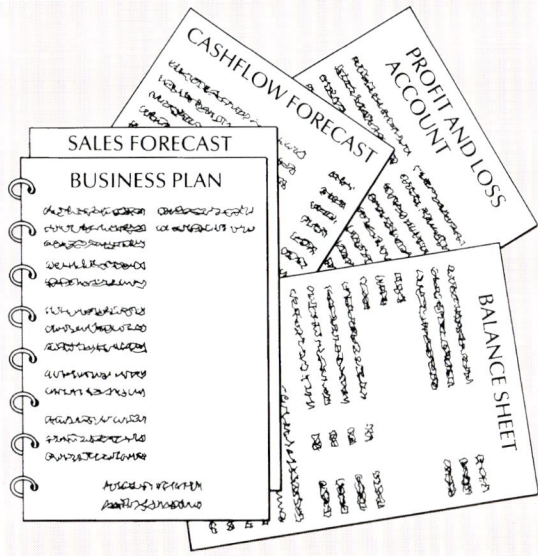

Fresh from Poly, Karen could not wait to put her Business Studies theory into practice. Careful saving during her sandwich work year, plus a £5,000 legacy, meant that she had the £10,000 she thought necessary as equity capital. The work year had been at Thomson Holidays and that – plus her love of travel – convinced her to start up a Travel Agency. Not just any one, mind, for she believed a market gap existed for Adventure Travel in her home city of Birmingham. She had been taught to make decisions on the basis of evidence, not hunch, so she had tested out and validated her hypothesis over the past two years by visiting every one of the 140 Agencies listed in Birmingham's Yellow Pages.

Now Karen had to prepare the documentation for the Business Plan to persuade her bank to lend her the extra fixed and working capital she would need. The keys to this, she knew, were a credible Sales Forecast, a Cash Flow Forecast, a Projected Profit and Loss Account for the first six months, and an estimated six months' Balance Sheet. To forecast sales she visited comparable Agencies in London, relying on her charm and the lack of threat of competition to persuade someone to volunteer their early sales performance. Two days of being charming yielded the information given overleaf. Karen decided that averaging the figures for all three firms would give her a realistic sales forecast.

The main start-up costs were estimated by her as follows:

Purchase of 5 year lease on shop	£2,500
Fixtures and fittings (to last 4 years)	£6,000
Advertising prior to launch	£3,500

The advertising would be treated as revenue expenditure, and therefore charged in full against the Profit and Loss account for the first trading period. All the start-up costs would be paid before the start of trading, i.e. in month zero. Fixed assets would be depreciated on a straight-line basis.

Running costs would include the 90% payment of revenue to the tour operator (as Travel Agents work on a 10% commission), plus overheads amounting to £800 a month. The 90% would be paid to the tour operator in the month after being received from customers. Overheads start in month 0 and must be paid in the month they are incurred.

Sales Revenue Data For The First Year's Operation Of Three Adventure Travel Agencies

	Adventure Hols Streatham	Go-Go Travel Hampstead	Action Vacs Acton	Average of all 3
Month 1	£2,400	£5,800	£800	**£3,000**
Month 2	£3,400	£8,200	£2,500	**£4,700**
Month 3	£5,800	£12,200	£4,800	**£7,600**
Month 4	£6,400	£16,800	£6,200	**£9,800**
Month 5	£7,200	£19,100	£7,300	**£11,200**
Month 6	£7,400	£20,700	£7,900	**£12,000**
Months 7–12 monthly average	£8,000	£23,000	£9,500	**£13,500**

Questions

1 What is a business plan? **(2)**

2 Why does a business need to draw up a plan? **(3)**

3 Why did Karen specifically need to produce a sales forecast, cash flow forecast and other financial information? **(2)**

4 What were Karen's main costs and how would she finance them? **(4)**

5 What other resources, besides finance, would Karen need to run a travel agency? Look at physical, human and time requirements. What problems are involved in estimating time spent on the business? **(4)**

Further work

1 To achieve element 7.1, you could use this case study to produce a financial plan which includes the following:

■ financing requirements

■ sources and methods of acquiring financial support.

You would need to research government help to small firms, and ideally visit an independent travel agency to discuss financial planning. If you did this you could probably produce your own financial plan for a travel agency. This could then go towards a full business plan in Unit 8. Karen's agency would help you to start your planning.

2 Using an appropriate spreadsheet package, produce a six-month cash flow forecast assuming that the bank is prepared to grant a £3,000 medium term loan. To obtain some of the Information Technology core skills, carry out a calculation using a spreadsheet; use the wordwrap facility to organise your information, orientate your page to landscape size, and print a draft version. Edit where necessary, and print a final version.

65 THE BUSINESS AT THE BOTTOM OF THE GARDEN

Elements: **8.1** *PC 2 3 4* **8.2** *PC 1 2 3 4 5 6 7 8* **8.3** *PC 1 2 3 4 5*
C 3.2 *1 2 3 4*

Key concepts: Background to business decisions, Producing a business plan and presenting it to an audience

It all started with a notice in a sweetshop window:

> **Garage To Let – No Rent, Just
> Two Hours DIY Per Week**

Pete saw it on his way home from work, and went straight round to the address. The owner, Maureen, showed him the garage at the foot of her garden – it was a corner house, so the garage had its own gate to the road. She explained that she never put her car away, and that her husband was as useless at Do It Yourself (DIY) as she was, so this unofficial untaxable arrangement seemed a solution. They shook hands on it, and agreed to start the arrangement from the following Monday.

Pete handed in his notice at the undertaker's the next day, collected his pay, and went off to buy some equipment. His idea was to set up as a self-employed carpenter, for he knew two probable regular customers already. Dave was a shop-fitting contractor (and often moaned about shoddy, expensive carpentry) and Leda was an interior designer. These two provided the bulk of the work at the start, though as word spread he received an ever greater share from new clients. This expansion had its downside, as in the case of the wealthy young home-owner who ordered a £18,000 oak kitchen – but stalled paying for five months. Pete reflected that if it had not been for his unusual freedom from rent and rates, this would probably have forced him out of business.

Yet here he was, just two years later, in a position where moving seemed the only option. Business had boomed in line with very buoyant property and retail markets – themselves a consequence of low interest rates (around 8%). Now, with an order book worth £60,000, the garage was proving far too small. He needed to hire four people to cope with demand, but it was a squeeze if two people worked in the garage at the same time. Furthermore, for the bigger jobs, there was often insufficient room inside to store the raw materials and work-in-progress.

Pete decided to talk the matter over with Maureen. She suggested an alternative:

> *'Why not build an extension at the back of the garage? If you built
> it so that it would be usable as a garden and tool shed in the future,
> it would add to the value of our property, and be useful to us. I
> think we'd have to come to a formal agreement though, about how
> long you'd stay in the garage; say four years?'*

The more he thought about this, the more attractive a proposition it seemed. Except that it would involve him in two months of work on the foundations, bricklaying and roofing. He jotted down a few estimates of the costs involved:

1 Bricks, cement, roof-tiles, guttering, window frames, and interior fitments … £3850.00

2 Hire of machinery … £1370.00

3 Four days of bricklayer's time, two days of a plasterer's, one day each of a plumber and a roofer (at daily rates of £100, £120, £80 and £60 respectively).

4 Loss of £30,000 of work of which 50% was materials, 30% was variable labour and expenses, and 15% was allocated annual overheads (including his own salary).

From this size of shed, he believed he would be able to cope with a 40% increase in work load by employing two more carpenters. Given the high levels of demand, Pete was confident that this extra capacity would be fully used, and that his cost structure would be unaffected.

Some phoning round revealed that factory units of various sizes were available on a local industrial estate. The smallest would double his maximum capacity to £30,000 of business per month, and would require an £18,000 payment for a 4 year lease. He hoped to achieve a capacity level of 90% over the year, but did feel apprehensive about employing the four extra carpenters he would need. After all, he had only ever had one person working for him, and that was an old school friend. Now Pete would have to take on the role of foreman in addition to that of salesman, designer, cost accountant, and craftsman. There was also the worry of the £1,000 additional monthly fixed costs he estimated would be involved.

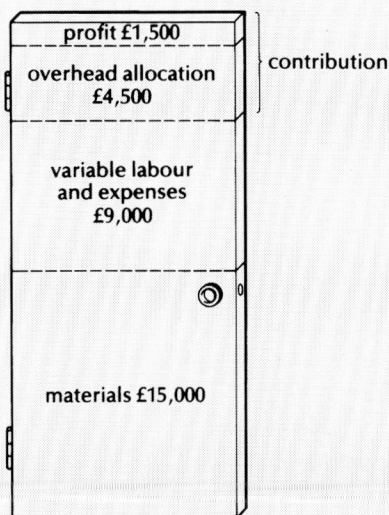

Breakdown of £30,000 of sales revenue

He now felt sure that he had sufficient information to help him decide which investment to make (if either).

Questions

1 Briefly explain the main forms of small business: private limited company, sole trader, partnership. **(6)**

2 Do you think Pete should turn his business into a private limited company? **(4)**

3 Work out the total cost of Pete's proposed extension. **(3)**

4 State three different types of resource that would be used to build the extension. **(3)**

5 Give two reasons why firms take out insurance. **(2)**

6 State three different types of insurance applicable to Pete's business. **(3)**

7 Pete has two options: extending his existing business or moving to a factory. What are the costs and benefits of each option? **(7)**

8 Give two reasons why firms draw up business plans. **(2)**

Further work

1 Pete was preparing work and collecting data for his business plan. Here are the requirements for a business plan, to help you plan yours.

- Make a reasoned decision on the type of product or service you will provide. (What are your objectives in starting up your business?)

- Decide on where to locate your premises.

- Choose a form of ownership and give reasons for your choice.

- Draw up a cash flow forecast for the first year of running the business. (Money in and money out.)

- List the different sources of finance available to cover your requirements and make a decision on which types you will use.

- Decide on which sort of marketing approach is likely to be effective, given the budget constraint.

- Look at constraints facing your business. Research legal requirements, health and safety, insurance, economic background, social and demographic trends.

2 By the time you have done your research and written up your business plan, you will have learnt a great deal about your particular plan. Give a presentation of your business plan to an audience concentrating on five areas: objectives, marketing plan, production plan, resource requirements, and financial support data. The marketing plan could also cover element 8.3.

THE PRINCE AND THE TURNSTILE

Elements: **8.2** *PC 1 2 3 4 5 6 8*
C **3.4** *PC 1 2 3*

Key concepts: Business plan, Resources, Profit, Objectives

When made redundant, 25 year old Jim Tilley was left with £5,000 and a fierce determination to be his own boss. As a fanatical supporter of Blyth Spartans Football Club, he had become used to helping out by maintaining and repairing their turnstiles. Now he would set up Tilley Turnstile Services and try to make a living out of his hobby.

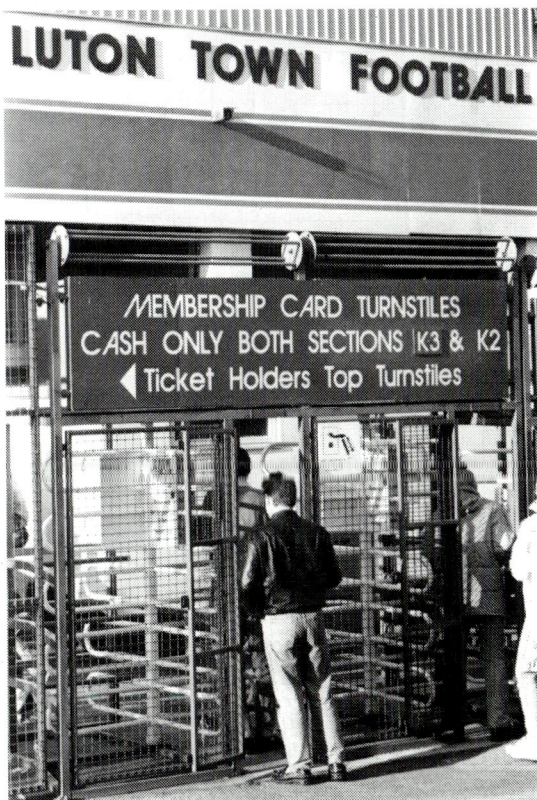

His first step was to get 1,000 brochures printed that explained the two main services: repair and maintenance. These he mailed out to the professional and leading amateur football clubs, plus other venues such as cricket clubs and racecourses. The week after completing the mailing was the worst of his life. He had no responses at all.

Then a letter arrived from Kilmarnock inviting him to come up and give a quote for a pre-season overhaul of their sixteen turnstiles. He was up in Scotland within three hours; by the end of the afternoon he had the contract. For £400 the club had its turnstiles made good and on arriving home three days later, Jim worked out that he had made £200 as pay/profit.

The next four weeks were crazily busy, as club after club invited Jim to work for them. He priced each job along the same lines as his first, working out all the direct costs, then adding 100%. With money flowing in, he bought a van and rented a factory unit on an industrial estate.

Then in late August the phones went dead as the pre-season work dried up. Eventually jobs came through from clubs that needed repair work to broken turnstiles, but the turnover was pretty low. Jim realised that he needed longer term work to fill in the gaps. He decided to move into the manufacture of turnstiles for new sports stadia or the replacement market.

First, however, he would need extra finance. Discussions with his local banks got nowhere, but a television programme led him to contact the Prince's Youth Business Trust. Jim was allocated an advisor who helped him construct a business plan as the basis for a loan application. The Trust itself lent £4,000 on a low interest rate and this commitment encouraged Barclays to lend the same amount.

Most of the £8,000 of new capital went into the machinery needed to make the turnstile structure. Jim planned to subcontract the production of many of the components, but he wanted full production control over the most critical parts. The Prince's Trust advisor helped to set up a software package to enable Jim to calculate the following data on unit production costs.

	Production Run			
	1	2–4	5–9	10+
Bought in components	£485	£455	£360	£320
Raw materials	£145	£125	£90	£80
Labour	£330	£330	£450	£480
Other direct costs	£100	£90	£80	£70

The advisor queried the rise in unit labour costs for 5+ units, but accepted the explanation that Jim would have to employ extra workers. These he expected to be less efficient than himself due to their lack of product familiarity and their lesser incentive to make the business successful.

The decision was made to price the turnstiles at 50% above total direct costs. Jim reasoned that his £2,000 per month of ongoing overheads had to be covered by the existing repair and maintenance business, so there was no point in counting them twice. The only specific turnstile overhead was £200 per month of interest and depreciation on the new machinery.

A new mailing to the same list of clubs plus a press feature in *Sports Management* magazine led to two orders. One, from the Greenacre Cricket Club, was for four turnstiles and the other for twelve turnstiles from Ayr racecourse. Fortunately the delivery dates were staggered, with Greenacre wanting the turnstiles installed within three months and Ayr within six months.

Even though the four turnstiles were Jim's first ever production run, the Greenacre job went remarkably smoothly. The only hiccup was over cash flow, as his suppliers demanded early payment whereas the Cricket Club proved to be very slow payers. Although Barclays helped by providing a £5,000 overdraft, the charges and interest costs involved took £500 off the profit on the job.

For the Ayr contract, Jim knew he would have to hire a welder and a fitter. This proved very time-consuming, as 40 people responded to the small advertisement he placed in the local paper. Even after two days of interviews he did not feel confident that he had picked the right people. The job had to be started, though, so it seemed silly to waste any more time. Two men were hired on the understanding that the job would cease when the contract was completed.

On the day they started, both workers were keen to learn about the job. By the end of their first week, however, Jim kept noticing how different they were. The fitter worked enthusiastically, helping in all sorts of ways as well as getting on with his work. Some of his suggestions for increasing efficiency were very astute. The welder, however, took frequent breaks and was never willing to do anything other than weld. The quality of the work was fine, but his attitude was infuriating.

As the weeks went by, Jim became ever more aware that the job was slipping behind schedule. Then vandalism at Cardiff F.C. forced Jim to spend a week in Wales. On his return, the fitter was spitting with rage at the welder's laziness and offhand manner. Jim was torn between the desire to sack the welder and the knowledge of the time it would take to replace him. He stumbled on without making a decision, living with conflict in his workplace until the Ayr job was finally completed, five weeks late.

The Ayr officials were so upset by the delay that they refused to pay in full; they deducted 5% from the bill as compensation. Jim squawked, but was too desperate to get paid to argue. The delay had pushed up his costs and sent him up to the overdraft ceiling. For a fortnight he was unsure of survival, but eventually the payment came that solved the cash shortage.

After that experience, Jim was far more careful with his recruitment procedure, always employing the same fitter whenever possible. In the second year, work flowed in more consistently, giving rise to the possibility of making a permanent appointment. Tilley Turnstile Services was on its way.

APPENDIX A: *Extracts from the business plan*

Sales Turnover to Date		Forecast Monthly Turnover (excluding turnstile manufacture)
July	£1,400	October – June (average) £4,500
August	£15,000	
September	£3,100	

Questions

1 What were three main objectives of Jim's business? (3)

2 How did Jim make sure that his business proposals were feasible? (2)

3 What physical, financial and human resources did Jim employ? (3)

4 In what sense can time be considered as a resource? Use an example from the case study to illustrate your answer (3)

5 Assuming the unit costs in the production run table, and the pricing policy of direct cost plus 50%, how much would Jim have made:

    a   on the Greenacre cricket club contract

    b   on the Ayr racecourse contract? (6)

6 Calculate the salary/profit Jim could expect to receive in his first year of trading. State clearly any assumptions you have made. (8)

Further work

1 Prepare a five-part business plan on the basis of Jim's proposal for a loan application. In order to meet the criteria for element 8.2 you would need:

- objectives
- outline marketing plan
- outline production plan
- resource requirements
- financial support data.

You should prepare your plan in written form, and then give an oral presentation to a simulated provider of finance.

2 Use this case study as the starting point to considering the main problems faced by new small firms.

67 THE BLACK HAIRDRESSERS

Elements: *8.1* PC 4567 *8.2* PC 1234567
AN *3.2* PC 123568 IT *3.2* PC 123456 *3.3* PC 12345

Key concepts: Time constraints identified on a flow chart, Resource requirements, Financial data, Forecasts to support a plan

It was a Business Studies project that made Kim think seriously about opening the hairdressers. She had always enjoyed fixing friends' hair, but knew that hairdressing trainees were badly paid, so saw no sense in thinking further about such a career. Then came the project.

She had set herself the objective of identifying where and how to open a profitable new hairdressers in Sparkbrook (Birmingham).

A survey among fifty fellow students revealed that 40% went to hairdressers regularly, but few were satisfied with the standard and atmosphere of the salons. She noticed that several had scrawled on the questionnaire comments like: 'All hopeless with Afro-Caribbean styles' which was a view she agreed with heartily. So Kim began to research the prospects for a black hairdressers.

She knew enough about marketing to understand the pros and cons of segmenting the market in this way. If there were no rivals, she would have a good chance of dominating the niche, with all the profit potential that implied. However, if her clients were mainly young (as seemed almost inevitable), she might end up segmenting a segment, and thereby have a large share of such a tiny market that overheads would be impossible to cover (see diagram).

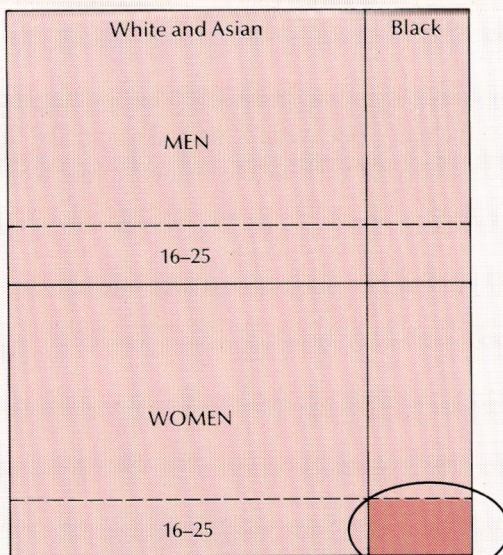

The gap Kim has identified

Segmentation of the market for hairdressing for adults

A trip to the library told her that 40,000 over-16s lived in her part of Sparkbrook, of which 25% were believed to be of Caribbean origin (and 50% were women). Kim then roped three friends into spending a day interviewing people in the nearby High Street. They approached 140 black women, and managed to get 80 interviews. Kim felt sure that they supported her strategy, and that with 60% saying they would definitely try a new, black salon, she had a potential base of 3,000 customers. Kim was then able to forecast her revenue, on the assumption that half the potential customers would come once every three months, and spend an average of £15 per visit.

Now, a year after getting her A-levels, her lifetime savings of £8,000 were to be sunk into the business (along with £4,000 from her parents and the same from the bank). She knew the site she wanted, but needed to make sure that her limited capital would cover not only the start-up period, but also the early months in case custom proved slow to develop. Her bank manager advised her to set 40% of her funds aside for working capital, i.e. for the day to day running of the business. Given her tight cash constraint, Kim decided to plan the start-up period with great care. She realised that the shorter she could make that period, the less time she would suffer cash flow difficulties.

These were the stages she knew she must go through:

A obtaining the site; this would take 2 weeks and would have to be completed before any other activity could begin;

B designing the layout, decor and equipment (3 weeks);

C rebuilding and redecorating (6 weeks);

D buying the equipment ready for installation as soon as C is completed (1 week);

E installation of equipment (1 week);

F hiring staff; this would take about 4 weeks, but could be started after the site was obtained;

G training staff; this would take 3 weeks and could only begin once the equipment had been installed;

H advertising when the salon is to open (2 weeks);

I run a one week half price opening offer.

Adding these up came to 23 weeks, which seemed worringly long, so Kim drew a network diagram to show how to schedule these events to enable completion to take the least possible time.

With just one week until opening time, Kim had just £3,500 left in the bank. Would this be enough to tide her over the half price week? She had calculated that her weekly overheads would be £900, but her £2 variable cost per customer would only generate £5.50 contribution this week.

Fortunately Kim pulled through the early problems and soon had a thriving ethnic hairdressers. Word-of-mouth proved her main advertising medium, and pulled people in from far enough afield to counteract the worries about segmenting the market excessively.

Questions

1 What is meant by a niche market? What are two possible problems that could result from trying to sell in a niche market? **(3)**

2 How did Kim calculate 3,000 potential customers? **(5)**

3 How much working capital did Kim provide? **(3)**

4 If Kim obtained 1,500 customers visiting four times per year, what would her weekly profit be? **(5)**

5 What human, physical, financial and time resources would Kim put into the business? **(4)**

Further work

1 To achieve core skills element 3.2 in Application of Number, you are required to use networks to solve problems. You could also incorporate Information Technology skills by drawing the network required by Kim, labelled to include the earliest start times and latest finish times of each activity. Indicate the critical path. In what ways could this diagram help Kim?

2 Produce a five-part business plan based on the black hairdressers, stating objectives, marketing plan, production plan, resource requirements and financial support data.

FAT SAM'S FRANCHISE

Elements: **8.1** *PC 134567* **8.2** *PC 12345678*
AN **3.2** *PC 12345*

Key concepts: Business plan, Objectives of business, Franchise

Fat Sam's Pasta Joint was a highly successful restaurant in Soho, London. It offered

'All the pasta you can eat for £2.95'.

This good value was combined with lively, bright design and atmosphere to make Fat Sam's a hugely popular place for young people. Fat Sam's owners realised that the same concept could work in many other locations, but they did not have sufficient capital to develop a large chain of restaurants themselves. So they appointed a Franchise Manager, who was set the objective of developing Fat Sam's into a hundred-strong chain.

The new manager decided on the following terms for anyone who wished to become a franchisee:

1   A £5,000 fee to be paid on signing a 5-year Franchise Agreement;

2   Fat Sam's to be paid 8% of the franchisee's sales turnover (including 3% to be used for advertising).

In return, Fat Sam's would provide assistance on siting, interior design and shop fittings, menu and provision supplies, and financial management advice. A franchisee would hardly need a chef, as all sauces could be supplied directly by Fat Sam's.

Although the company advertised their franchises in the magazine 'Franchise World', the first person to apply was a waitress working in the Soho branch. Gill had no business experience, but she was sure she understood how to create the fun atmosphere needed for success, and was willing to take out a £100,000 second mortgage on her house to fulfil a lifetime dream of being her own boss.

She already knew that Fat Sam's took an average of £7 revenue per customer, with variable costs per head of £1.80 for food and 50 pence for drink. Even a novice entrepreneur could appreciate that a mark-up of over 200% presented a promising prospect.

Within a week, the Franchise Agreement had been approved by Gill's solicitor and was signed. She was sure that a good site existed in the centre of the town nearest her house (Colchester) and as it had no competing pasta restaurant, Fat Sam's agreed with her choice. Fat Sam's calculated that the site would take five months to be fully decorated, fitted and therefore become operational. The start-up costs were estimated at £100,000 (including the franchise fee).

Within a few weeks, Gill was becoming increasingly worried by the dithering of the Franchise Manager who was supposed to be helping her. Progress was slow, and many of the interior fittings were being supplied at what Gill thought were outrageous prices. Yet as the suppliers were the only ones who could supply her with fittings in the correct Fat Sam's colours and designs, she was stuck. After seven months, her money had run out, and the opening was still not in sight. She borrowed £25,000 more from her family, and two months later the outlet was finished.

Having spent out all £125,000 she was desperate to start trading in order to bring in some cash. It came like a thunderbolt to hear from the Franchise Manager that he had still not managed to obtain the licence needed to serve alcoholic drinks, but she could not wait. Fat Sam's Pasta Joint opened in Colchester without any advertising, and with signs up apologising for the fact that only the soft drinks on the menu could be served. In such circumstances, it was quite pleasing that 800 customers were served in the first week – only 200 down on her forecast. Of course, the extra start-up expenditure meant higher interest charges on her borrowings, so her fixed costs were higher than originally planned, at £2,898 per week.

Sadly, the poor start meant that Gill's restaurant was rarely full, which undermined the bustling atmosphere she knew she needed. So not even the arrival of the drinks licence (one month after starting) stopped a relentless decline in the Colchester outlet's revenue. A friend worked out the following chart to show her

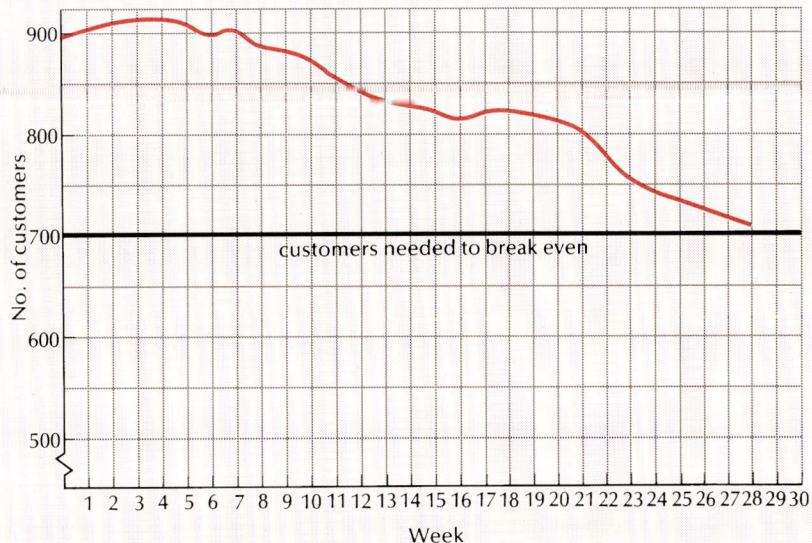

Sales Graph for Colchester Outlet – four period weekly moving average

how her customer base was moving towards the break-even level.

Forty weeks after she started trading, Gill's bank manager persuaded her to give up. Her bitterness towards Fat Sam's and their Franchise Manager turned into rage as she was forced to sell her house. The price it fetched was enough to repay all her debts, but she was left homeless and virtually penniless.

(The above account is true in every detail, though the name of the firm has been changed for legal reasons.)

Questions

1 Explain the meaning of a franchise and break even level. **(2)**

2 What resources did the franchise provide for Gill to help with production, design and marketing? **(5)**

3 In what ways was the franchise very disadvantageous for Gill? **(5)**

4 Give examples of people and organisations that Gill could have consulted before rushing into the franchise. **(3)**

5 Before the delays, Gill had budgeted for weekly fixed costs of £2,500. What is meant by fixed costs? What fixed costs would Gill have incurred? **(4)**

6 If Gill had an average of 1,000 customers per week, assuming a 50-week year, and fixed costs of £2,500, how much profit would she have made in her first year? **(6)**

Further work

1 Use this case study as a starting point for your own business plan. A restaurant could be chosen, and you would need to:

- explain your objectives
- select the type of business, for example sole trader, partnership, private limited company
- select premises
- consider competition and market potential
- consider marketing
- think about resource requirements
- consider legal and insurance implications
- consider financial requirements.

Draw up a conclusion on whether your restaurant would survive. Research should include a visit to a restaurant to obtain primary data to help with your plan.

69 THE MARKETING PLAN

Element: **8.3** *PC 1 2 3 4 5*
AN 3.2 *PC 1 2 3 5*

Key concepts: Sales and marketing plans, Marketing budget

The launch of the low interest rate Visa card had been a great success. Rarely had a new financial product from a small bank caused such a stir. All the newspapers covered the story and it even received a mention on BBC TV News. The media story was simple: if Brooklyn Bank could offer a credit card charging an annual interest rate of 10%, why were the big banks charging 20%? Many suspected that it was a case of **market penetration** by the Brooklyn Bank and that the interest rate would rise later on. The company assured its customers that this was not so.

Three months after the launch, with the £120,000 advertising campaign completed, Bill Stein – the UK Banking Director – conducted a review. His sales target had been for 100,000 customers, a modest share of the 16 million credit cardholders in Britain. In the event 320,000 people contacted Brooklyn for an application form; half were converted into customers. Their rate of usage of the card enabled him to estimate a gross profit of £20 per customer per year.

One week before, he had commissioned a report from his data processing section to analyse all the customer application forms. This provided a full demographic breakdown – valuable material to help construct a marketing plan for the next two years.

Extracts from breakdown of customer demographics

Age breakdown		Social class (occupation)	
Category	%	Category	%
18 – 24	3	AB	40
25 – 34	23	C1	38
35 – 44	38	C2	18
45 – 54	24	DE	4
55+	12		

Bill's first task was to clarify his objectives. Brooklyn had started up in the UK with one branch to service American customers in the City of London. The successful launch of the Visa card provided a foothold among ordinary British consumers. This enabled him to consider two types of goal:

1 customer targets for the Visa card, such as 250,000 within two years;
2 targets for developing new products for the customer list built up by the Visa card, such as selling pension plans.

After discussion with his marketing manager and advertising agency, a decision was made to concentrate on the Visa card for the coming year, then develop new products the year after. This would prevent his limited staff resources being spread too thinly, and should ensure continuation of the successful start made by the credit card. He was able, therefore, to produce this brief statement of Brooklyn's marketing objective for the coming year:

'To gain 5,000 new customers per month, with minimal losses of existing customers, in order to achieve an average of 190,000 customers during the coming year.'

Having identified the objective, Bill next worked out his marketing budget. His American parent company's rule-of-thumb was that marketing expenditure should be set at 10% of the expected annual gross profit. A quick calculation persuaded him that he could not afford television advertising, so he decided to focus upon upmarket (broadsheet) newspapers.

Before further planning, Bill had to tackle a classic problem of advertising strategy: should he focus upon coverage or repetition? With a limited budget, if he used all the broadsheet dailies and Sundays he could afford no more than one advertisement every two months. By only advertising in *The Daily Telegraph* he could cover some 42% of the target market once a week for a whole year. After much thought, he decided that his product's **Unique Selling Point** (USP) was so strong as to make repetition less important than coverage.

Bill's final major decision concerned distribution. Should he be relying solely on advertising plus word of mouth to bring in new customers, or would it be wise to get a distribution outlet such as Independent Financial Advisors (IFAs) and accountants, or building societies too small to have their own credit card? He spent a week taking IFAs and building society bosses out to lunch. This convinced him of the enthusiasm of these potential distributors, but also made it clear that their commissions would take half the gross profit margin on the cards they sold. In addition, they would expect Brooklyn to provide the brochures and **point-of-sale** display materials to encourage consumer interest.

Questions

1   What is meant by market penetration, unique selling point and point of sale?   **(3)**

2   Give three reasons why people use credit cards as a means of payment.   **(3)**

3   How much should Brooklyn budget for their marketing expenditure in the coming year? Justify your answer.   **(5)**

4   Assuming that half the people who contacted Brooklyn for an application form were converted into customers, how many would be in the 35 – 44 age range?   **(4)**

5   How could Brooklyn use the customer demographics breakdown in its sales and marketing plan?   **(5)**

Further work

1   In order to meet the criteria for element 8.3, a sales and marketing plan can be prepared on the basis of this case study. The purposes of your plan should be clearly stated. Your plan should be for the next six months. You will need to outline your planning activities on timing, distribution, advertising and promotions.

MRS AHMED'S COUSIN

Elements: **4.1** *PC 45* *BTEC Law Option* **9.2** *PC 123* **9.3** *PC 123*

Key concepts: Legal relationships in business, Contractual agreements, Employee rights

Mrs Ahmed shrieked when the needle hit her finger. As her cousin helped her to the medical room, she realised that she had nodded off at her workbench. The rushed order for 15,000 pairs of jeans had meant 10-hour days and 6-day weeks for the past month. Mrs Ahmed had not even wanted the extra work, for although the money was needed, a 40-hour week was as much as she could cope with. When she turned the overtime down, the proprietor of Mile End Textiles (MET) had threatened her with dismissal. With no shortage of clothing machinists seeking work locally, she had to accept.

At their thirty-minute lunch break, the other workers asked anxiously about the damaged finger and talked yet again about the harshness of their working lives. Half were on a flat rate of £2.64 per hour, while the others were on **piecework**. The flat rate represented the wages council minimum, but now that the government was abolishing the councils, there was a chance that the rate would fall rather than rise. The biggest staff grievances were that none received holiday pay and there was no bonus rate for overtime. Mrs Bradfield thought it typical of the manager's meanness, while Mrs Ahmed's cousin pointed out that:

> *'It makes little sense, as it means that we are always tired and never have anything to look forward to.'*

As the discussion continued, Mrs Ahmed turned to her cousin and asked her to tell everyone what she had learned about the **wage differentials** in the factory. This was risky, as her cousin was supposed to keep secret the things she found out in her new post as office assistant. She hesitated, but was soon persuaded to say that:

> *'The men are all on much more than the women. In the warehouse they earn £3.50 an hour and the mechanics are on £4.80. It's the same in the office, with Dave the book-keeper getting more than Sarah, our materials buyer.'*

The all-female machinist section was outraged to hear that the warehousemen were earning so much extra. Making jeans was hard, skilful work, whereas the warehousemen could work at their own pace and the forklift trucks took most of the physical labour out of the job. Several muttered about joining a union, but they all knew that the MET management would never give it recognition.

That afternoon the cousin was summoned to see the proprietor. He said straight away that her conversation had been overheard and that she was being dismissed for breach of trust. She pleaded to have her job back, as it had taken her four years at MET to make the switch to the office. Her regrets were too late.

After ten months of applications, interviews and rejections, it was a radio programme that made Mrs Ahmed wonder whether her cousin had been placed on an **employers' blacklist**. She persuaded the cousin to write to the local Textile Employers' Federation for a copy of any computerised files held on her. To her surprise the Federation did send information, and it contained a damning comment about 'her disruptive influence'. Clearly, to have any chance of getting another job in the industry she would have to get that phrase removed. In despair, she turned to the Citizen's Advice Bureau.

Questions

1   Explain what is meant by the terms piecework, wage differentials, employers' blacklist.   **(3)**

2   On what basis could the company be taken to court for sex discrimination?   **(3)**

3   What possible reasons could the firm give for paying the mechanics and warehousemen more than the women on the factory floor?   **(4)**

4   What would be two consequences for the firm of the warehousemen and women on the factory floor having equal pay?   **(4)**

5   What kind of redress is available to employees who feel they have been wronged at their workplace?   **(3)**

6   What liability has an employer towards an employee?   **(3)**

Further work

1   Draw up a contract between an employer and an employee of Mile End Textiles. In your contract you should state what rights the employee should have from the employer, and what the employer should expect from an employee.

2   What are the legal requirements of a valid contract? Examples of negotiated agreements, used in business, should be analysed so that the legal requirements of a valid contract can be identified and illustrated. Examples could include:

   ■   a contract of employment

   ■   a contract to supply a product from one company to another.

What would be the effect of defects in the contractual agreement, for example the absence of an essential piece of information?

71 A PROBLEM OF PRODUCTION AND STOCK SCHEDULING

Elements: B **12.1** *PC 123*   **12.3** *PC 123*
              IT **3.1** *PC 123*   **3.2** *PC 1234567*

Key concepts: Production planning, Stock control, Co-ordinating business functions

The marketing manager of a lawnmower manufacturer forecasts the following sales pattern for the coming year:

Monthly Sales (000 units)

Jan	55
Feb	60
Mar	95
April	140
May	110
June	80
July	70
Aug	65
Sept	75
Oct	80
Nov	60
Dec	45

Maximum production capacity is 90,000 units per month and only 80,000 units of finished stock can be stored. The management aim to keep a minimum (buffer) stock level of 40,000 units at all times; so the year starts and should finish with that amount of stock. The production manager must schedule output for the coming year bearing all these factors in mind.

With a view to the longer term, though, the production manager believes she must discover whether a different strategy would be more profitable. At present, it is inevitable that the expensive factory overhead costs are being fully utilised for only part of the year. Perhaps it would be more economic to sell off some of the machinery, convert part of the factory to warehousing, and then use a full-time workforce to produce flat out all year? Surely that would be more efficient than the time-consuming and expensive process of recruiting and training temporary workers every winter.

She decided to spend more time planning out her idea, and then to discuss it with the firm's chief accountant.

Questions

1   Draw a line graph to show monthly sales. Plot the sales on a spreadsheet package if possible and use the chart option to produce your graph. Add a title and label the axes. Create a text file and explain the seasonal variation in predicted lawnmower sales. Merge the paragraph with the text and print out a hard copy.   **(12)**

2   Explain the meaning of a buffer stock. What will determine the minimum and maximum stock levels that a manufacturer wishes to hold?   **(6)**

3   Assuming that the production manager's plan is implemented, produce a short production plan in the form of a report from the production manager to the managing director. The plan should include the following:

■   how the conversion of part of the factory to warehousing would help with the low stocks at the beginning of the year in relation to sales forecasts

■   how the conversion would affect cash flow.   **(12)**

4   Explain why there is a need to co-ordinate sales, marketing, stocks, production and finance. Construct a diagram to show the linkages between these functions.   **(5)**

Further work

1   Work out a recommended production level for each month, bearing in mind the maximum production capacity of 90,000 units per month and the maximum and (desired) minimum stock levels. Use this layout to work out your answer:

	Stocks at start (thousands)	Sales (thousands)	Production level (thousands)	Stocks at end (thousands)
Jan				
Feb				
Mar				
etc.				

72 FORD'S MODEL T – THE BIRTH OF MODERN INDUSTRY

Elements: *BTEC **12.1** PC 123 **12.2** PC 12*
                *AN **3.3** PC 23456 IT **3.3** PC 12345*

Key concepts: Mass production, Co-ordinating business functions

At the turn of the century, production of cars was mainly done by skilled workers who crafted the car with the aid of quite simple machinery. Henry Ford's small car factory followed this pattern, until demand for his newest model (the Model T) forced him to look for ways of speeding up output. Ford's twelve to fifteen young engineers were given the freedom to test the performance of new machine tools against their existing methods. If they could prove the superiority of their new system, the factory layout would be changed in whichever way would allow output to be expanded most rapidly. They soon found that the easiest way to increase output per worker was by getting parts moving automatically from one production stage to another. At first this was done with downward sloping chutes, then later with conveyor belts. When cost-saving measures were introduced, Ford passed these on as price cuts to his customers. As demand increased further, they found it possible to subdivide different units of work into smaller and smaller operations. At first, unskilled workers were used to produce these parts repeatedly; then the engineers set about devising machinery that would simplify the work even further.

By 1910, Ford's success had enabled him to afford to construct a massive new factory at Highland Park. By 1913, many of the main components were being constructed on assembly lines. In late 1913, experiments were carried out on a moving line for the car chassis. This proved highly successful. By June 1914, a chain-driven line (as is still used in many car factories) had cut assembly time from 12 hours to 93 minutes. Within a year, Ford had introduced moving assembly lines throughout the plant.

Yet the ever-increasing mechanisation of the plant made it a progressively more unpleasant place to work. The constant pressure to keep up with the pace of the line, plus the appalling noise and dust levels, resulted in Ford's labour turnover reaching 380%. A 13% pay rise (to $2.34 per day) had no impact on the problem, so in January 1914 Ford created world headlines by adopting the unprecedentedly high figure of $5 per day (more than many Americans and British earned per week).

The five-dollar-a-day wage ensured that Fordism became widely discussed and admired by managements, workers and consumers throughout Europe; and

Ford became a folk hero in America. He had shown that mass production could enable high wages to be paid, yet consumer prices cut (see Appendix A). The fact that Ford offered no choice of colour or model design was not seen as a disadvantage at a time when people were thrilled to be able to afford their first car. At their height, Ford's Highland Park and the new, massive River Rouge plants produced two million Model T's in one year – giving Ford 50% of the US car market in the early 1920s. It was only later in that decade that customers began to switch to the wider range of models provided by General Motors. Model T production ended in 1927, by which time Ford had produced over fifteen million.

APPENDIX A: *Model T pricing and sales 1909–1916*

Year	Retail Price	Sales
1909	$950	12,292
1910	$780	19,293
1911	$690	40,402
1912	$600	78,611
1913	$550	182,809
1914	$490	260,720
1915	$440	355,276
1916	$360	577,036

Questions

1 Distinguish between job, batch and flow production. **(3)**

2 Why was flow production particularly appropriate to car production? **(2)**

3 What were two advantages and two disadvantages of the mass production system introduced by Henry Ford? **(4)**

4 Why did Henry Ford pay such high wages? **(2)**

5 One famous saying attached to the Ford Model T car was that customers could choose any colour of car as long as it was black. Give two reasons why there was no alternative colour. **(4)**

6 Which comes first: marketing or production? Justify your answer. **(4)**

7 Explain how the following two aspects of car production show the need to co-ordinate marketing and production:

   a design

   b quality control. **(6)**

Further work

1 **a** Draw a demand schedule that plots price against quantity for Ford's Model T. When the graph is drawn make sure that it has a title, labelled axes, a key, and it shows the use of colour. You could plot your demand curve by using a suitable graphical package. Incorporate text with the graph to show that you are able to combine information from different sources.

   b Underneath your graph draw two conclusions from the data.

   c Outline three factors that might have been operating to distort the relationship between price and demand during this period.

BUDGETING IN HARROGATE

Elements: **6.3** *PC 23467*   *BTEC* **11.2** *PC 1234*
        IT **3.4** *PC 12345*   **3.5** *PC 1234*

Key concepts: Forecast and actual figures, Use of spreadsheets, An evaluation of Information Technology in the workplace

Cleeton is a long established family firm based in Harrogate, Yorkshire. Its production of ropes and cables began in 1863 and has changed little since then. The only striking change in recent years has been the appointment of a young Finance Director, given the task of masterminding a steady increase in the firm's profitability.

Last December he brought in a new computerised budgeting system to provide managers with a monthly print-out of actual, compared with forecast, revenues and costs. At the same time, he encouraged the Sales Director to introduce a more flexible pricing policy, allowing sales representatives to offer discounts in order to get business.

Now, in April, he is reviewing his initiatives at the monthly Board meeting:

'Our policy changes have been working very well. Sales are up, market share is up and profits are up... Our new budgeting system has been especially successful, encouraging staff to keep costs down (though variable costs, I am delighted to say, have been pushed up by our buoyant sales level). With the economy of our major export market, Germany, so strong at the moment, the future looks very bright.'

Other Board members, still unfamiliar with the format of the budgeting spreadsheet, could only nod their approval

Budget and variance statement – Cleeton Ltd.

| | All figures in £000s | | | | | | | | |
| | January | | | February | | | March | | |
	B*	A	V	B	A	V	B	A	V
Sales revenue	80	92	12	100	110	10	120	122	#
Materials	40	48	(8)	50	57	(7)	60	63	#
Other direct costs	10	12	(2)	13	15	(2)	15	17	#
Overheads	20	21	(1)	24	24	–	27	24	#
Profit	10	11	1	13	14	1	18	#	#
Year to date	10	11	1	23	25	2	41	#	#
Last year		5			20			40	

*B = Budget   A = Actual   V = Variance

Questions

1   What is a budget? Why do firms budget? (3)

2   Explain the term variance. Put Cleeton's budget and variance statement into a spreadsheet and calculate the missing variances for March shown by #. (10)

3   What is a flexible pricing policy? How would such a policy affect the accuracy of the figures in the spreadsheet? (4)

4   **a**   Comment on the performance of the company from the accounting information alone. (3)

   b   What other information would be useful to complete your picture of the company's performance? (3)

5   Give two possible reasons why the actual figures for overheads vary from the budget figures. (2)

Further work

1   To achieve the final core skill Application of Number elements, it is necessary to prepare written work on elements 3.4 and 3.5. The March figures in the case study were omitted by computer error. Explain how this error may have occurred. What routine systems should be in place to make sure that mistakes like this do not happen? State the general advantages to be gained from computerising accounting information in comparison with non-IT means of information handling.

It would be appropriate to visit a firm to see how it computerises its accounts, and then produce a wordprocessed report on:

■   how information is protected from accidental deletion and tampering

■   how facilities offered by software improve a company's efficiency by saving time, increasing accuracy, and reducing cost

■   how errors and faults are dealt with to ensure that there is no damage to to persons, equipment or stored information

■   how information technology equipment is used in accordance with health and safety requirements.

A bank would be an ideal place to visit as accountancy and security are paramount. (Also see further work case study 20: Production Management.)

2   In order to meet the requirements of BTEC option element 11.2 you could do the following desk research using an Accountancy textbook:

a   a description of the main types of budget

b   a description of how budgets are structured and compiled

c   an analysis of how budgets are monitored.

74 BOOMTIME FOR BANKCHECK

Elements: **4.3** *PC 1* BTEC option **15.1** *PC 12* **15.3** *PC 1 2 3 4*

Key concepts: Mismanagement, Leadership role, Recruitment, Communications

It had been a marvellous recession for Iain Truscott. His company BankCheck supplied ultraviolet banknote scanners, and demand soared as a wave of forged notes hit Britain. At first BankCheck's 40 employees were delighted at the job security implied by the firm's success. Then they found themselves overstretched as more and more orders needed to be processed. After three months of hectic work, mistakes began to be made with deliveries and invoices, so Iain advertised for more personnel: two sales and two clerical staff, plus three distribution workers. The result was an unwelcome deluge of 600 applicants.

By the time the new recruits started work, demand was already forcing still more appointments to be made. Iain could see this process continuing, so he hired a personnel officer to look after these matters. Yet with every extra appointment Iain was frustrated to find that even more of his time was required to induct the individual into his business and his ways of working. The situation became even worse when he found that the new personnel officer was failing to recruit the right kind of people. BankCheck's success had been built up by experienced, practical workers; yet many of the new recruits were graduates who had bright ideas but were unenthusiastic about applying the procedures that Iain had laid down.

Meanwhile, several of the original staff found jobs with competitor firms that were willing to offer responsible managerial posts to people from BankCheck To stop this exodus, Iain offered substantial bonus payments to key personnel based on workload (as measured by the number of subordinates the manager was directly responsible for). This worked well at first, but less so as staff numbers rose towards 70.

The situation came to a head at the company's finest hour. Iain had just signed a £2 million contract with the National Dairy Federation to supply a portable banknote scanner to every milkman in the country. The extra work involved in supplying and training each milkman proved too much, and two key managers fell ill. Neither had kept their staff informed of their wider plans, so it was very hard for anyone to take over.

After eight weeks of chaos, in which Iain dashed around the country trying to keep things running, the Dairy Federation warned that if BankCheck could not sort out their administration, the contract would be cancelled and the firm would be sued. Other clients were just as angry, including some very long-standing ones.

Iain knew he must act fast, but felt too drained to think clearly about what to do, so he called in a management consultant.

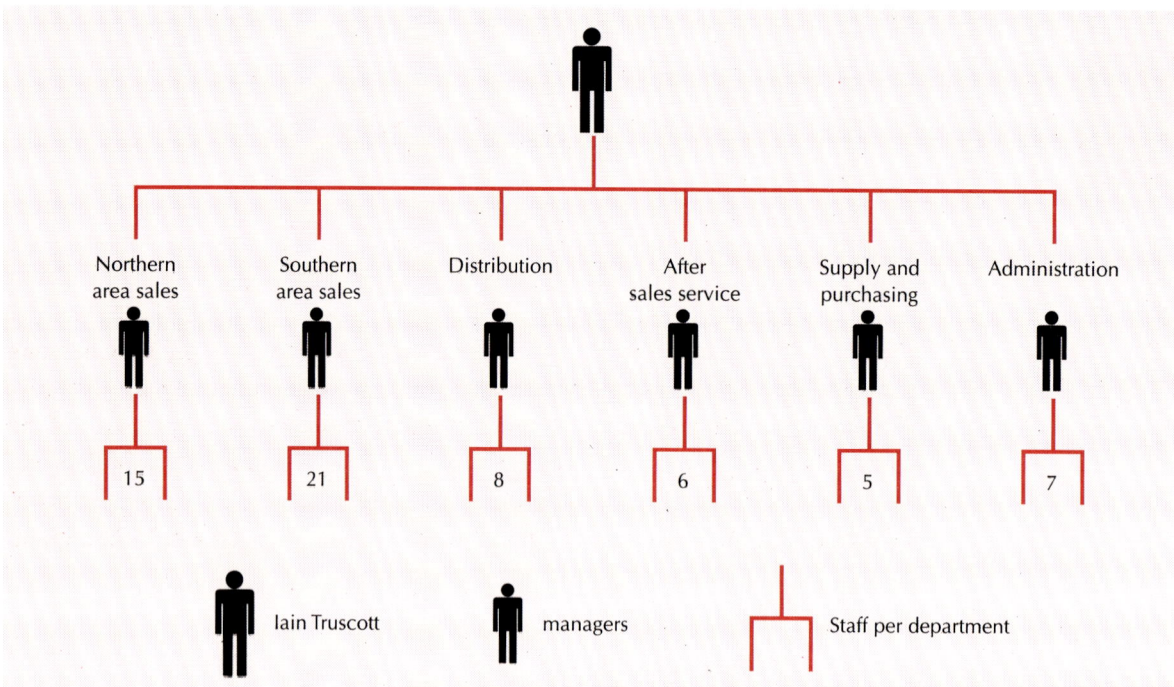

Northern area sales — 15

Southern area sales — 21

Distribution — 8

After sales service — 6

Supply and purchasing — 5

Administration — 7

Iain Truscott   managers   Staff per department

Questions

1 What are three costs involved in recruiting? (3)

2 What could Bankcheck have done to make sure that it had fewer, but still very well qualified, candidates for the post? (4)

3 What is meant by management style? How would you describe Iain's management style? (3)

4 What communication difficulties were there at Bankcheck? How could internal communication be improved? (5)

5 Iain could be referred to as a 'firefighter', one who goes from crisis to crisis putting fires out but never dealing with long-term issues and strategies. To what extent do you feel that this was true? (5)

Further work

1 In order to meet the requirements for BTEC option element 15.3, you are required to:
- use secondary sources to identify and compare different management styles
- identify leadership tasks of management
- identify the types of channels for effective communication
- examine barriers to effective communication.

Use this case study to illustrate mismanagement. Explain how poor management and communication led to workplace difficulties.

PROBLEMS OF POLLUTION IN A CHEMICAL PLANT

Elements: CGLI **14.1** PC 1 2 **14.2** PC 1 2 3 4 **14.3** PC 1
          RSA **9.3** PC 1 2 3 4

Key concepts: Environment, Social responsibility, Pressure groups

Chemdex Chemicals is situated on Teesside, in the northeast of England. It employs 1,200 fulltime workers – half the number of five years ago. Yet Chemdex is still the main local employer in an area where male unemployment is 19%. As with other local labour forces, the level of unionisation has fallen; just 41% of the workforce belong to a trade union. Chemdex produces weedkillers, pestkillers and chemical dyes for use in paint. Over recent years, fierce competition from Germany and from ICI has often pushed Chemdex into losses, as is shown by the graph below.

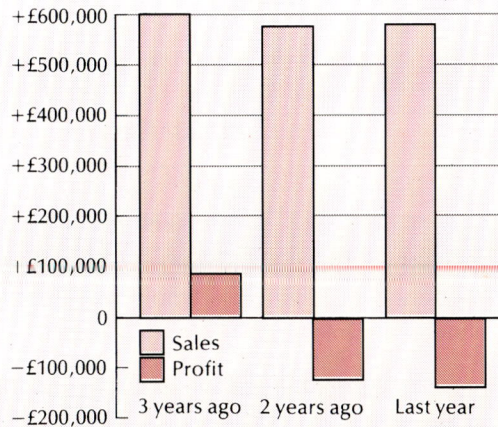

Trend in Chemdex sales and profit

The firm has recently launched a new, highly effective weedkiller (Weedex). Sales are building up rapidly, and the product is soon to be featured on BBC TV's *Gardeners' World*. The firm's management is already talking about the new product as the company's saviour.

Yet many in the factory are worried about the fumes given off in the production process. They frequently escape from the safety valves, leaving a fine blue powder everywhere in the factory, and even on the washing of the local houses. Following furious complaints from its members, the factory workers' union AGU has just held a meeting at which eighteen operators have complained of blinding headaches, and seven say they have fainted when overcome by the air pollution.

AGU's membership also includes the maintenance mechanics, who tell the meeting that they believe the entire Weedex plant has been designed so poorly and constructed so shoddily that leaks are inevitable. The meeting votes that the shop stewards should discuss the situation with the management, and ask for an independent report on the nature of the blue powder.

The union's request that this issue be discussed at the Works' Council is an irritant to a management that is wrapped up in the success of the Weedex launch. Latest forecasts show that in the coming year it should transform a £100,000 loss into a £400,000 profit. That would provide the funds for a desperately needed factory modernisation programme. The Works Manager is aware that the Weedex production equipment is leaky and unstable, but the Managing Director only seems interested in discussing ways of boosting output.

Frustration has led the Works Manager to ask the Chief Scientist at Chemdex to write a report on the chemical, and send a copy to the Managing Director. This has been completed and shows that the blue chemical is copper hydrocyanide. The concluding paragraph reads:

> 'The quantities found in the atmosphere within the
> factory represent a serious, if long term, health hazard.
> As the situation is in direct contravention of the Health
> and Safety at Work Act, I strongly recommend the
> immediate adoption of lightweight oxygen masks for all
> factory workers in contact with Weedex.'

At the Works' Council, the Managing Director starts by saying to the employee representatives that the success of Weedex is vital, and that if its launch is disrupted and thereby falters, the whole weedkilling division will be closed, causing four hundred job losses. He also declares that:

> 'We are not willing to discuss the blue powder at all, as it is
> precisely the ingredient that our competitors would like to identify.'

At the subsequent union meeting, there are many grumbles about the bullying tactics of the Managing Director, but the threat of redundancies is enough to weaken the workers' resolve. This would probably be where the matter rested were it not for a local journalist's enterprise in talking to local mothers and doctors. The local newspaper's headline 'Children Turning Blue!' is even picked up by the national media. As environmentally conscious supermarket stockists of Weedex start phoning for details, the Managing Director springs into action. The company puts out a press release saying that they are already implementing a 'green strategy' to make production 'even safer'.

Within a week, filtration devices costing £25,000 are fitted that halve the air pollution, and plans are underway for a new, safer production line to be built alongside the existing one.

Questions

1 In what ways were Chemdex's activities affecting the environment? **(3)**

2 With reference to the chart, explain why Weedex was so important to the company. **(4)**

3 How was the pollution at Chemdex monitored internally? **(3)**

4 What external means of monitoring environmental problems are in existence? **(2)**

5 What is meant by social responsibility? To whom do you think Chemdex should have a social responsibility? **(3)**

6 Chemdex eventually spent money to reduce pollution. What pressures acted upon the company? **(3)**

7 What were the main objectives of:

   a the trade union

   b the media

   c Chemdex? **(7)**

Further work

1 In order to fulfil the criteria for RSA element 9.3, you have to evaluate the effects and impact of two business organisations on their environment. This case study could be used for a comparison with a local firm.

2 Investigate the environmental policies of leading companies. Research material can be obtained by using the *Business Studies* magazine, volume 6, number 1, October 1993, published by Anforme, or by visiting or writing to a suitable company.

Companies which could be considered include Safeway, McDonalds, ICI, British Coal, British Steel, Boots, The Electricity Council, British Airways, Shell and Norsk Hydro.

Elements: BTEC option **14.1** *PC 123*   **14.2** *PC 1234*   **14.3** *PC 12*
                 14.4   *PC 12*

Key concepts: Evaluating alternative locations, Business opportunities within
                         Europe, Marketing overseas

The success of 'Stun' in the United States has already become a standard business case history. Started as an ethnic, black leisurewear business, it grew on the back of the athletics and basketball successes of its sponsored sports stars. Unusually for a fashionable sportswear firm, Stun had always used the slogan 'The value of style' to highlight that it offered the customer performance at reasonable prices. Sales of $380,000 in its first year ballooned to $56 million by year five. Now, two years later, with US sales still rising at a compound rate of 50%, the 'Stun' directors want to make a decisive move into Europe.

Their strategy is to set up a single marketing and distribution centre which will be given responsibility for covering the entire European Union. The warehousing and transport systems must be capable of handling and storing large volumes of shoes imported from Mexico. The Directors believe that the single European market's removal of costly and time-consuming border controls has opened up the opportunity of distributing goods cheaply to a market of 320 million people. Stun's rivals such as Nike and Reebok operate on a national basis, with offices, depots and staff overheads in each country in Europe. So Stun wants to gain a competitive advantage by benefiting from the economies of scale associated with a single, large operation.

Their problem is to decide where. A consultant has collected data and provided a shortlist of four sites: Dover in Southeast England, Hamburg in North Germany, Antwerp in Belgium, and Lille in Northeast France. All four sites are near to ports that could cope with the shoes shipped from Mexico. They also have very good motorway and rail links. Yet there are many other points of difference. The consultant has set out the key points in a report; extracts from this are shown below.

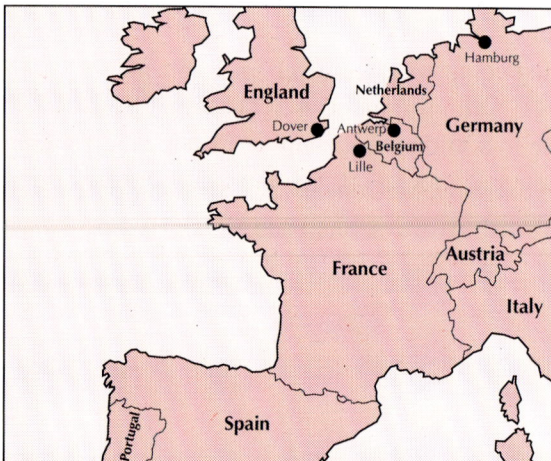

Main resource needs

Office space	10,000 sq feet	Marketing staff	45
Warehousing	80,000 sq feet	Warehouse staff	30
		Other staff	50

Main Resource (Indirect) Costs

	Dover	Hamburg	Antwerp	Lille
Office ($ per sq ft)	14	10	8	8
Warehouse ($ per sq ft)	5	3	2	2
Marketing staff ($ p.a.)	32,000	52,000	40,000	45,000
Warehouse staff ($ p.a.)	15,000	25,000	20,000	18,000
Other staff ($ p.a.)	30,000	40,000	30,000	30,000
Overhead costs ($ p.a.)	570,000	575,000	450,000	500,000
Corporation tax (%) (tax on profit)	35%	48%	40%	38%

From their research into potential European revenues, Stun's Directors forecast first year gross profits of $15 million, after allowing for direct production, distribution and marketing costs. In addition the Dover site would carry a cost penalty of an estimated $2 million for a year's time delays and charges relating to crossing the English Channel.

There are other, less quantifiable factors to consider. As more of the East European countries are allowed to enter the Community, the nearness of the German site would be most useful. Dover also has its trump cards. As the least regulated of all the member states, the Directors are aware that Britain would be the easiest location for redundancies or dismissals, should either be necessary. No less important is that senior American managers are more willing to move to England than to continental Europe. Offset against these advantages for Dover is this warning from Stun's consultant: 'Do bear in mind that Britain is a reluctant European Union member, therefore it may not join in with key future developments such as a common currency.'

Stun's Directors have a few calculations and a great deal of thinking to do.

Questions

1 What are five general factors which influence the location of industry?　　(5)

2 Construct a grid which shows the strengths, weaknesses, opportunities and threats to Stun of a Dover based location. Include information from the text and the consultant's report.　　(8)

3 Take any three of the main resource costs listed in the consultant's report, and give possible reasons why costs vary between the four locations.　　(6)

4 On the basis of the numerical data available, calculate which of the four sites would be the most profitable for the company.　　(6)

5 What difficulties might be faced when selling a product like leisure wear into different European markets?　　(5)

Further work

1 Assume that Dover was not chosen for the location of the company. To help meet the criteria for BTEC element 14.3, you are required to prepare a feasibility study on a possible location for a company in a named country in the EU. Your study could include:

- the problems that result from entering an overseas market
- the range of supporting services that would be needed overseas
- legal requirements in a different country.

Your information could be obtained from official and unofficial sources from member states, EUROSTAT, and financial institutions. The latest edition of the *Regional Marketing Pocket Book,* published by the Advertising Association in association with NTC Publications Ltd, has a chapter on Europe which includes demographic figures, GDP by EU region, richest and poorest regions, and unemployment rates.

2 In order to complete element 14.1 you will need to write a short report examining two areas of Europe in terms of natural and human resources and economic activity. You could compare and contrast Scotland and Denmark, Northern Ireland and Portugal or the South East of England and the North of France. Your choice may depend on your sources of information. The latest edition of the *Lifestyle Pocket Book* covers the UK and has a chapter on Europe which includes spending categories, demographic statistics and unemployment figures. A CD Rom facility would give you background information on population, GDP, and political features.

GNVQ GLOSSARY

Action plan – you should plan your tasks at the start of a unit element, and for all your activities and projects. Then fill out an official action plan form. Action plans are not required for every single element but it is a good habit to get action planning from a very early stage. It is also good practice to check your action plans with your teacher or tutor. The way in which performance criteria will be met is noted in your plan. You should renew each of your action plans against the performance criteria and range as you work through the element to make sure there are no gaps and to update the plan if necessary.

Assessor – the person who is responsible for assessing your work and ensuring that it meets the performance criteria and national standards for GNVQ.

Core Skills Units – these are three units which form an integral part of your GNVQ. They concentrate on general skills that can be applied to any job or career not just those in business. You will complete them as you are working through your mandatory and optional units. The core skills are divided into:

Communication skills: letter writing, interviewing etc.

Information Technology skills: using spreadsheets, wordprocessing, etc.

Application of Number: mathematics, statistics, etc.

Cumulative Assessment Record (CAR form) – you should complete a CAR form for each element of each unit. This form records details of the work in your portfolio to be assessed against that element.

Element – each GNVQ unit is divided into three or more sections called elements, e.g.Unit 1 element 1.1 'The purposes and products of business'. The elements relate to particular topics and contain the performance criteria, range and evidence indicators.

Evidence – the proof you have completed the work and covered the performance criteria and the range for an element. Evidence is based on projects and assignments and needs to be contained in a portfolio. It may include written work, notes, letters, cassettes, videos, case studies etc..

Evidence indicators – a part of an element which suggests the kinds of evidence you need to collect to meet the performance criteria and range. An example is, Unit 2 element 2.1 'Investigate administrative systems'. The evidence indicators for this state: 'An account of an administration system in a business organisation showing how the system meets the needs of the organisation and reporting on users' opinions. A task or project can be developed from the evidence indicator. The outcome from the task or project can form part of your portfolio.'

External verifier – a person associated with an awarding body who maintains a consistent level of assessment between different GNVQ centres. This person will visit your centre two or three times each year.

Grading criteria – the overall grade of your qualification will be decided by how well you use a range of skills including planning and handling information. The grading criteria are national standards used to allocate merit or distinction grades.

Internal verifier – a person in a GNVQ centre who ensures a consistent level of assessment between different assessors.

Performance criteria (PC) – these are statements which describe what you must do to cover all the aspects of the element, for example element 4.2 PC2 states 'Job roles within structures are described'. To gain credit for an element you must meet all of the performance criteria for that element.

Portfolio of evidence – this is a collection of your evidence which you should keep in a folder or other container ready for assessment. Your work should be clearly labelled and cross referenced to the performance criteria. Action plans and Cumulative Assessment Records should also be part of your portfolio.

Range – a list which tells you what has to be covered and what knowledge is required to achieve the performance criteria and the unit test. For example, for element 4.2 PC2 the range statement is 'Job roles: director, manager, team member'.

Unit – each GNVQ course at advanced level consists of 8 mandatory units and three optional units chosen from a list provided by your awarding body. The 8 mandatory units for Business are:

> Business in the economy
>
> Business systems
>
> Marketing
>
> Human resources
>
> Employment in the market economy
>
> Financial transactions and monitoring
>
> Financial resources
>
> Business planning

Each unit consists of three or more elements. There are also three core skills units to be completed for your GNVQ award which cover Communication skills, Information Technology and Application of Number.

Unit test – these are short tests which are designed to test your understanding across the whole range.

SOURCES OF INFORMATION FOR BUSINESS ASSIGNMENTS

Name, Address and Telephone Number	Type of information
Advertising, Institute of Practitioners in 44 Belgrave Square London SW1X 8QS Tel. 071 235 7020	Good library on advertising; hold reports on measuring advertising effectiveness
Advertising Standards Authority (ASA), Brook House, 2/16 Torrington Place London WC1E 7HN Tel. 071 580 5555	The role of the ASA in policing advertising standards
Advisory, Conciliation and Arbitration Service (ACAS) Library and Information Service, Room 111 27 Wilton Street London SW1X 7AZ Tel. 071 210 3613	Human resources, especially legal requirements, redress and employee relations
Banking Information Service 10 Lombard Street London EC3V 9AP Tel. 071 626 8486	Helpful on business plans and preparing requests for loans
British Franchise Association Thames View, Newtown Road Henley-on-Thames Oxon RG9 1HG Tel. 0491 578049	Useful contact for recent case studies of new business start-up
British Standards Institution 2 Park Street London W1A 2BS Tel. 071 629 9000	Information on BSI Kitemark, BS 5750 and BS 7750 (environmental assurance)
Central Office of Information Hercules Road London SE1 7DU Tel. 071 928 2345	Facts on government policies and advertising
Central Statistical Office (CSO) HMSO Publications Centre 51 Nine Elms Lane London SW8 5DR Telephone enquiries: 071 873 0011 (24 hours) Telephone orders: 071 873 9090 (24 hours)	Government statistical publications such as the Annual Abstract of Statistics and Social Trends

Name, Address and Telephone Number	Type of information
Chambers of Commerce, Association of British 9 Tufton Street London SW1P 3QB Tel. 071 222 1555	For address of your local Chamber of Commerce
City Business Library 1 Brewers Hall Garden London EC2V 5BX Tel. 071 638 8215	Excellent secondary material on markets and economic data
Commission for Racial Equality Elliot House 10-12 Allington Street London SW1E 5EH Tel. 071 828 7022	Legal requirements and obligations to employees
Companies House 55-71 City Road London EC1Y 1BB Tel. 071 253 9393	Annual accounts of all limited companies available publicly
Companies House Crown Way, Maindy Cardiff CF4 3UZ Tel. 0222 388588	Annual accounts of all limited companies available publicly
Confederation of British Industry (CBI) Centrepoint, 103 New Oxford Street London WC1A 1DU Tel. 071 379 7400	Data on business performance nationally
Consumers' Association 2 Marylebone Road London NW1 4DF Tel. 071 486 5544	Publishers of *Which?* magazine – covering many issues in marketing ethics and honesty
Data Protection Registrar Wycliffe House, Water Lane Wilmslow Cheshire SK9 5AF Tel. 0625 535777	Responsible for operating the Data Protection Act
Design Council 28 Haymarket London SW1Y 4SU Tel. 071 839 8000	For the role of design in boosting business export potential

Name, Address and Telephone Number	Type of information
Equal Opportunities Commission Overseas House, Quay Street Manchester M3 3HN Tel. 061 833 9244	Information on workplace legal obligations and redress
European Commission, Information Office 8 Storey's Gate London SW1P 3AT Tel. 071 973 1992	For EU policies and EU opportunities within the Single Market
Eurostat Publications, Office of Official Publications of the European Union HMSO Books, 51 Nine Elms Lane London SW8 5DR General enquiries tel. 071 873 0011 (24 hours)	Statistics on the European Union
Health and Safety Executive, Press Office 1 Chepstow Place London W2 4TF Tel. 071 221 0870	Workings of the Health and Safety Act and the Health and Safety Executive
HMSO Books, see under Central Statistical Office	
Industrial Society 3 Carlton House Terrace London SW1Y 5AF Tel. 071 839 4300	For unbiased information on human resources (especially employee relations)
Industrial Tribunals, Central Office 93 Ebury Bridge Road London SW1W 8RB Tel. 071 730 0252	To ask for nearest local industrial tribunal hearings
Institute of Management Third Floor, 2 Savoy Court, Strand London WC2R 0EZ Tel. 071 497 0580	Workplace performance of business
Judge Institute of Management Studies Mill Lane Cambridge CB2 1RX Tel. 0223 338171	Research papers on Japanese manufacturing in the UK
Market Research Society 15 Northburgh Street London EC1V 0AH Tel. 071 490 4911	Information on market research methods and the value of research

Name, Address and Telephone Number	Type of information
NTC Publications Ltd, PO Box 69 Henley-on-Thames Oxfordshire RG9 1GB Tel. 0491 574671	Lifestyle and Drink Pocket books
Office of Fair Trading 15-25 Bream's Buildings London EC4 1PR Tel. 071 242 2858	Reasons for government intervention to support competition
OFWAT Centre City Tower 7 Hill Street Birmingham B5 4UA Tel. 021 625 1450	Water industry regulator; a type of government intervention
Personnel Management, Institute of IPM House, 35 Camp Road London SW19 4UX Tel. 081 946 9100	Informative library for human resourcing and workplace performance; publish *Personnel Management* magazine
Small Firms Service Department of Trade and Industry Kingsgate House 66-74 Victoria Street London SW1E 6SW Tel. 071 215 5000	Government policy and assistance to small firms
Society of Motor Manufacturers and Traders Forbes House, Halkin Street London SW1X 7DS Tel. 071 235 7000	Monthly data on car and truck sales (giving good scope for trend analysis and prediction of consumer demand)
Stock Exchange Old Broad Street London EC2N 1HP Tel. 071 588 2355	Sources of finance for Public Limited Companies
Trades Union Congress Congress House, Great Russell Street London WC1B 3LS Tel. 071 636 4030	Role and impact of trade unions in business